Energy Demand in Asian Developing Economies

Energy Demand in Asian Developing Economies

M. Hashem Pesaran   Ron P. Smith   Takamasa Akiyama

A World Bank Study.
Published by the Oxford University Press for the World Bank and
the Oxford Institute for Energy Studies
1998

Oxford University Press, Walton Street, Oxford OX2 6DP
Oxford New York
Athens Auckland Bangkok Bogota Bombay
Buenos Aires Calcutta Cape Town Dar es Salaam
Delhi Florence Hong Kong Istanbul Karachi
Kuala Lumpur Madras Madrid Melbourne
Mexico City Nairobi Paris Singapore
Taipei Tokyo Toronto
and associated companies in Berlin Ibadan

Oxford is a trade mark of Oxford University Press

© *1998 The International Bank for Reconstruction and Development/*
The World Bank 1818 H Street, N.W., Washington, D.C. 20433

Reprinted with corrections←1999.

British Library Cataloguing in Publication Data
A catalogue record for this book is available from the British Library

ISBN 0-19-730020-0

"*The findings, interpretations, and conclusions expressed in this paper are entirely*
those of the author(s) and should not be attributed in any manner to the World
Bank, to its affiliated organizations, or to members of its Board of Executive Direc-
tors or the countries they represent. The World Bank does not guarantee the accuracy
of the data included in this publication and accepts no responsibility whatsoever
for any consequence of their use. The boundaries, colours, denominations, and
other information shown on any map in this volume do not imply on the part of
the World Bank Group any judgment on the legal status of any territory or the
endorsement or acceptance of such boundaries."

Cover design by Holbrook Design Ltd, Oxford
Typeset by Newgen Imaging Systems (P) Ltd, Chennai, India
Printed by Bookcraft, Somerset

Contents

List of Figures

List of Tables

Preface

This book and the energy databank were produced as a part of the World Bank research project "Energy Demand in Asian Developing Economies: Structure, Trends, Impacts, Prospects and Strategies". We are grateful to the World Bank for financial support and for permission to publish the study. All conclusions and opinions are those of the authors and not the World Bank. We are also grateful to a number of anonymous referees who commented on earlier versions.

The energy databank has been constructed by M. Hashem Pesaran in collaboration with Takamasa Akiyama and Ron Smith. Jonathan Coleman and Jamshid Heidarian helped with the construction of the underlying spreadsheets, and James Mitchell and Brian Holley helped with getting the spreadsheets ready for conversion into the databank format.

The computer program for estimation of the pooled mean group estimators was initially written by Kung So Im and subsequently rewritten and completed by Yongcheol Shin. This program is written in Gauss, and we are particularly grateful to Yongcheol Shin for making the program user-friendly. The estimation of the structural cointegrating VAR model of inter-fuel substitutions in Chapter 8, as well as the graphs were implemented using the Windows version of *Microfit 4.0* (1997). The data and the Gauss program for pooled mean group estimation are available from the Oxford Institute for Energy Studies on request.

James Mitchell provided valuable assistance with the preparation of some of the graphs and tables, and Ann Widdop did an excellent job of keyboarding the manuscript.

M. Hashem Pesaran
Ron Smith
Takamasa Akiyama

March 1997, Revised August 1997, and April 1998
Cambridge, London and Washington D.C.

0.1 Glossary

0.1.1 Sectors

IT: Industrial
TT: Transport
RE: Residential
CO: Commercial, Public and Agriculture

0.1.2 Fuels

CL: Coal
EL: Electricity
NG: Natural Gas
PP: Petroleum Products

See Section 3.2 for more detail

0.1.3 Key Variables

E_{fsit}: Total Energy demand for fuel f in sector s of country i in year t
POP_{it}: Population in country i year t
e_{fsit}: Per-capita energy demand ($= E_{fsit}/POP_{it}$)
P_{fit}: Price of fuel f in country i in year t
w_{fit}: Value share of fuel f in total value of energy consumption
y_{it}: Per-capita income in country i year t
CPI_{it}: Consumer Price Index
P_t^*: Foreign Price Index in domestic currency

0.1.4 Parameters and Operators

φ: Speed of adjustment, $\lambda = 1 - \varphi$
θ_j: Long-run coefficient variable j, for example for $j = y$, θ_y long-run income coefficient
Δ: First difference operator
∇: Deviation from year mean operators

0.1.5 Models Selection Criteria and Estimators etc.

AIC: Akaike Information Criterion
SBC: Schwarz Bayesian Criterion
ARDL(p, q_1, q_2): Autoregressive Distributed lag Model or order p on the dependent variable, q_1 on the first independent variable and q_2 on the second independent variable
DFE: Dynamic Fixed Effect Estimator
LL: Maximised Log Likelihood

LR: Likelihood Ratio test
MG: Mean Group estimator
OLS: Ordinary Least Squares estimator
PMG: Pooled Mean Group estimator
SBC: Schwarz Bayesian Criterion
SFE: Static Fixed Effect Estimator
SURE: Seemingly Unrelated Regression Estimator

CHAPTER 1

Introduction

The importance of research on energy demand in developing countries hardly needs emphasizing. Firstly, developing countries are playing an increasingly important role in the world energy markets. Their consumption of commercial energy has increased substantially over the past two decades. Excluding the former Soviet Union (FSU) and the Eastern European countries, the share of non-OECD countries in global energy consumption has increased from 16 per cent in 1971 to 29 per cent in 1993 (IEA, 1996).[1] This rising trend has been particularly pronounced amongst the developing countries of East and South-East Asia, and is likely to continue well into the next century despite the 1997 financial crisis in the region. The strength of future energy demand by developing countries will, however, depend on a host of factors such as expected income levels, real energy prices, and the speed with which there will be shifts towards energy-intensive activities due to factors such as urbanization and industrialization, increased motorization and use of electrical appliances by households, as well as the continued trend away from traditional non-commercial, for example biomass, energy sources to commercial fuels. The trend in energy consumption in the developing economies is likely to be particularly strong in the case of petroleum and electricity because of the expected rapid growth in personal and commercial transport needs and further electrification of production and consumption activities in these economies.

Secondly, the growing concern over the environment and the global nature of the environmental problems has focused attention on the pattern and the trend of energy demand in the developing economies. More than one-half of the total carbon dioxide emissions currently originates in the energy sector and a large and increasing share of the flow will be from the developing economies. The share of non-OECD (excluding FSU and the Eastern European countries) in global emissions of carbon dioxide is projected to increase from 33 per cent in 1993 to around 45 per cent by 2010, while the share of OECD is expected to decline from 50 per cent to 42 per cent over the same period (IEA, 1996).[2] For example, with capital being scarce and the highly-polluting indigenous coal in

---

[1] A useful descriptive review of the sectoral trends in energy demand in developing countries over the period 1978–1984 is given by Sathaye, Ghirardi and Schipper (1987).

[2] Also see Vouyoukas (1992).

1

abundant supplies in countries such as China and India, it seems almost certain that on present energy policies coal consumption in these economies will continue to rise substantially over the next decade, with important implications for the CO_2 emission abatement policies discussed at the Rio and Kyoto summits. A detailed analysis of energy demand and the possibilities of inter-fuel substitution in the major coal producing countries such as China and India is therefore of great importance both for a better understanding of the global environmental problems and the energy needs of these economies.

Thirdly, with volatile international energy markets and the threat of a possible further hike in oil prices on the horizon over the next two decades, domestic energy policy has once again become a top priority in many developing countries. The proposed research can also help provide a framework for the analysis of energy policy in developing countries. By identifying the main determinants of the pattern and the structure of energy demand in a number of key developing economies it is hoped that a deeper understanding of the issues surrounding the energy policy in developing countries can be achieved.

Finally, the increasing importance of the share of developing economies in the global energy markets also means that economic growth and the energy and environmental policies taken in these economies will most likely have a significant impact on world prices of primary energies and the global environment. A fuller and more detailed understanding of the trends of energy demand in developing economies is clearly of crucial importance in obtaining more reliable forecasts of international energy prices and demands at the world level.

1.1   An Overview of the Literature

In spite of the importance of the above issues, there exists only a very limited number of studies on the structure and characteristics of energy demand in developing economies. Most studies of energy demand are confined to OECD countries, where the required data are more readily available. The books by Pindyck (1979) and Griffin (1979) represent good examples of the early work carried out on energy demand. Both books focus on the experience of industrialized countries, although Pindyck also presents some estimates of energy demand obtained using data from a few less developed countries. These studies give only very limited attention to the problem of dynamic adjustments of energy demand to income and price changes, and by pooling the data from different countries and time periods implicitly assume a high degree of homogeneity of behaviour across these economies; an assumption which seems to be less warranted as far as the developing countries are concerned. A reasonably comprehensive review of this early literature is given by Bohi (1981). More recent reviews can be found in the two edited volumes by Hawdon (1992) and

Barker *et al.* (1995). Watkins (1992) presents a wide ranging review of energy demand modelling over the past two decades, but does not have much to say on the topic of energy demand in developing countries. The more recent survey of international energy elasticities by Atkinson and Manning (1995) provides a comprehensive summary of over 30 different studies of energy demand carried out over the past two decades. Once again the bulk of these studies are concerned with energy demand in industrialized countries.

The few studies of energy demand in developing countries that are available are primarily concerned with the identification of general trends in energy consumption and energy intensities possibly disaggregated by fuel types and sectors of economic activity. Prominent among these studies are the Sectoral Energy Demand Studies sponsored by UNDP, which employs the so-called "end-use" or "techno-economic" methodology. This approach relies on a high level of disaggregation of the sectoral energy demands and links the energy demand of each sector (regarded as homogeneous "modules") to a number of technical and economic indicators. It differs from the traditional econometric approach in two important respects. Firstly, it operates at a much finer level of disaggregation than is feasible using the econometric approach. Secondly, it relies on energy surveys, technical studies, energy audits and so on to calibrate the energy demand relations. A more detailed discussion of the relative merits and limitations of the two approaches to the modelling of energy demand is given in Chapter 3. In contrast, there are only a limited number of studies of energy demand in the developing countries that attempt a formal econometric analysis of responses of energy demand to changes in income, prices or the structure of output. These include the work of Uri (1979) on inter-fuel substitution and Williams and Laumas (1981) on energy and non-energy demands in the manufacturing sector in India, Igbal (1986) on capital energy substitution in the manufacturing sector of Pakistan, Siddayao *et al.* (1987) on energy demand in the food processing and textile industries in Bangladesh, Philippines and Thailand. The book by Siddayao (1985) also provides econometric estimates of the elasticities of energy demand for a certain number of the Asian countries and presents an interesting discussion of the main issues and problems involved in energy demand analysis in developing economies. Sterner (1989) studies energy demand in Mexican manufacturing. Ibrahim and Hurst (1990) estimate aggregate oil and energy demand functions for a selection of developing countries during the 1970s and early 1980s. Moss and Tybout (1992) and Guo and Tybout (1992) consider the problem of inter-fuel substitution in the Chilean and Colombian manufacturing sectors. Westley (1992) examines electricity demand in Latin America, focusing in particular on Costa Rica and Paraguay. More recently, Gately and Streifel (1996) also provide a detailed study of oil product demand in 37 developing countries. Useful surveys of oil demand elasticities and oil product demand elasticities for a number of developing countries are provided by Dahl (1993, 1994).

In analysing energy demand in developing countries a variety of different approaches have been employed. These have differed in method, ranging from those which relied primarily on time series econometric methods to those largely based on engineering information, as well as hybrid studies which have combined various approaches. The studies have also differed in the degree of disaggregation, by fuel or by the sector using the fuel, and in the countries that have been studied. Chateau and Lapillonne (1991) set out the main objections to the econometric approach. They argue that long reliable and consistent historical series are usually limited thus constraining the level of disaggregation and the choice of explanatory variables to that imposed by the existing statistical series. They also argue that estimated econometric parameters are not stable over time and that technical changes and in particular energy savings cannot be well reflected in econometric models. In this paper we examine the extent to which these problems can be addressed by the effective use of a panel of data. This raises a number of conceptual issues, particularly with regard to the appropriate way to apply econometric methods to diverse data: "to pool or not to pool?" We will address some of these methodological issues in this book.

The vast bulk of the studies have concentrated on the OECD countries and there have been fewer studies of other parts of the world. In particular, there have been relatively few studies of Asian countries. The studies that have been available, tend either to focus on a particular country or a particular fuel, e.g. electricity in Ishiguro and Akiyama (1995b), or a particular sector. The piecemeal approach has the disadvantage that it loses the insights that come from comparison of the results across countries, sectors and fuels. However, as was noted above the more comprehensive approach has been inhibited by the lack of consistent data at a disaggregated level across countries.

1.2   The Approach of this Study

This study presents the first comprehensive econometric analysis of energy demand in Asian developing economies using a consistent and comparable data set. Analysis of energy demand in Asia is particularly important for two reasons. First, this is a region of very rapid growth, by large countries, such as China, as well as smaller countries. This means that the individual countries have to take actions to ensure adequate energy supplies, it means that the world energy market must adjust to large new demands of indeterminate size and composition, and it has implications for the environment. Understanding and forecasting Asian energy demand is thus important to both national and global decision makers. The second reason is that the Asian countries are very diverse ranging from rich industrialized countries like Korea, which recently joined the OECD, to very poor rural countries like Bangladesh. Their differences are economic, political, demographic, geographic and historical.

Notwithstanding this diversity in experience, it is interesting to ask how much similarity or commonality there is in the responses of these countries to aspects of their economic environment. In particular, we will be interested in how similar the responses of their energy demands are to income and prices. If there is considerable similarity behind the diversity, this is not only interesting in its own right, but it improves the precision with which we can estimate these responses and it improves the predictions we can make for countries such as China for whom we have limited and relatively poor data. The degree and nature of any similarities or homogeneities is of course central to the methodological issue we raised above, "to pool or not to pool".

In this study we employ recently developed econometric methods for the analysis of dynamic heterogeneous panel data models to investigate the pattern and structure of energy demand in ten Asian developing economies, namely Bangladesh, India, Indonesia, South Korea, Malaysia, Pakistan, Philippines, Sri Lanka, Taiwan and Thailand. The choice of these countries is based on their importance in energy consumption, and data availability.[3] The share of these countries in the world commercial energy consumption has increased from 9.2 per cent in 1981 to 13.4 per cent in 1991, and in 1991 they account for almost half of the total commercial energy consumption of the non-OECD countries (see Table 2.1). There are also important and interesting differences among these economies in their pattern of energy consumption by fuels and by sectors of economic activity. In India the share of industry in total energy consumption is well over 50 per cent, while in Indonesia and the Republic of Korea, shares of industry, transport and residential sectors broadly speaking are very similar. Finally, coal is the predominant source of primary energy in India, while in the other countries it is mainly petroleum products.

Our econometric analysis is based on a consistent and comparative time series data, disaggregated by activity and type of fuel and which uses the theoretically appropriate measures of income and price. This data set, which was specially constructed for the project, allows the investigation of a range of questions that have not been covered in the literature.[4] The most important of these is the extent of heterogeneity in energy demand across countries: the importance of the differences in the effect of price and income across countries, sectors and fuels. Other panel data studies use pooled estimators which impose short-run as well as long-run homogeneity of price and income effects. This explicit treatment of heterogeneity allows us to identify common features in the data rather than impose them as existing studies tend to do. This study introduces a new econometric estimator (the pooled mean group estimator) which captures long-run features that may be homogeneous across countries,

---

[3] Originally we had also intended to include China in our sample, but were unable to do so due to lack of reliable time series data on energy prices. We do, however, examine trends in energy intensities in China.

[4] The database is described in Appendix A.

while allowing for possible heterogeneity in the short-run dynamics and error variances. Unlike most previous studies, the procedures used here can allow for completely general technological trends and coefficient heterogeneity (standard estimators can allow for one or the other) and provide valid estimates irrespective of whether the variables are trend-stationary or first-difference stationary. Therefore, the econometric issues concerning unit-roots and cointegration are fully taken into account.

At each level of aggregation, there are extensive specification searches over dynamics, explanatory variables and functional form for a variety of estimators. The study provides full results and extensive diagnostics. This transparent approach allows readers to select their preferred model on the basis of statistical and theoretical criteria. While such an approach is not uncommon in the analysis of a single time-series, to our knowledge it has never been applied to a large panel, because of the substantial technical difficulties involved. This study provides an illustration of how to overcome these difficulties.

The study shows that inter-fuel value-share demand functions, of the type commonly estimated, perform poorly for these countries, failing a variety of statistical tests and rejecting price homogeneity. This appears to be the result of the assumption, typically made in the literature, that income and prices are exogenous. This assumption is not required by the "long-run structural modelling" approach, which is also used. This approach provides estimates of the inter-fuel demand functions which both have good statistical properties and are consistent with the consumer demand theory.

The study evaluates the alternative models on the basis of forecasts for four years of data which were not used at the estimation stage. While forecast evaluation on single time-series is not uncommon, application to large panels is rare. It provides detailed forecasts to the year 2015 based on forecasts of the exogenous variables provided by international organizations in the summer of 1997. Again because of the transparent approach, the detailed documentation allows readers to easily construct alternative forecasts.

1.3   Outline and Summary

This study is in three parts. Part I discusses measurement issues and reviews the trends in energy intensities in the eleven Asian developing countries over the period 1973–1990. Part II reviews the theoretical and econometric issues and Part III gives the empirical results. The data and a Gauss program for pooled mean group estimation are provided on disk.

Chapter 2 discusses measurement issues and presents the data. A major contribution of the project was the construction of an energy databank for Asian developing countries covering eleven countries over the period 1971–1992.

The central part of the databank is a consistent set of energy balances disaggregated by fuel and use and a detailed set of prices also disaggregated by fuel and type of use. In addition there are a set of activity measures. At an aggregate level these include GDP measured at international prices. For the industrial sector they include the index of industrial production, value added and wage data. For the transport sector they include various measures of travel and freight activity. Not all data are available for all countries for all years, in particular data on prices are lacking for China and most of the econometric analysis is confined to ten countries. All the empirical analysis focuses on final energy consumption, rather than energy supply, i.e. it excludes energy used to generate energy. The chapter presents measures of energy use per capita and energy intensity (the energy–GDP ratio) for these countries and compares them to the OECD countries. The energy intensity measure uses GDP at international prices which avoids the problems associated with energy intensities relative to GDP at national prices. The general pattern is great stability in energy intensities within countries, unlike OECD countries where energy intensities fell and growth in per-capita energy use has been modest, but there are quite large variations between these Asian countries. Per-capita energy use is growing rapidly in all of these countries.

Part II of the book, presents the economic and econometric methodology used to analyse the data. Chapter 3 reviews the economic theory of consumer demand and the special problems involved in applying it to energy demand. One of the important issues is the appropriate response to cases where there is a conflict between the theoretically desirable specification and the data. Chapter 4 examines the dynamic specification of energy demand equations and explains the Autoregressive Distributed Lag (ARDL) model that is largely used in this report. Chapter 5 discusses alternative methods for pooling the data. The data available in this case, a panel of data on energy demand for ten countries over 18 years, allow us to examine the similarities and differences between countries. In this report we introduce a new estimator, the Pooled Mean Group estimator, which makes long-run slope coefficients the same across countries, but which allows short-run slope coefficients, intercepts and error variances to differ across countries. This provides a compromise between allowing every coefficient to differ across countries and constraining all coefficients other than the intercept to be the same. The chapter also discusses methods of allowing for a completely general technological trend by demeaning the data.

Part III contains the empirical analysis of the data for 1973–1990, which were the latest available when the project started. Chapter 6 examines the aggregate data. Chapter 7 examines the data disaggregated into four sectors: industry, transport, residential and commercial (which includes agriculture and public). Chapter 8 examines the data disaggregated into three fuels: petroleum products, electricity and the total of natural gas and coal consumption. Chapter 9 examines the data for four major industries, namely chemicals, iron and steel, non-metallic minerals and paper, pulp and printing, which together account for the bulk of energy consumption in the industrial sector of the economies in the region. In each case a range of alternative specifications are considered in terms of alternative functional forms, dynamic specifications and possible explanatory variables. In addition, in each case individual country-specific estimates are provided as well as a range of alternative pooled estimators.

This comprehensive analysis produces a very wide range of detailed results. The most notable results are as follows. Average estimates, i.e. for the region as a whole, tend to be very sensible and often quite robust to alternative specifications. At the aggregate level they suggest an elasticity of about 1.2 with respect to per-capita GDP and an elasticity of about −0.3 with respect to energy prices. However, there is very substantial heterogeneity across countries and it is difficult to determine the extent to which countries are really different and the extent to which the small sample available and poor quality data are making the estimates for particular countries unreliable. Price elasticities tend to be negative in most countries and for most sectors, with the averages or pooled estimates giving sensible results.

This heterogeneity in national estimates is a common feature of every level of disaggregation. As one moves to more disaggregated data, there seems to be more noise in the data and the precision of the estimates reduces. There is some indication that price elasticities are larger at disaggregated levels but they are not very precisely determined. At the sectoral levels GDP elasticities differ, substantially across sectors and countries, with no obvious pattern. However the average is somewhat above unity, and thus consistent with the aggregate results. At the more detailed industrial level, elasticities with respect to industrial production seem to be below unity. The higher GDP elasticity is thus probably reflecting the growing share of those sectors in GDP.

In the analysis of the value shares of individual fuels in total energy demand a traditional vector partial adjustment model gave very poor results, with most countries rejecting homogeneity of degree zero in prices. This seemed to be a consequence of the inappropriate assumption of exogeneity of total energy demand and fuel prices. When the long-run structural parameters of the fuel share equations were estimated from a cointegrating vector autoregressive (VAR) model which treated all the variables as endogenous, much better results were obtained with price homogeneity and symmetry being accepted in almost all countries. The results suggested that for the low income countries electricity and petroleum products did not substitute much with each other, but that both tended to substitute with other fuels, i.e. coal and natural gas. Coal and natural gas use are largely determined by supply features, in particular availability of indigenous resources. For the more industrialized countries there was evidence of substitution between electricity and petroleum products.

Chapter 10 evaluates the models by out of sample forecasts for 1991–1994, which were not used in estimation, and provides forecasts of energy demand till the year 2015 using summer 1997 forecasts from international organizations for output and energy prices. We are primarily interested in forecasting aggregate demand for each of these countries and the region as a whole. In forecasting an aggregate, one has a choice between forecasting using the estimates for the dis-aggregate categories and aggregating the forecasts or forecasting using the estimates for the aggregate equation. In general, there is no presumption that one method is better than the other. In this case, given the greater noise in the disaggregate data and the heterogeneity of some of the disaggregate results, it seemed better to forecast using the aggregate equations. Two sets of forecasts are presented. One uses the individual country estimates, the other uses Pooled Mean Group estimates which impose common long-run elasticities, but allow short-run coefficients, intercepts and error variances to differ across countries. The models predict the data for 1991–1994 quite well. In only one country, the Philippines, is predictive failure significant. The PMG model pre-dicts somewhat better than the country-specific model, and the dynamic PMG forecast for total demand in these ten countries is quite close to the actual figure for 1994. The longer-term forecasts suggest that on plausible assump-tions about growth the average per-capita energy consumption in the region will double between 1994 and 2005 and double again between 2005 and 2015. Since these forecasts were constructed growth in some of the countries has been disrupted by the financial crisis that began in the late summer of 1997. However, we believe that given the fundamentals in these countries, this shock will be transitory and that our long-term forecasts for the region as a whole remain valid.

The final chapter draws conclusions and policy implications. The policy implications are quite stark. The detailed examination of the evidence suggests that the average GDP elasticity is over unity, around 1.2, and the average price elasticity is quite small, around −0.3. Given the high growth rates of these countries these estimates suggest that demand is likely to grow rapidly and that it would require implausible increases in national energy prices to restrain it to any significant extent. While the estimates for individual countries are more uncertain, what matters for the global energy market and the global environment is the average for the region as a whole.

Part I

Data and Measurement Problems

CHAPTER 2

Measurement Issues and Energy Use

2.1 Introduction

Long time series of consistent and comparable data on energy demands and supplies are essential both for estimating reliable econometric energy models and for developing appropriate energy policies. In this chapter we first describe a new energy databank that we have constructed for eleven developing Asian countries. This databank covers energy balances of all the major Asian developing economies over the period 1970–1993, together with real energy prices, and comparable measures of economic activity needed for estimation of income and price elasticities by econometric techniques. The databank can be accessed in a user-friendly manner, and could be an important resource for empirical analysis of energy demand and supplies in Asia.

This chapter also discusses the difficulties involved in measurement of energy intensities and real energy prices for the purpose of cross-country comparisons. We avoid problems associated with cross-country comparisons of energy intensities by using real output series from Penn World Tables which are computed using international prices (see Summers and Heston (1991)). Using these measures we show that there has been little change in energy intensities across the eleven Asian economies over the period 1973–1990, with Bangladesh having the lowest energy intensity and China followed by Korea the highest. In contrast, the energy use per capita in these economies has increased substantially since 1973, despite the significant increases in energy prices.

To deal with the cross-country comparability of real energy prices, we shall consider two different measures of real energy prices. A standard measure defined as the ratio of domestic energy prices to a general price index (such as the CPI), and a supplementary measure defined as the ratio of domestic energy prices in US dollars relative to the general level of prices in the US (taken to be the foreign price level). Under the Purchasing Power Parity hypothesis these relative price measures are perfectly correlated, but in general they capture different aspects of the substitution process between energy, non-energy domestic goods and non-energy imports.

The plan of this chapter is as follows. The next section describes the energy databank. Section 2.3 discusses the particular data set to be used in this study.

13

Section 2.4 deals with the issues that arise in cross-country comparisons of energy intensities and real energy prices. Section 2.5 provides an over-view of the trends in energy intensities in Asian economies and a number of selected OECD countries over the period 1973–1990.

2.2 Energy Databank for Asian Developing Economies

This databank was produced as part of the World Bank research project Energy Demand in Asian Developing Economies: Structure, Trends, Impacts, Prospects and Strategies. The details of the databank, its sources, and how it can be accessed is described in Appendix A. Here a brief overview is provided.

2.2.1 Content of the Databank

The databank consists of three main modules: *Energy Balances, Energy Prices,* and *Activity Measures.* Each module contains annual observations over the period 1970–1993 for the following eleven countries:[1]

Bangladesh (BGD)   Pakistan (PAK)
China (CHA)   Philippines (PHI)
India (IND)   Sri Lanka (LKA)
Indonesia (IDN)   Taiwan (TWN)
South Korea (KOR)   Thailand (THA)
Malaysia (MYS)

2.2.2 Energy Balances

This module provides consistent energy balances, disaggregated by fuel types, sources of supply and end use, measured in thousand Tons of Oil Equivalent (TOE). The method of conversion from original units to TOE is described in IEA(1996). See the data sources.

The Fuels included are the relevant country-specific subset of: Coal, Crude oil, Petroleum products, Gas, Nuclear, Hydro/other, electricity, and total energy. The sources of supply which make up Total Primary Energy Supply include: Indigenous production, Imports, Exports, International Marine Bunkers, and Stock changes. Total Primary Energy Supply is then related to Total Final Consumption by taking account of the use of energy in the energy producing industries. Total Final Energy Consumption is then broken down into use by fuel by the Agriculture, Industry, Transport, Public, Commercial and Residential Sectors. The Transport and Industrial sectors are further disaggregated in the case of some countries.

---

[1]Energy prices are not available for China.

2.2.3 Energy Prices and Consumer Price Indices

The energy price component of the databank contains time series data for the individual countries (excluding China) on the prices of various fuels in both local currency per TOE and real local currency per TOE. This list of prices differs depending on the range of products available in each country. It includes average energy prices, electricity, coal/anthracite, natural/town gas, oil products and disaggregated oil products such as gasoline, diesel, kerosene, fuel oil.

2.2.4 Activity or Output Measures

The activity data consist of sectorally disaggregated data on:

The Index of Industrial Production;
Value Added in Current Prices;
Value Added in Constant Prices;
The Wage Bill.

The sectoral disaggregation is based on the ISIC and the match to the energy balance data is described in Appendix A.

There are also various measures of activity for the transport sector, such as number of passengers disaggregated by different modes of transport (road, rail, air and sea), number of passenger miles travelled etc. These measures are available only for some countries, over short periods, and are not used in this study.

2.2.5 National Product

The full Penn World Tables, described in Summers and Heston (1991) is also supplied as a part of the energy databank for convenience. This module provides annual observations on GDP and its components at international prices, population and exchange rates.

2.3 Data Used in this Study

The variable we are interested in explaining and predicting in the present study is final energy consumption measured in Tons of Oil Equivalent (TOE). This will usually be divided by population to give a per-capita series and since it is measured in physical units it is comparable across countries. Particular economies can then be compared in terms of their energy intensities: the ratio of total energy consumption to GDP. The measurement of energy consumption is relatively straightforward, since there are natural physical units; though there are difficulties both in establishing coefficients of equivalence between fuels and with the implicit assumption that it is the energy content that is the defining characteristic of a fuel. In many cases fuels differ in other characteristics than their energy content, which makes them poor substitutes. In some cases the data supplied in the energy databank had to be adjusted. For example, the Bangladesh 1990 figure for energy consumption recorded in the databank is very low, because natural gas consumption by industry is entered as zero, although there seems no apparent interruption in natural gas supplies. We adjusted the data by interpolation at a sectoral level: setting natural gas residential demand to 261, public and commercial to 72, chemical industry to 1345.1 and other industries to 400. These numbers make total demand equal total supply for natural gas in 1990. This example indicates the value of the disaggregated information for cross-checking.

Since there were no energy price data for China we were forced to confine our econometric analysis to the ten remaining countries. For the purpose of cross-country comparability we also decided to work with a balanced panel and used the common time period 1973–1990 for all the ten countries where we had a complete set of time series data on energy use, output and prices.

Given the potential importance of the aggregation problem in the analysis of energy demand we shall also use data disaggregated by four major sectors:

Industrial (IT);
Transport (TT);
Residential (RE);
Commercial (CO);[2]

and four fuel types:

Coal (CL);
Electricity (EL);
Natural Gas (NG);
Petroleum Products (PP).

We shall denote the total final energy consumption by TC. The set of data series and their mnemonics for each country are:

Fuels		Coal	Electricity	Natural gas	Petroleum products	Total
Sectors		*CL*	*EL*	*NG*	*PP*	*TO*
Industrial	*IT*	*CLIT*	*ELIT*	*NGIT*	*PPIT*	*TOIT*
Transport	*TT*	*CLTT*	*ELTT*		*PPTT*	*TOTT*
Residential	*RE*	*CLRE*	*ELRE*	*NGRE*	*PPRE*	*TORE*
Commercial	*CO*	*CLCO*	*ELCO*	*NGCO*	*PPCO*	*TOCO*
Total	*TC*	*CLTC*	*ELTC*	*NGTC*	*PPTC*	*TOTC*
Real energy prices	*RP*	*CLRP*	*ELRP*	*NGRP*	*PPRP*	*AERP*

---

[2] This is a residual category and also includes energy use in the public and agricultural sectors.

AERP is average real energy price, in local currency per TOE deflated by the CPI, similarly for the fuels. Natural Gas is not used for transport anywhere. There is another category, non-energy use of petroleum products, mainly used as feedstocks for the chemical sector. This is included in PPTC and TOTC, but not in the sectoral figures. This category is of importance only in Taiwan and Korea.

Other variables used in this study are *RGDPL*, real GDP per capita in international prices, *POP* population, *EX* the spot exchange rate against the U.S. dollar, each of these is taken from the PWT and *CPI*, the consumer price index for the particular country and *CPIUS*, the US CPI.

We will denote total energy demand by upper case, *E*, and per-capita energy demand with lower case. Thus the per-capita energy demand data are four dimensional, with typical element e_{fsit} energy demand in country i ($i = 1, 2, \ldots, 10$); for year t, $t = 1973 \ldots 1990$; for fuel f, $f = 1(CL)$, $2(EL)$, $3(NG)$, $4(PP)$; for sector s, $s = 1(IT)$, $2(TT)$, $3(RE)$, $4(CO)$. We will denote aggregates by dropping the appropriate subscript; so $e_{fit} = \sum_{s=1}^{4} e_{fsit}$ is total per-capita energy consumption in country i in year t for fuel f aggregated over all sectors, e_{sit} is total per-capita consumption for sector s aggregated over fuels and e_{it} is total per-capita energy consumption of country i in year t aggregated over all fuels and sectors. When we use averages rather than aggregates, they will be denoted by a bar. The original price data is 3 dimensional with the typical element, P_{fit}, but we can construct indices for each sector, P_{sit}, by appropriate weighting of prices of fuels used in the sector under consideration.

2.4 Measurement Issues

2.4.1 Measures of Energy Use

The measure of energy use that we will be concerned with is the total final consumption of "modern" energy in a country, i.e. it excludes "traditional" biomass based sources of energy. The alternative measure of modern energy use is total primary energy supplies. The difference between them is determined by the nature of the power generation and distribution system. The OECD, for instance, uses the supply based measure to estimate energy intensities. Since these countries differ very substantially in the nature of their power generation and distribution systems, it seems better to focus on demand.

2.4.2 Output Measures

The measurement of GDP raises much more fundamental difficulties than the measurement of energy consumption. Because relative price structures differ across countries, identical physical activities (e.g. production of a particular amount of steel) will contribute different amounts to different countries'

GDPs. The best way to avoid this problem is to measure the volume of production in a common set of "international prices". This is the procedure that we have adopted and our GDP measure is the estimate in international prices from the Penn World Table. Energy intensities calculated using these measures of GDP avoid the effects of variations in relative prices on output. Since this series is in international prices, it is comparable across countries. For the measurement of energy intensity, the PWT measure of GDP in international prices is appropriate. However, it should be noted that the PWT measure of GDP does not correspond to the measure that would appear in the national budget constraint and this has implications for the measurement of value shares that we discuss below.

2.4.3   Real Energy Prices

The basic price data in the databank is the nominal price in local currency for a TOE of a particular fuel. The prices are provided at a quite detailed level of disaggregation by fuel as well as there being an average energy price for each country. Even at a disaggregated level, there is a degree of approximation because prices for the same fuel may differ over activities (e.g. industrial and residential costs of electricity will differ); because non-proportional pricing (e.g. a two part tariff) is common for energy; and because prices may differ by location. A number of prices were missing in the databank. Coal prices were completely missing for Sri Lanka and average energy prices were used instead. For a number of other countries (Indonesia till 1983, Malaysia till 1982, Pakistan till 1979 and Thailand till 1982), coal prices were missing for some years, and for those years average energy prices were used, scaled by the ratio of coal to average energy prices in the first year for which there were data on both. When Natural Gas prices were not available, either LPG, Propane or Butane prices were used.

Thus the basic prices we have are those for the four fuels, $P_{itf}, f = 1, 2, 3, 4$ and the average energy prices given in the databank, P_{it}. Two measurement issues arise. Firstly what are the appropriate relative prices for energy as compared to alternative goods and secondly what are the appropriate energy price indices to construct. Consider the first of these. The local currency price per TOE needs to be deflated by a domestic price index to give a constant price series. The deflator we have available is the Consumer Price Index, CPI_{it}. We will denote relative series, e.g. deflated by the CPI in lower case, thus $p_{it} = P_{it}/CPI_{it}$. This is likely to be an inadequate measure of the range of alternatives that are substitutes for energy either in consumption or the production process. In particular, it is likely to underestimate the role of traded goods. Thus one would expect that demand would also be sensitive to the price of energy relative to the domestic price of foreign products $P_{it}^* = EX_{it} \times USCPI_t$, the product of the exchange rate for the currency of country i per US dollar times the US CPI.

The second real energy price is thus $p_{it}^* = P_{it}/P_{it}^*$. In the empirical work we include both relative prices for energy (namely, p_{it} and p_{it}^*), which in terms of the theory discussed in Chapter 3, can be interpreted as total expenditures being allocated amongst three categories of goods: energy, non-energy domestic goods and non-energy imported goods.

There are a number of different ways that energy price indices can be constructed for aggregate or sectoral demands. At the aggregate level one could use the average energy prices, P_{it}, supplied in the databank. But there are no corresponding sectoral price indices available in the databank. A simple alternative procedure would be to construct implicit unit values both at the aggregate and the disaggregated levels. At the aggregate level the relevant unit energy values are given by:

$$P_{it}^u = \sum_{f=1}^{4} P_{fit}E_{fit}/E_{it},$$

and at the sectoral levels they are given by:

$$P_{sit}^u = \sum_{f=1}^{4} P_{fsit}E_{fsit}/E_{sit}.$$

The aggregate unit value should be close to the average energy price. Other possibilities are Stone price indices which are constructed as weighted geometric means of the different fuel prices. The Current Stone index uses value share weights from the current year:

$$\ln(P_{it}^c) = \sum_{f=1}^{4} w_{fit} \ln P_{fit},$$

in the case of the aggregate; and the Moving Stone index uses the average value share weights for the previous two years:

$$\ln(P_{it}^m) = \sum_{f=1}^{4} [(w_{fi,t-1} + w_{fi,t-2})/2] \ln P_{fit},$$

where $w_{fit} = P_{fit}E_{fit}/\sum_{f=1}^{4} P_{fit}E_{fit}$. Similar indices can be constructed for the sectors.

The logarithm of the Stone index is the weighted average of the logarithms of the prices for four fuels (petroleum products, coal, electricity and natural gas), with the weights being value shares in total expenditure on fuel. Since the prices are used to form the weights in the index, the value shares, errors in the levels of prices may bias the movement of the index over time. In constructing a price index, one has to trade off two features. The weights should be relatively stable, otherwise price and quantity changes get intertwined, and at the same time the weights should accurately reflect the consumption patterns of the consumers over the period under consideration. These two criteria tend to conflict. The Current Stone index, uses the value shares in the current year. The Moving Stone index uses the average share over the previous two years, with the shares in the first two years set at the weights in the first year. This has the advantage that it avoids problems of endogeneity; the weights are smoother, changing less than the current year weights; and the indices can be generated recursively for forecasting.

At an aggregate level we investigated the differences between the various price indices by estimating fixed effect dynamic regressions of the form:

$$\Delta \ln p_{jit} = \alpha_i + \beta \Delta \ln p_{0it} + \gamma (\ln p_{jit-1} - \ln p_{0it-1}) + \delta \ln p_{0it-1} + u_{it},$$
$$i = 1, \ldots, N; \quad t = 1, \ldots, T \tag{2.1}$$

where p_{0it} is the price series from the databank deflated by the CPI (P_{it}/CPI_{it}) and p_{jit} is another relative price series, for example the unit energy values or the two Stone price indices discussed above. The use of the two price series, p_{0it} and p_{jit}, in estimation of energy demand equations will result in similar long-run estimates if $\delta = 0$, $\gamma \neq 0$ and the regression fits reasonably well. When these conditions are met the two price series will be proportional in the long run and could be used as proxies for one another. For the real unit value series, the t-ratio of δ was -0.41, and the regression had $\bar{R}^2 = 0.977$. For the real current Stone index the equation $\bar{R}^2 = 0.926$ and the t-ratio on δ was 0.38. For the real moving Stone index the regression's $\bar{R}^2$ was 0.943 and the t-ratio on δ was -0.169. Thus there seem to be relatively little differences between these three price measures at an aggregate level. However, when the same procedure was applied to energy prices relative to foreign prices: $P_{it}/(EX_{it} \times USCPI_t)$, we obtained $\bar{R}^2 = 0.714$ and the t-ratio on $\delta = -7.01$.

In practice, changing the weights makes relatively little difference in most cases. This is primarily because most of the energy prices tend to move together, so that even the large variations in the weights that occur make little difference to the index. Were relative price movements more extreme, this would not be the case. The fact that there is little variation in relative prices will however make it difficult to measure inter-fuel substitution.

The relative price that matters to an individual decision-maker is the local currency price of energy relative to the local currency prices of all other goods and this is what the constant price series measures. However this is not comparable across countries. This does not matter for individual time series for each country, but it does matter when the data are pooled or run in cross-section. If the logarithm of the relative price is used any constant currency conversion factor will be picked up by the intercept in country-specific or fixed effect models. In cross-section regressions we use the exchange rate for a single year or the average over the sample to convert all the prices into a common currency measure. Clearly the choice of exchange rate is arbitrary and the results will be sensitive to the year chosen, but it seems impossible to avoid this problem.

2.4.4   Share of Energy Use in Output

The theoretical model discussed in Chapter 3 suggests that the appropriate dependent variable in a model determining the demand for energy and all other goods is the value share of energy in *GDP*. This was constructed as the ratio of real expenditure on energy to total real GDP: (AERP × TOTC)/(POP × RGDPL). AERP is the average energy real price, the price of a *TOE* in domestic currency divided by the *CPI*. TOTC is total consumption in *TOE*. The product of these is divided by the product of population and per-capita *GDP*. The numerator is in domestic prices deflated by the *CPI* while the denominator is in constant international prices. Thus this is not a true share, since the denominator does not correspond to the measure in the national budget constraint. It should give a reasonable indication of the movement of the share over time, but it is not comparable across countries: all the coefficients in this equation will be scaled by the ratio of national to international constant prices. Unlike traditional logarithmic equations, where only the intercept is affected by such scale effects, in value share equations all coefficients are affected.

2.5   Trends in Energy Intensities

Table 2.1 gives per-capita *GDP*, per-capita energy demand and energy intensity, measured as the ratio of energy consumption to *GDP*, for each of the eleven Asian countries in our sample over the 1973 and 1990 period. Table 2.2 gives the same data for a selection of *OECD* countries. In the Asian sample, the range of initial incomes is very large, with four countries under $1,000 and three countries over $2,000. Although it is not shown in Table 2.1, there is also a marked disparity in growth rates among the Asian countries over this period, ranging from 0.82 to 6.9 per cent per annum. Compared to the *OECD* countries, the Asian sample initially showed much lower amounts of per-capita energy consumption. However, by 1990 Taiwan and Korea were close to Italy in per-capita energy consumption. It is clear from the *OECD* figures that climate has an important effect, with colder countries tending to have higher per-capita energy consumption. Most of the differences between per-capita energy consumption in Asian and *OECD* countries, however, are accounted for by differences in per-capita income. The differences in energy intensities across countries are, however, much less than in per-capita energy consumptions. The energy intensities (measured in *TOE* per 10,000 US dollars) seem to be positively related to per-capita income, but this relationship is not very strong over the combined group of Asian and *OECD* countries. Plots of energy intensity

Table 2.1: Per-capita income, per-capita energy consumption and energy intensities in Asian developing countries.

Country	Per-capita income[1]		Per-capita energy consumption[2]		Energy intensities[3]	
	1973	1990	1973	1990	1973	1990
Bangladesh	759	1,390	0.02	0.04	0.21	0.30
China	740	1,324	0.24	0.44	3.26	3.34
India	786	1,262	0.09	0.14	1.14	1.13
Indonesia	833	1,973	0.06	0.18	0.78	0.93
Korea	2,063	6,665	0.54	1.64	2.60	2.47
Malaysia	2,559	5,117	0.33	0.75	1.30	1.47
Pakistan	907	1,394	0.09	0.17	1.02	1.20
Philippines	1,532	1,761	0.17	0.16	1.12	0.91
Sri Lanka	1,252	2,096	0.09	0.09	0.68	0.42
Taiwan	2,912	8,067	0.66	1.64	2.28	2.04
Thailand	1,652	3,570	0.17	0.37	1.06	1.04

[1] Per-capita income in 1985 International $, Laspeyres Index, Source: Penn World Tables.
[2] Per-capita final energy consumption in TOE per 1000 people.
[3] Energy intensity in TOE per 10,000 US $.

Table 2.2: Per-capita income, per-capita energy consumption and energy intensities in selected OECD countries.

Country	Per-capita income[1]		Per-capita energy consumption[2]		Energy intensities[3]	
	1973	1990	1973	1990	1973	1990
US	14,356	18,073	6.34	5.39	4.41	2.98
Canada	11,852	17,179	6.10	6.12	5.15	3.56
Sweden	11,371	14,741	4.40	3.81	3.87	2.58
West Germany	10,318	14,331	4.04	3.97	3.92	2.77
Japan	8,537	14,317	2.35	2.50	2.75	1.75
France	10,312	13,896	2.74	2.54	2.65	1.83
UK	9,598	13,223	2.70	2.57	2.82	1.94
Italy	8,266	12,486	1.86	2.07	2.25	1.66
Greece	5,218	6,768	1.04	1.49	2.00	2.20
Mexico	4,609	5,825	0.84	1.16	1.81	1.99
Turkey	2,472	3,743	0.53	0.75	2.20	2.00

[1] Per-capita income in US $. Laspeyres index, 1985 international prices. Source: Penn World Tables.
[2] Energy intensities are TOE per 10,000 US $. Source: Penn World Tables and IEA Energy Balances.
[3] Per-capita energy consumption is TOE per 1000 people. Source: OECD IEA Energy Balances of OECD Countries 1993–1994, Paris 1996, p. 225 for Total Final Energy Consumption, Penn World Tables for population figures.

against per-capita income in 1973 and 1990 are given in Figures 2.1 and 2.2. The extreme outlier is China, which has an energy intensity of 3.3, similar to that of the rich countries, but with a per-capita income of the poor countries. In 1973, Turkey, Korea and Taiwan also had relatively high energy intensities, over 2, for their income, between $2,000 and $3,000. Whereas in 1973 there

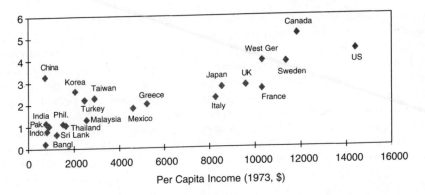

Figure 2.1: Scatter of energy intensities against per-capita income in 1973.

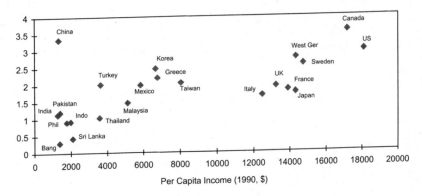

Figure 2.2: Scatter of energy intensities against per-capita income in 1990.

appears to be a single relationship over the sample, by 1990 there are clearly two separate relationships, with the same slope but different intercepts. Countries with income over $10,000 have lower energy intensities than one would expect from extrapolating the relationship from low income countries.

In 1973, most developing Asian countries had energy intensities close to unity. The exceptions are Bangladesh with an energy intensity of 0.2 on one extreme, and China with an energy intensity of around 3.3 on the other extreme. Taiwan and Korea also had relatively high energy intensities (2.28 and 2.60, respectively), partly reflecting their higher per-capita income, and the more industrial structure of these economies. By contrast the rural structure of Bangladesh, where traditional biomass sources of energy are more important as energy sources than traditional fuels, could explain the rather low energy intensity. The high energy intensity of China is more difficult to explain and could be due to difficulties of measuring output in a centrally planned economy, and the fact that China's industrial structure had been biased towards heavy industry, combined with inefficient energy use. Over the period to 1990, most countries reduced their energy intensities, the exceptions in the Asian sample were Indonesia, Malaysia, Pakistan and Bangladesh though the latter still had by far the lowest energy intensity. In most cases the changes were not very large, although Malaysia was tending to rise more. Thus one gets the impression of energy intensities being relatively stable over this period, largely determined by country-specific factors, such as the sectoral composition of output (see Figure 2.3). This relative stability of energy intensities in the Asian economies is in marked contrast to the OECD countries, where energy intensities fell more sharply over the period, falling in every country but Mexico (see Figure 2.4). So for instance while Japan had a much higher energy intensity than Korea or Taiwan at the beginning of the period, by the end of the period it had a much lower one.

The reduction in energy intensity in the rich countries is the result of a mix of factors including changes in industrial structure away from traditional energy-intensive heavy industry towards more information-intensive industries and increased energy efficiency in response to higher prices and as a result of

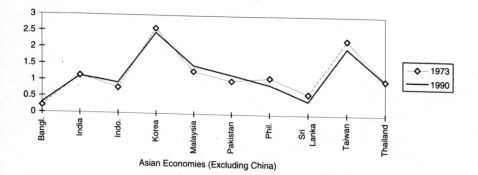

Figure 2.3:   Energy intensities in ten Asian economies – 1973 and 1990.

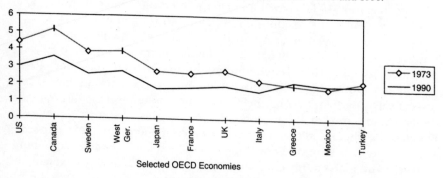

Figure 2.4:   Energy intensities in selected OECD economies – 1973 and 1990.

technological change. Over the period 1973–1990, real energy prices (relative to the CPI) rose in all of the ten Asian Developing countries for which we have data (see Figures 2.5a and 2.5b). They rose at more than 5 per cent a year in Bangladesh, Sri Lanka and the Philippines and by less than 2 per cent a year in Malaysia, Taiwan and Thailand. This average conceals substantial variations within the period. The typical pattern for the real energy price in these countries is to rise rapidly from 1973, then peak in the early to mid 1980s and then to fall substantially. The only exception to this pattern is India, where prices rose fairly steadily over the whole period. However, the large variation in price seems not to have had much impact on energy intensities.

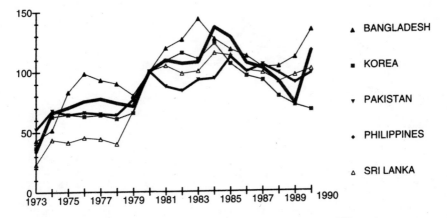

Figure 2.5a: Average real energy prices. (1980 = 100)

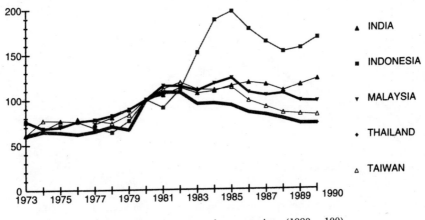

Figure 2.5b: Average real energy prices. (1980 = 100)

The movements of real energy prices by industrial sectors across the ten Asian countries are displayed in Figures 2.6–2.15. Generally speaking, and perhaps not surprisingly, real energy prices tend to follow similar patterns across the main industrial sectors. The exceptions are the industrial sector in the case of Indonesia and Sri Lanka, where since 1979 real energy prices have risen much faster in this sector as compared to the other sectors. The transport sector in Thailand also seems to be an outlier, in the sense that since 1971 real energy prices in Thailand's transportation sector have fallen quite sharply, while real energy prices in other sectors have remained relatively high.

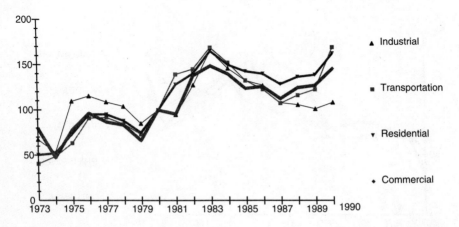

Figure 2.6:   Real energy Stone prices by industrial sector in Bangladesh. (1980 = 100)

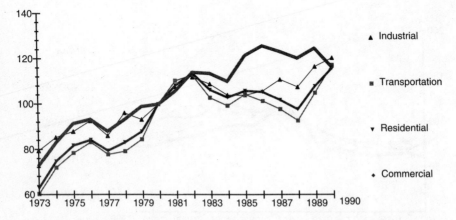

Figure 2.7:   Real energy Stone prices by industrial sector in India. (1980 = 100)

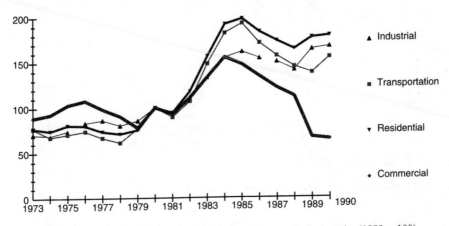

Figure 2.8: Real energy Stone prices by industrial sector in Indonesia. (1980 = 100)

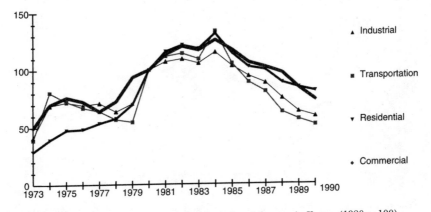

Figure 2.9: Real energy Stone prices by industrial sector in Korea. (1980 = 100)

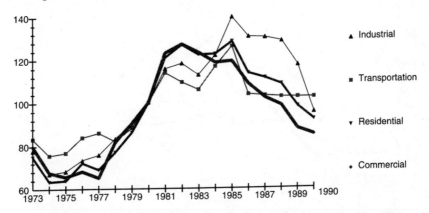

Figure 2.10: Real energy Stone prices by industrial sector in Malaysia. (1980 = 100)

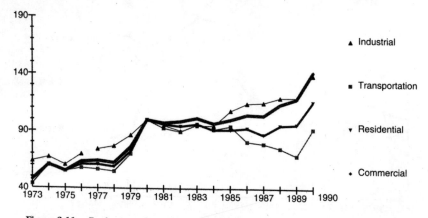

Figure 2.11: Real energy Stone prices by industrial sector in Pakistan. (1980 = 100)

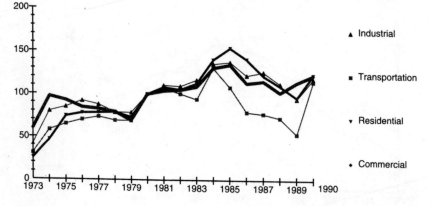

Figure 2.12: Real energy Stone prices by industrial sector in Philippines. (1980 = 100)

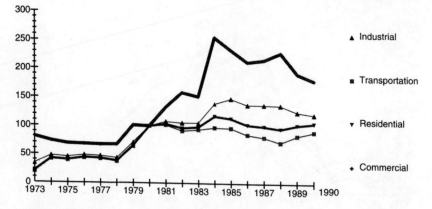

Figure 2.13: Real energy Stone prices by industrial sector in Sri Lanka. (1980 = 100)

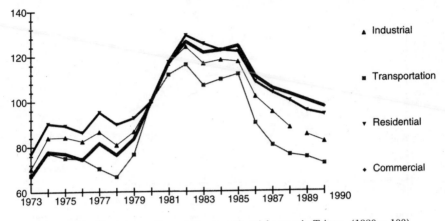

Figure 2.14: Real energy Stone prices by industrial sector in Taiwan. (1980 = 100)

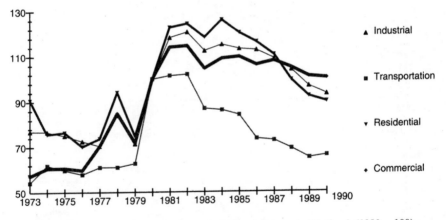

Figure 2.15: Real energy Stone prices by industrial sector in Thailand. (1980 = 100)

Figures 2.16–2.25 show the movement of real energy prices by fuel types across the different countries as well as the average real energy prices. In most countries electricity and petroleum prices tend to dominate the price movements of the other fuels. However, overall the fuel prices tend to move together.

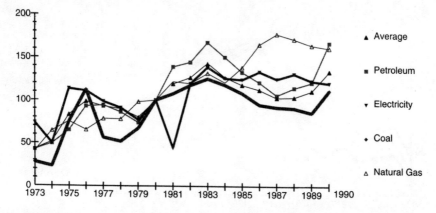

Figure 2.16:   Average and fuel specific real energy prices in Bangladesh. (1980 = 100)

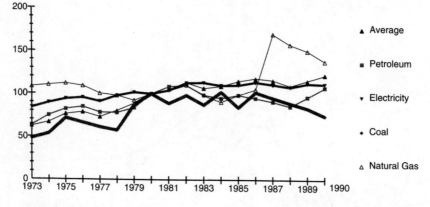

Figure 2.17:   Average and fuel specific real energy prices in India. (1980 = 100)

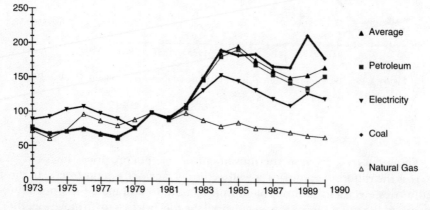

Figure 2.18:   Average and fuel specific real energy prices in Indonesia. (1980 = 100)

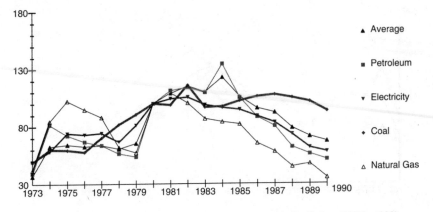

Figure 2.19:   Average and fuel specific real energy prices in Korea. (1980 = 100)

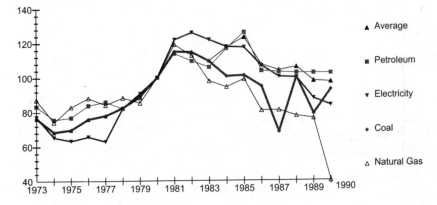

Figure 2.20:   Average and fuel specific real energy prices in Malaysia. (1980 = 100)

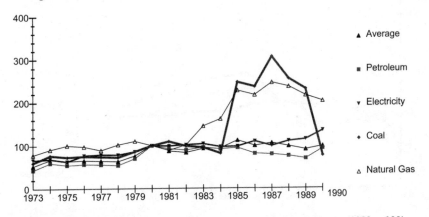

Figure 2.21:   Average and fuel specific real energy prices in Pakistan. (1980 = 100)

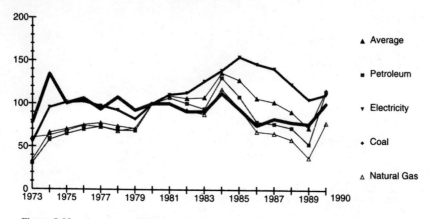

Figure 2.22: Average and fuel specific real energy prices in Philippines. (1980 = 100)

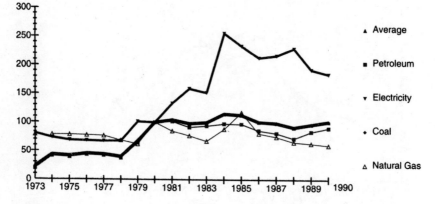

Figure 2.23: Average and fuel specific real energy prices in Sri Lanka. (1980 = 100)

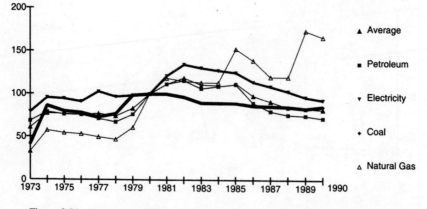

Figure 2.24: Average and fuel specific real energy prices in Taiwan. (1980 = 100)

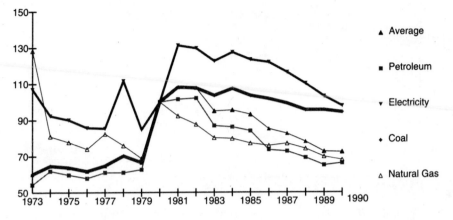

Figure 2.25: Average and fuel specific real energy prices in Thailand. (1980 = 100)

Countries differed in the degree of intra-period variations in energy intensity, with Bangladesh and Sri Lanka showing the most variation. The pattern of energy intensities by sector and fuel in each country is shown in Figures 2.26–2.47. In these figures for expositional clarity energy intensities are measured in TOE per 100,000 US dollars. The fuels are stacked starting with natural gas then coal, petroleum products and electricity, giving total energy intensity as the sum of the intensities of the four fuels. There are large differences between countries in the use of particular fuels. Typically petroleum products is the largest source of energy, though Bangladesh and Pakistan use a considerable amount of natural gas, India, South Korea and Taiwan a considerable amount of coal. The share of electricity is typically small, but has been growing steadily in all the countries.

The energy use by sectors is also displayed in a stacked form, starting with the industrial sector, followed by transportation, residential and commercial (including public and agriculture). What is striking from the graphs is that the relative importance of different sectors differs substantially across countries. In Bangladesh a very high proportion of energy demand comes from industry, though this reflects the low demand relative to GDP from the other sectors. Korea has a large, though falling, proportion from residential demand, Sri Lanka, Malaysia, Pakistan and Thailand a large proportion from transportation. However, although the variation across countries in the importance of the relative sectoral demands is large, the variation across time within countries is less marked.

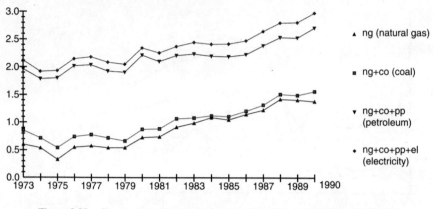

Figure 2.26: Energy intensities by fuel type in Bangladesh. (TOE per $100,000)

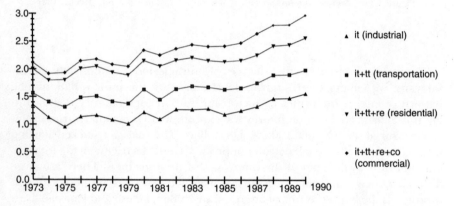

Figure 2.27: Energy intensities by sector in Bangladesh. (TOE per $100,000)

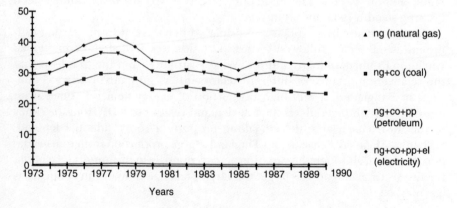

Figure 2.28: Energy intensities by fuel type in China. (TOE per $100,000)

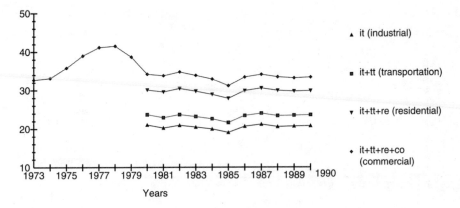

Figure 2.29: Energy intensities by sector in China. (TOE per $100,000)

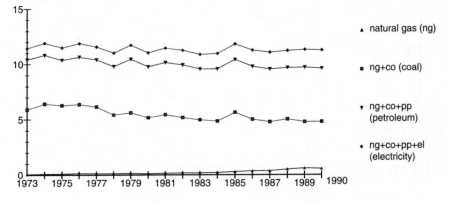

Figure 2.30: Energy intensities by fuel type in India. (TOE per $100,000)

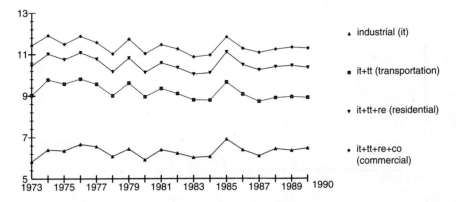

Figure 2.31: Energy intensities by sector in India. (TOE per $100,000)

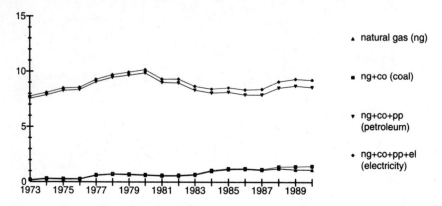

Figure 2.32:   Energy intensities by fuel type in Indonesia. (TOE per $100,000)

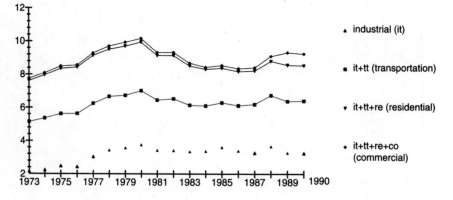

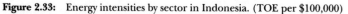

Figure 2.33:   Energy intensities by sector in Indonesia. (TOE per $100,000)

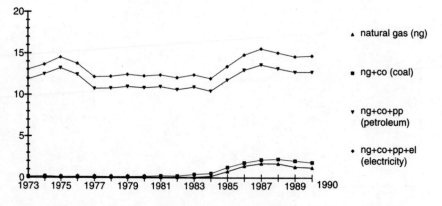

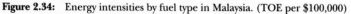

Figure 2.34:   Energy intensities by fuel type in Malaysia. (TOE per $100,000)

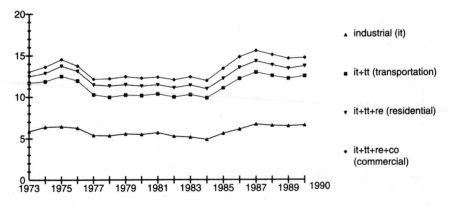

Figure 2.35: Energy intensities by sector in Malaysia. (TOE per $100,000)

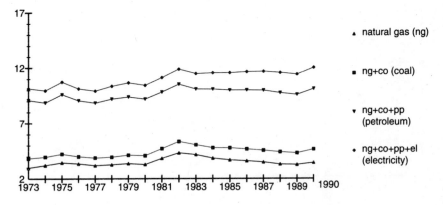

Figure 2.36: Energy intensities by fuel type in Pakistan. (TOE per $100,000)

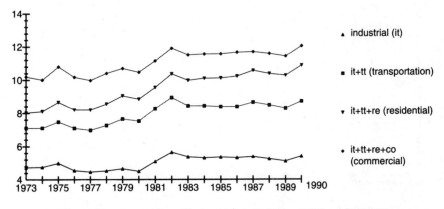

Figure 2.37: Energy intensities by sector in Pakistan. (TOE per $100,000)

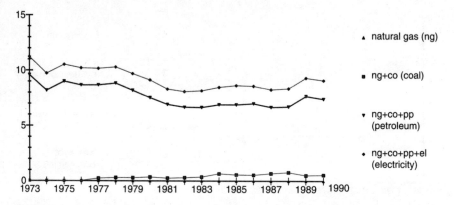

Figure 2.38:   Energy intensities by fuel type in Philippines. (TOE per $100,000)

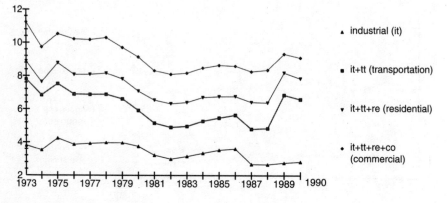

Figure 2.39:   Energy intensities by sector in Philippines. (TOE per $100,000)

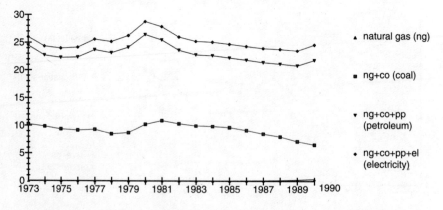

Figure 2.40:   Energy intensities by fuel type in South Korea. (TOE per $100,000)

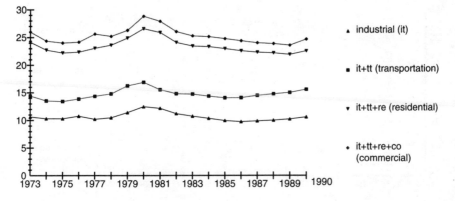

Figure 2.41:   Energy intensities by sector in South Korea. (TOE per $100,000)

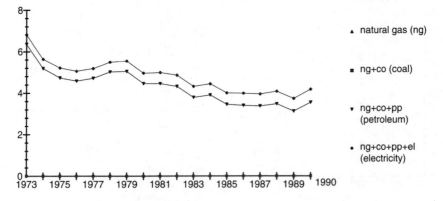

Figure 2.42:   Energy intensities by fuel type in Sri Lanka. (TOE per $100,000)

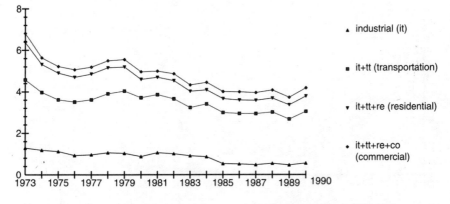

Figure 2.43:   Energy intensities by sector in Sri Lanka. (TOE per $100,000)

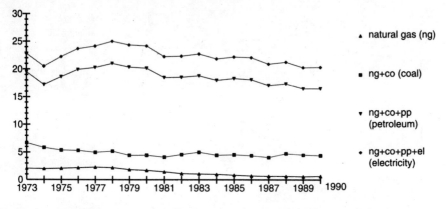

Figure 2.44:   Energy intensities by fuel type in Taiwan. (TOE per $100,000)

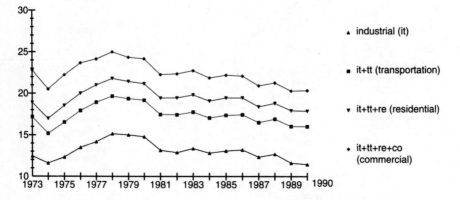

Figure 2.45:   Energy intensities by sector in Taiwan. (TOE per $100,000)

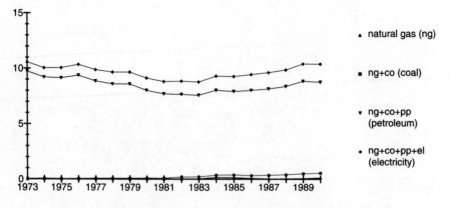

Figure 2.46:   Energy intensities by fuel type in Thailand. (TOE per $100,000)

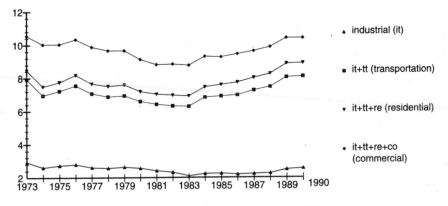

Figure 2.47: Energy intensities by sector in Thailand. (TOE per $100,000)

This descriptive analysis indicates a number of interesting features in the changing patterns of energy intensity in the Asian Developing countries. Firstly, China and Bangladesh are outliers with exceptionally high and exceptionally low energy demands for their levels of GDP. Secondly, the cross-section pattern is for energy intensity to tend to rise with GDP, but whereas the rich countries have tended to reduce their energy intensities over time, the poorer countries in our sample have not. Rather for our sample, despite the increases in income energy intensity has remained relatively stable. Thirdly, a large number of idiosyncratic factors other than income and price seem to influence energy demand. These factors include supply factors (particularly the effect of planning on Chinese consumption); climate through its effect on the use of energy for heating and cooling; the availability and use of traditional biomass fuels; population density through its effect on the use of energy for transportation. Fourthly, although petroleum products tended to be the dominant energy source, countries differed substantially in the fuels they used. Similarly countries differed substantially in the sectoral breakdown of energy use.

Part II

Methodology

CHAPTER 3

Modelling Energy Demand

3.1 Introduction

Modelling of energy demand, whether for residential, industrial or transportation purposes, is complicated by the fact that demand for energy is a derived demand; in the sense that a given amount of a particular type of energy is usually demanded for use in conjunction with a particular type of capital equipment or consumer durable such as industrial machineries, household appliances, or motor vehicles. Seen from this perspective, modelling of energy demand is best approached from a structural viewpoint where demand for a particular fuel is linked to the type of capital equipment in use, the energy efficiency of the equipment, and the degree of its utilization. In this approach the demand for fuel i, say, is given by

$$E_{it} = \sum_j e_{ij} \varphi_{jt} K_{jt},$$

where K_{jt} is the quantity of capital equipment of type j in use at time t, φ_{jt} is the degree of its utilization at time t, and e_{ij} is the technical energy coefficient of fuel i when used in conjunction with the capital equipment of type j. This structural characterization of energy demand clearly highlights the three main ways that demand for a particular fuel can be affected: namely through changes in the utilization of the existing capital stock, by altering the energy efficiency of the existing equipments through retrofitting, and by investing in new capital equipment. Changes in energy coefficients can be brought about by better insulation of homes, regular servicing of the machinery, or by retrofitting of existing equipments with energy-saving devices. The effect of changes in real energy prices and incomes on energy demand can then be studied by analysing the short-term and long-term responses of the different components of the demand (namely φ_{jt}, e_{ij}, and K_{jt}) to price and income changes.

This structural engineering process approach while theoretically attractive, is highly data-intensive and so far has found only limited applications even in the case of the OECD countries.[1] Nevertheless, it provides an appropriate

---

[1] For an early discussion of the structural approach to modelling energy demand see Fisher and Kaysen (1962). More recent expositions and applications can be found in Griffin (1979, Chapter 2), and Bohi (1981, pp. 23–27).

framework for understanding the time lags involved between income and price changes and their eventual impacts on energy demand. It is reasonable to expect that the short-run effects of price and income changes on E_{it} will be primarily through the utilization variable, φ_{jt}, while the medium- and long-term responses will be through changes in the energy coefficients, e_{ij}, and the turnover of the capital stock, K_{jt}. More practical alternatives are the end-use and the econometric approaches.

3.2   The End-Use Approach

The end-use or techno-economic approach relies on energy surveys, technical studies and energy audits for the calibration of the energy model's parameters. The primary motivation behind this approach is to forecast trends in energy demand at a disaggregated level. More recently the approach has also been used for historical analysis and assessment of energy conservation policies.[2] The focus of this approach is the disaggregation of the sectoral demand into "homogeneous modules", so that energy demand of each module can be easily linked to technical and economic factors that govern energy demand of the sector. Simple examples of such homogeneous modules include gasoline demand of households in a particular region, or the fuel-oil demand of iron and steel industries in a given country. In familiar economic jargon the "modules" in the end-use approach correspond to "optimal" grouping or aggregation of energy demand by households or firms as far as their demand for a particular type of energy is concerned. As Chateau and Lapillonne (1991), the two main pioneers of the approach, state:

> These "modules" aim at representing the largest grouping of energy consumers which behave homogeneously and whose demand dynamics can be analyzed properly in the long term, in other words, energy demand grouping whose dynamics are not affected by internal changes. (p. 4)

The idea that demand analysis should be based on as homogeneous a grouping of consumers (or producers) as is feasible is clearly important for a valid empirical analysis and is a concern which is common to both the econometric and the end-use approaches. The main difference between the two approaches lies in the way energy demand relations are estimated. The econometric approach almost exclusively relies on historical observations, while under the end-use approach the so-called "techno-economic" methods are

---

[2]See Chateau and Lapillonne (1982) and the United Nations publications in the Energy Resources Development Series, particularly the publication number 33 entitled Sectoral Energy Demand Studies: Applications of the End-Use Approach to Asian Countries.

used that rely more on energy surveys, technical studies, energy audits to "estimate" energy demand relations. The end-use approach represents a simple application of the "calibration" technique often used in the analysis of Computable General Equilibrium models. The strength of the end-use approach lies in the fact that it searches for the optimal level of aggregation of sectors by considering the trade-offs that exist between data availabilities and aggregate categories that form sufficiently homogeneous consumer groups. Contrary to what is often the case under the econometric approach, the level of disaggregation in the end-use approach is not imposed by the availability of historical time series. It is, however, important to recognize that the strength of the approach is at the same time its weakness.[3] The choice of elasticities in the end-use approach is frequently based on *ad-hoc* considerations, and it is often difficult to provide an objective evaluation of the forecasts or the assessment of energy conservation policies generated by the approach. It is also not easy to impose the various homogeneity and symmetry restrictions from the theory of consumer behaviour on demand relations calibrated by the end-use approach. This is particularly important in the analysis of sectoral inter-fuel substitutions (see Chapter 8). One strength of the end-use approach is in estimating energy demand in sectors or industries where a technical relationship between output and energy use is well established. Examples are transportation, steel industry, and cement production. For these sectors and sub-sectors, potential for energy saving can also be more readily evaluated using the end-use approach.

3.3 The Econometric Approach

This is the traditional approach to modelling energy demand and can be applied only if there exist reasonably long historical observations on energy consumption, population, income and prices. The starting point of this approach is formulation of suitable energy demand equations, normally derived as decision rules of optimizing consumers (individuals/households) and/or producers (firms). In practice energy demand is disaggregated by four end uses (residential, industrial, transportation, and commercial), and four fuel types (coal, electricity, natural gas and petroleum). Energy demand equations are derived following a two-stage budgeting procedure where in the first stage

---

[3]For example, under the end-use approach income (or output) elasticities of energy demand are estimated as the ratio of the annual average growth rate of the energy consumption to that of output, which, as Chateau (1991) acknowledges will be valid only under very restrictive conditions (i.e. both the energy consumption and output should show considerable variations, there should be no significant energy price changes, and there should exist empirical evidence of strong correlation between energy consumption and output). To ascertain whether all these conditions are satisfied or not is not a straightforward matter and often requires historical observations of the type that the end-use approach aims to do without. The problems are far more serious when one comes to estimate price elasticities.

total expenditures (costs) of households (firms) are allocated across broad commodity (input) groups with energy being one of these groups. In the second stage the composition of expenditures across the commodities within each group is determined. In the case of energy, this means that first the allocation of expenditures between energy and non-energy commodities is determined, and then the total expenditure on energy is broken down across the different fuel types.[4] This two-stage procedure is theoretically justified only under a number of rather restrictive aggregation and separability assumptions. In what follows we briefly set out the standard derivations of energy demands for households and firms, and highlight the assumptions that underlie them.

3.3.1   Modelling Household Energy Demand

Most derivations of the household energy demand function in the literature are based on a static formulation of the consumer's decision problem and relate the share of expenditure on each commodity group such as energy to total expenditure and relative prices. Two popular econometric formulations of this approach are the indirect translog utility specification due to Christensen, Jorgenson and Lau (1975), and the Almost Ideal Demand System due to Deaton and Muellbauer (1980).[5] Both of these specifications are static in the sense that they are derived from constrained optimization of a single-period utility function assumed to be separable across durable and non-durable goods.

Translog Specification

Suppose a consumer is interested in allocating a given total expenditure, Y_t, across m commodity groups, $X_{1t}, X_{2t}, \ldots, X_{mt}$, with price indices $P_{1t}, P_{2t}, \ldots, P_{mt}$, where $Y_t = \sum_i P_{it} X_{it}$. The translog formulation of the indirect utility function for this problem is given by:

$$\ln V_t = \alpha_0 + \sum_{i=1}^{m} \alpha_i \ln \left(\frac{P_{it}}{Y_t} \right) + \frac{1}{2} \sum_{i=1}^{m} \sum_{j=1}^{m} \beta_{ij} \ln \left(\frac{P_{jt}}{Y_t} \right) \ln \left(\frac{P_{it}}{Y_t} \right) \tag{3.1}$$

$$+ \sum_{i=1}^{m} t \beta_{i\tau} \ln \left(\frac{P_{it}}{Y_t} \right), \tag{3.2}$$

---

[4]Most studies focus on one or the other of these two stages. For example, the pioneering study of energy-capital complementarity in US manufacturing considers the demand for total energy, while the studies by Uri (1979) and Bacon (1992) focus on the second stage and only examine the possibilities of inter-fuel substitutions.

[5]Other important examples include the linear expenditure system due to Stone (1954), and the Rotterdam model due to Theil (1975–76) and Barten (1977).

where the last term involving the time trend is intended to capture gradual changes in tastes. The application of Roy's identity to this indirect utility function yields the following system of budget-share equations:

$$w_{it}^* = \frac{P_{it}X_{it}}{Y_t} = -\frac{\partial \ln V_t / \partial \ln P_{it}}{\partial \ln V_t / \partial \ln Y_t} \tag{3.3}$$

$$= \frac{\alpha_i + \sum_{j=1}^m \beta_{ij} \ln (P_{jt}/Y_t) + \beta_{i\tau} t}{\alpha + \sum_{j=1}^m \beta_j \ln (P_{jt}/Y_t) + \beta_\tau t}, \tag{3.4}$$

where w_{it}^* is the "equilibrium" or "long-run" level of expenditure share of the i-th commodity group and

$$\alpha = \sum_{j=1}^m \alpha_j, \quad \beta_i = \sum_{j=1}^m \beta_{ij}, \quad \text{and} \quad \beta_\tau = \sum_{i=1}^m \beta_{i\tau}. \tag{3.5}$$

The long-run income and price elasticities can be obtained from the parameters of the share equations. The long-run income elasticity of demand for good j is given by

$$\eta_{jt}^* = 1 + \frac{\sum_{i=1}^m \beta_i - \sum_{i=1}^m \left(\beta_{ji}/w_{it}^*\right)}{\alpha + \sum_{i=1}^m \beta_i \ln (P_{it}/Y_t) + \beta_\tau t}. \tag{3.6}$$

Similarly, the price elasticities are given by:

(i) Long-run own price elasticity

$$\eta_{jj,t}^* = -1 + \frac{\left(\beta_{ji}/w_{jt}^*\right) - \beta_j}{\alpha + \sum_{i=1}^m \beta_i \ln (P_{it}/Y_t) + \beta_\tau t}. \tag{3.7}$$

(ii) Long-run cross-price elasticities

$$\eta_{ji,t}^* = \frac{\left(\beta_{ji}/w_{jt}^*\right) - \beta_j}{\alpha + \sum_{i=1}^m \beta_i \ln (P_{it}/Y_t) + \beta_\tau t}. \tag{3.8}$$

These elasticities are "partial" in the sense that they assume total expenditure is given and therefore do not allow for the effect of simultaneous changes in incomes and prices. Relevant expressions for total price elasticities can be readily derived and are given in the literature.

Almost Ideal Demand Formulation

The formulation of the Almost Ideal Demand (AID) System is somewhat simpler and gives the following expression for the "equilibrium" expenditure share of the i-th commodity group:

$$w_{it}^* = \alpha_i + \sum_{j=1}^m \beta_{ij} \ln P_{jt} + \delta_i \ln(Y_t/P_t), \quad i = 1, 2, \ldots, m, \tag{3.9}$$

where as before P_{jt} is the price deflator of the commodity group j, Y_t is the per-capita expenditure on all m commodities, and P_t is a general price index. The exact expression for $\ln P_t$ is given by

$$\ln P_t = \alpha_0 + \sum_{k=1}^{m} \alpha_k \ln P_{kt} + \frac{1}{2} \sum_{k=1}^{m} \sum_{j=1}^{m} \beta_{kj} \ln P_{kt} \ln P_{jt}. \qquad (3.10)$$

However, its use gives rise to non-linear systems of share equations which are complicated to estimate. A possible alternative often employed in the literature would be to approximate it using the Stone formula:[6]

$$\ln P_t = \sum_{j=1}^{m} w_{jt}^0 \ln P_{jt}. \qquad (3.11)$$

Typically, the weights w_{jt}^0 refer to the budget shares in some base year, but in the case of the developing economies where the fuel shares may undergo important changes over relatively short time periods, a moving window weighting scheme is more satisfactory. In the present study we employ the following two-year moving window:

$$w_{jt}^0 = (w_{j,t-1} + w_{j,t-2})/2, \quad t = 3, 4, \ldots, T, \qquad (3.12)$$

and use w_{j1} for the first two observations in the sample (namely $w_{j1}^0 = w_{j2}^0 = w_{j1}$).

Consumer theory imposes the following restrictions on the parameters of the long-run share equations in (3.9):

- Adding-up restrictions: $\sum_{i=1}^{m} \alpha_i = 1$, $\sum_{i=1}^{m} \beta_{ij} = 0$, $\sum_{i=1}^{m} \delta_i = 0$,
- Homogeneity restrictions: $\sum_{j=1}^{m} \beta_{ij} = 0$,
- Symmetry restrictions: $\beta_{ij} = \beta_{ji}$.

The adding-up restrictions are not testable, and are imposed indirectly by first estimating the $m - 1$ share equations, and then estimating the parameters of the remaining equation from the adding-up restriction. In system estimation of the share equations the results are invariant to the choice of the $m - 1$ commodities included in the analysis.

The coefficients are not elasticities and elasticities are discussed further in an appendix. Under the AID's formulation the long-run income elasticity of demand for good j is given by

$$\eta_{jt}^* = 1 + \frac{\delta_j}{w_{jt}^*}, \qquad (3.13)$$

---

[6]Pashardes (1993) provides an empirical evaluation of Stone's approximation in the context of a static AID system.

and the long-run own and cross-price elasticities are given by

$$\eta^*_{jj,t} = -1 + w^0_{jt} + \frac{\beta_{jj}}{w^*_{jt}}, \tag{3.14}$$

$$\eta^*_{ji,t} = w^0_{jt} + \frac{\beta_{ji}}{w^*_{jt}}. \tag{3.15}$$

Dynamic Specifications

Static versions of the above formulation (which assumes $w^*_{it} = w_{it} = P_{it}X_{it}/Y_t$) have been extensively applied in energy demand studies with some success. Nevertheless, it is important that the limitations of this approach are recognized. By assuming that the utility function underlying the consumer's decision is separable over durable and the non-durable goods, the approach ignores the joint nature of the determination of demand for energy and the stock of household appliances. The static fuel share approach also ignores the dynamics of the adjustments in the process of inter-fuel substitutions, and the costs involved in the adjustment of stock of appliances to income and relative price changes. Both of these limitations can lead to gross underestimation of the long-run response of energy demand to relative price changes, especially if only time series data are used in the estimation of the elasticities.

To deal with some of these shortcomings, joint models of appliance choice and use have been developed in the literature (see, for example, Hausman (1979), Dubin and McFadden (1984), Dubin (1985), and Baker *et al.* (1989)). These models are estimated using US and UK micro data sets, and their application to developing economies is likely to face severe data problems.

An alternative modelling strategy which we propose to follow in this study is to embed the static share equations within a dynamic framework, thus allowing an explicit distinction between the short-run and the long-run impacts of income and price changes on energy demand as a whole and on inter-fuel substitutions.[7] The resulting dynamic system of share equations can then be estimated for each country separately using time-series data, or by pooling the time-series observations across all the ten countries under investigation. In the latter case the dynamic nature of the share equations generates a number of important econometric issues that need to be addressed at the estimation stage. These econometric problems are discussed in some detail in the next two chapters. But in embedding the equilibrium or long-run share equations given by (3.9) in a dynamical system a number of considerations should be borne in mind. It is important that the theoretical restrictions of homogeneity

---

[7]For an application of this approach in empirical demand analysis see Anderson and Blundell (1983a, 1983b), and for a more general discussion covering recent developments in the cointegration literature see Pesaran (1997).

and symmetry, and the fact that the (fuel) shares should add up to unity in the short run as well as in the long run are taken into account.

In the general case where $m \geq 2$, derivation of theory-consistent dynamic models for the budget shares is best accomplished by an explicit solution of a multivariate cost of adjustment optimization problem. There are many different ways that this problem can be formulated. Here we adopt the simple one-period quadratic formulation of the problem and assume that actual expenditure shares, $\mathbf{w}_t = (w_{1t}, w_{2t}, \ldots, w_{mt})'$, adjust to their long-run values, $\mathbf{w}_t^* = (w_{1t}^*, w_{2t}^*, \ldots, w_{mt}^*)'$, by minimizing the quadratic objective function[8]

$$G_t = \tfrac{1}{2}\left(\mathbf{w}_t - \mathbf{w}_t^*\right)' \mathbf{A}\left(\mathbf{w}_t - \mathbf{w}_t^*\right) + \tfrac{1}{2}\left(\mathbf{w}_t - \mathbf{w}_{t-1}\right)' \mathbf{B}\left(\mathbf{w}_t - \mathbf{w}_{t-1}\right), \qquad (3.16)$$

subject to the adding-up condition

$$'\mathbf{w}_t = 1, \qquad (3.17)$$

where is an $m \times 1$ vector of ones, and $\mathbf{A}$ and $\mathbf{B}$ are known $m \times m$ coefficient matrices. This is a multivariate generalization of the simple partial adjustment model, and explicitly imposes the additivity condition in every period. The first term in (3.16) measures the cost of being out of equilibrium, and the second term measures the cost of change. The solution to the above optimization problem is given by

$$\mathbf{w}_t = \Lambda \mathbf{w}_t^* + (\mathbf{I} - \Lambda)\mathbf{w}_{t-1}, \qquad (3.18)$$

where $\mathbf{I}$ is an $m \times m$ identity matrix,

$$\Lambda = \mathbf{H} - \frac{\mathbf{H}\mathbf{A}^{-1}\,'\mathbf{H}}{'\mathbf{H}\mathbf{A}^{-1}},$$

and

$$\mathbf{H} = (\mathbf{A} + \mathbf{B})^{-1}\mathbf{A}, \qquad (3.19)$$

The above dynamic share equations have a number of important desirable properties:

(i) As required they satisfy the additivity condition $'\mathbf{w}_t = 1$ in every period.
(ii) Share of each commodity group depends on the equilibrium levels of expenditure shares of all the commodity groups.
(iii) The additivity condition imposes important restrictions on the columns of the adjustment coefficient matrix, namely that the coefficients in the columns of Λ should all add up to zero, or in matrix notations, we should have $'\Lambda = \mathbf{0}$. This involves an important saving in the number of the parameters that need to be estimated. This restriction also has the important implication that the adjustment coefficient matrix, Λ, cannot be diagonal, which renders the usual practice of using univariate partial adjustment models in the case of systems of share equations inappropriate.

---

[8]For a multivariate and multi-period version of the cost of adjustment problem under the rational (consistent) expectations hypothesis see, for example, Binder and Pesaran (1995).

(iv) The actual shares, $\mathbf{w}_t$, eventually converge to their long-run levels $\mathbf{w}_t$, assuming that the eigenvalues of Λ lie in the range $(0,2)$.

Assuming that the equilibrium shares $\mathbf{w}_t^*$ are determined by the AID's model, and substituting w_{it}^*, $i = 1, 2, \ldots, m$ from (3.9) in (3.18), the resultant dynamic system of share equations can be written as the multivariate partial adjustment model:

$$\Delta \mathbf{w}_t = \Lambda \left(\mathbf{w}_{t-1} - \quad - \quad \ln (\mathbf{P}_t) - \quad \ln (Y_t/P_t) \right), \quad (3.20)$$

where $= (\alpha_1, \alpha_2, \ldots, \alpha_m)'$, $= (\delta_1, \delta_2, \ldots, \delta_m)'$, $\ln(\mathbf{P}_t) = (\ln(P_{1t}), \ln(P_{2t}), \ldots, \ln(P_{mt}))'$, and $= (\beta_{ij})$ is an $m \times m$ matrix of price coefficients. This system of equations can now be estimated subject to the short-term and long-term additivity conditions, namely $'\Lambda = \mathbf{0}$.

As in the univariate case the above model can be generalized to the following first-order multivariate error correction model:

$$\Delta \mathbf{w}_t = - \Lambda \left(\mathbf{w}_{t-1} - \quad - \quad \ln (\mathbf{P}_{t-1}) - \quad \ln (Y_{t-1}/P_{t-1}) \right)$$
$$+ \Gamma_1 \Delta \ln (\mathbf{P}_t) + \Gamma_2 \Delta \ln (Y_t/P_t) + \varepsilon_t, \quad (3.21)$$

where Γ_1 and Γ_2 are $m \times m$ and $m \times 1$ coefficient matrices that capture the short-run dynamics of price and income changes and ε_t is an $m \times 1$ vector of serially uncorrelated disturbances. The adding-up restrictions $'\mathbf{w}_t = 1$ also impose the following restrictions on the short-run coefficients:

$$'\Lambda = 0, \qquad '\Gamma_1 = 0, \qquad '\Gamma_2 = 0, \quad (3.22)$$

and on the disturbances:

$$'\varepsilon_t = 0. \quad (3.23)$$

One simple method of imposing these adding-up restrictions is to estimate the multivariate error correction model (3.21) in $m - 1$ of the shares, and estimate the parameters of the remaining share equation from the adding-up restrictions. In system estimation of the share equations the results are invariant to the choice of the $m - 1$ commodity groups included in the analysis. For an application of such a system approach see Pesaran and Shin (1997b).

In the simple case where $m = 2$, the relationship between the "equilibrium" share of expenditure on energy, w_{1t}^*, to the actual expenditure share, w_{1t}, is given by:

$$\Delta w_{1t} = w_{1t} - w_{1,t-1} = \varphi \left(w_{1t}^* - w_{1,t-1} \right). \quad (3.24)$$

Using the Almost Ideal Demand system formulation, (3.9), to determine the equilibrium budget shares the equation to be estimated is given by

$$\Delta w_{1t} = - \varphi w_{1,t-1} + \varphi \alpha_1 + \varphi \beta_{11} \ln(P_{1t})$$
$$+ \varphi \beta_{12} \ln(P_{2t}) + \varphi \delta_1 \ln(Y_t/P_t). \quad (3.25)$$

The share equation for the non-energy commodity group can then be derived consistently noting that $w_{2t} = 1 - w_{1t}$, or

$$\Delta w_{2t} = - \varphi w_{2,t-1} + \varphi(1 - \alpha_1) - \varphi\beta_{11} \ln(P_{1t})$$
$$- \varphi\beta_{12} \ln(P_{2t}) - \varphi\delta_1 \ln(Y_t/P_t). \tag{3.26}$$

In practice one only needs to estimate either (3.25) or (3.26). The existence of a long-run relationship between w_{1t}, $\ln(P_{1t})$, $\ln(P_{2t})$, and $\ln(Y_t/P_t)$ requires a non-zero value for the partial adjustment coefficient, φ. Notice also that when $\varphi \neq 0$, (3.25) can be written in the following algebraically equivalent error correction forms:

$$\Delta w_{1t} = \varphi\alpha_1 - \varphi(w_{1,t-1} - \beta_{11} \ln(P_{1t}) - \beta_{12} \ln(P_{2t}) - \delta_1 \ln(Y_t/P_t)) \tag{3.27}$$

or

$$\Delta w_{1t} = \varphi\alpha_1 - \varphi(w_{1,t-1} - \beta_{11} \ln(P_{1,t-1}) - \beta_{12} \ln(P_{2,t-1})$$
$$- \delta_1 \ln(Y_{t-1}/P_{t-1})) + \varphi\beta_{11}\Delta \ln(P_{1,t})$$
$$+ \varphi\beta_{12}\Delta \ln(P_{2,t}) + \varphi\delta_1\Delta \ln(Y_t/P_t). \tag{3.28}$$

This latter representation provides a transparent decomposition of the short-run and long-run influences of price and income changes on energy demand. Its implied long-run income and price elasticities are the same as those of the static AID's model, and in this simple case are given by

$$\eta_1^* = 1 + \delta_1/\bar{w}_1, \tag{3.29}$$
$$\eta_{11}^* = -1 + \bar{w}_1 + \beta_{11}/\bar{w}_1,$$

where for simplicity they are evaluated at the sample mean of the energy expenditure share. The short-run income and price elasticities, also evaluated at sample means are given by:

$$\eta_1 = 1 + \varphi\delta_1/\bar{w}_1, \tag{3.30}$$
$$\eta_{11} = -1 + \bar{w}_1 + \varphi\beta_{11}/\bar{w}_1.$$

Despite its theoretical appeal the partial adjustment model is rather restrictive and can impose untenable restrictions on the relationships between the short-run and long-run elasticities. For example, in the present application we have $(\eta_1 - 1) = \varphi(\eta_1^* - 1)$, and $\eta_{11} = \varphi\eta_{11}^* - (1 - \bar{w}_1)(1 - \varphi)$. Relaxation of these restrictions yields the first-order error correction model

$$\Delta w_{1t} = \varphi\alpha_1 - \varphi(w_{1,t-1} - \beta_{11} \ln(P_{1,t-1}) - \beta_{12} \ln(P_{2,t-1})$$
$$- \delta_1 \ln(Y_{t-1}/P_{t-1})) + \gamma_{11}\Delta \ln(P_{1,t})$$
$$+ \gamma_{12}\Delta \ln(P_{2,t}) + \gamma_{13}\Delta \ln(Y_t/P_t), \tag{3.31}$$

which can also be written equivalently as

$$\Delta w_{1t} = \varphi\alpha_1 - \varphi(w_{1,t-1} - \beta_{11}\ln(P_{1t}) - \beta_{12}\ln(P_{2t}) - \delta_1\ln(Y_t/P_t))$$
$$+ (\gamma_{11} - \varphi\beta_{11})\Delta\ln(P_{1,t}) + (\gamma_{12} - \varphi\beta_{12})\Delta\ln(P_{2,t})$$
$$+ (\gamma_{13} - \varphi\delta_1)\Delta\ln(Y_t/P_t). \tag{3.32}$$

A test of the simple partial adjustment model against the unrestricted first-order error correction model may now be carried out by testing the restrictions:

$$\gamma_{11} = \varphi\beta_{11}, \qquad \gamma_{12} = \varphi\beta_{12}, \qquad \gamma_{13} = \varphi\delta_1.$$

Higher order error-correction models can also be considered, but given the limited time-series observations available on energy consumption in Asian developing economies we shall confine our analysis to at most the first-order error correction model given by (3.32). Notice also that (3.32) can be written as a first-order autoregressive distributed lag (ARDL(1, 1, 1, 1)) model in w_{1t}, $\ln(P_{1t})$, $\ln(P_{2t})$ and $\ln(Y_t/P_t)$:

$$\lambda(L)w_{1t} = a + b_1(L)\ln(P_{1t}) + b_2(L)\ln(P_{2t})$$
$$+ b_3(L)\ln(Y_t/P_t) + \varepsilon_{1t}, \tag{3.33}$$

where

$$\lambda(L) = 1 - \lambda L, \tag{3.34}$$
$$b_i(L) = b_{0i} + b_{1i}L, \quad i = 1, 2, 3,$$

L is the one-period lag operator $(Lw_{1t} = w_{1,t-1})$, and ε_{1t} is a serially uncorrelated error term. The relationships between the 8 "reduced" form parameters, λ, a, b_{0i}, b_{1i}, $i = 1, 2, 3$ and the 8 "structural" form parameters α_1, φ, β_{11}, β_{12}, δ_1, γ_{11}, γ_{12}, and γ_{13}, are given by

$$\lambda = 1 - \varphi, \quad a = \alpha_1\varphi, \quad b_{0i} = \gamma_{1i}, \quad i = 1, 2, 3,$$
$$b_{1i} = \varphi\beta_{1i} - \gamma_{1i}, \quad i = 1, 2, 3, \quad b_{03} = \varphi\delta_1 - \gamma_{13}.$$

In their unrestricted forms, the ARDL(1, 1, 1, 1) model, (3.33), and the error correction model, (3.31), are observationally equivalent. But as will be argued in the next chapter, for purposes of estimation and hypothesis testing, the ARDL specification is more convenient to use in practice. The long-run homogeneity restriction $\beta_{11} + \beta_{12} = 0$, can also be readily imposed on the ARDL specification, and is given by $b_{01} + b_{11} + b_{02} + b_{12} = 0$. Notice also that in this simple case where $m = 2$, by additivity restriction we have $\beta_{21} = -\beta_{11}$, and therefore the symmetry hypothesis (namely $\beta_{21} = \beta_{12}$) will be automatically satisfied when the homogeneity hypothesis is satisfied.

3.3.2   Modelling Industrial Energy Demand

Derivation of energy demand equations for the industrial sector proceeds along similar lines as in the previous section, and follows a two-stage budgeting procedure. In the first stage total industrial energy demand is obtained, treating energy as a factor of production. In the second stage, total energy expenditure is broken down into expenditures on oil, coal, natural gas, and electricity. In both stages the factor input demands will be derived assuming cost minimization for a given level of industry output. As with the residential sector, the static fuel share equations will be incorporated into a dynamic framework allowing for the possibility of a slow adjustment of factor inputs to price and output changes. Total energy use in the industrial sector is determined as a part of an individual firm's factor input decisions. Different energy demand specifications are obtained depending on the particular form of the production (or cost) function assumed, the treatment of capital and labour as variable or quasi-fixed inputs, and the nature of the adjustment costs. Using a translog cost function, energy demand equations for the industrial sector can be easily derived in an analogous manner to that set out in the previous section for the residential sector. In our derivation we treat all factor inputs as variables, but distinguish the long-run determinants of the energy demand as predicted by economic theory from its short-run determinants which we model using an error correction mechanism.[9] Starting with the following translog cost function

$$\ln C_t = b_0 + \sum_{i=1}^{n} b_i \ln P_{it} + \frac{1}{2} \sum_{i=1}^{n} \sum_{j=1}^{n} b_{ij} (\ln P_{it}) (\ln P_{jt})$$

$$+ b_q \ln Q_t + \frac{1}{2} b_{qq} (\ln Q_t)^2 + \sum_{i=1}^{n} b_{iq} (\ln P_{it}) (\ln Q_t),$$

in natural logarithms of firm's output, $\ln Q_t$, and the n factor input prices, $\ln P_{it}$, $i = 1, 2, \ldots, n$, the "equilibrium" or "long-run" factor share equations can be obtained via Shepard's lemma, and are given by:

$$S_{it}^* = b_i + \sum_{j=1}^{n} b_{ij} \ln P_{jt} + b_{iq} \ln(Q_t), \quad i = 1, 2, \ldots, n,$$

where $S_{it} = P_{it} X_{it} / \sum_{j=1}^{n} P_{jt} X_{jt}$, X_{it} is the quantity of i-th factor input used to produce Q_t, and S_{it}^* denotes the equilibrium value of S_{it}. As before equilibrium

---

[9]Other approaches to modelling of industrial energy demand, referred to as second and third generation models, can be found in Watkins (1992). In these models dynamics are introduced into the analysis by treating capital and labour as quasi-fixed. See Pindyck and Rotemberg (1983) for details.

factor shares, S_{it}^*, can be incorporated into an error correction model of the type:

$$\Delta \mathbf{S}_t = -\Lambda_f \left(\mathbf{S}_{t-1} - \mathbf{b} - \mathbf{B} \ln \mathbf{P}_{t-1} - \mathbf{b}_q \ln \left(Q_{t-1} \right) \right)$$
$$+ \Gamma_{if} \Delta \ln \mathbf{P}_t + \Gamma_{2f} \Delta \ln Q_t + \varepsilon_{tf},$$

where $\mathbf{S}_t = (S_{1t}, S_{2t}, \ldots, S_{nt})'$, $\ln \mathbf{P}_t = (\ln P_{1t}, \ln P_{2t}, \ldots, \ln P_{nt})'$, and the short-run coefficient matrices Λ_f, Γ_{1f}, Γ_{2f} and ε_{tf} will be subject to the adding-up restrictions similar to those in (3.22) and (3.23). The above error correction model can also be used to estimate short-run and long-run output and price elasticities.

3.4   Choice of Functional Form

In addition to the share equations derived in the previous section, many other functional forms have also been used in empirical energy demand analysis; the most prominent example of which is the double-log formulation

$$\lambda(L) \ln(X_{1t}) = a + b_1(L) \ln (P_{1t}) + b_2(L) \ln (P_{2t})$$
$$+ b_3(L) \ln(Y_t/P_t) + u_t, \tag{3.35}$$

where X_{1t} is energy consumption (in TOE per capita), P_{1t} and P_{2t} stand for prices of energy and non-energy goods, Y_t/P_t represents a measure of activity (which could be output, real disposable income or real total expenditures), $\lambda(L)$, $b_1(L)$, $b_2(L)$ and $b_3(L)$ are finite-order lag polynomials such as those specified by (3.34), and u_t is a serially uncorrelated error term. To facilitate comparisons of the above log-linear model with the share equation specification given by (3.33), using the identity relations

$$\ln(w_{1t}) = \ln(X_{1t}) + \ln(P_{1t}/P_t) - \ln(Y_t/P_t), \tag{3.36}$$

and

$$\ln P_t = w_1^0 \ln P_{1t} + \left(1 - w_1^0\right) \ln P_{2t}, \tag{3.37}$$

we also note that (3.35) can be written in the algebraically equivalent form:[10]

$$\lambda(L) \ln(w_{1t}) = a + \left(b_1(L) + \left(1 - w_1^0\right) \lambda(L) \right) \ln(P_{1t})$$
$$+ \left(b_2(L) - \left(1 - w_1^0\right) \lambda(L) \right) \ln (P_{2t})$$
$$+ (b_3(L) + \lambda(L)) \ln(Y_t/P_t) + u_t. \tag{3.38}$$

Therefore, the log-linear model can also be viewed as a log-share version of (3.33).

---

[10]This derivation assumes that the weights used in the construction of the Stone price index are fixed.

Although venerable, the log-linear model has a number of important limitations. It is not consistent with optimization, it does not handle zero energy demands, it does not aggregate consistently, and one of its important implications, namely that price or income elasticities are constant over large ranges of energy use, is implausible. Watkins (1992) provides a good exposition of the limitations of the constant elasticity model. Nevertheless, the log-linear model serves a useful baseline model against which the performance of the share equations could be judged. The ARDL share equation given by (3.33) has the virtue of being theory consistent, but it may not fit the data as well as the log-linear model. If this happens we are faced with a hard choice; whether to choose the log-linear model and ignore its theoretical shortcomings or to adopt the theory-consistent share equation model despite its relative poor fit to the data. A better fitting log-linear model may also be viewed as signalling important deficiencies in the functional form of the indirect utility or cost functions that underlie the share equation model. This suggests a third possible response, namely abandoning both models in favour of a different specification for the share equation model. One approach would be to introduce non-linearities in the determination of the budget or factor shares. The budget shares implied by the AID's model, for example, have the undesirable property that they will rise (fall) without bounds with real total expenditures (Y_t/P_t) if $\delta_i > 0$ $(\delta_i < 0)$.[11] To overcome this problem one could consider replacing the log-linear term $\delta_i \ln(Y_t/P_t)$ in (3.33) by the non-linear function

$$\frac{\delta_{i0}}{1 + \psi_0 (Y_t/P_t)^{\psi_1}}.$$

Under this specification the effect of rising income on the budget share either tends to zero or to δ_{i0} depending on whether ψ_1 is positive or negative. Other functional forms bounded in Y_t/P_t, such as $1/(Y_t/P_t)$, could also be employed and we experiment using the reciprocal in the fuel demand equations below.

3.5   The Identification Problem

All empirical demand analyses are potentially subject to the identification problem familiar from the simultaneous equation literature in econometrics. In the context of modelling energy demand identification is not a problem if changes in domestic energy prices follow closely their international levels and/or energy supplies are infinitely elastic. In the case of most of the ten Asian developing economies in our sample these conditions are likely to be satisfied for petroleum products, and possibly for coal, but not necessarily for

---

[11]This problem is unlikely to arise in the case of the price variables so long as the homogeneity condition is imposed. Under the homogeneity hypothesis an ever increasing (decreasing) relative price is needed for the shares to rise (fall) without bounds, which seems less likely.

electricity and natural gas whose supplies in the short run are likely to be constrained by domestic economic factors, and limited possibilities for imports. On the other hand, the fact that in many countries prices of public utilities such as gas and electricity tend to be set by governments, often independently of market conditions, should help identification. Under these circumstances prices entering the demand equation could be treated as pre-determined, at least as far as the short-run effects are concerned.

3.6 The Aggregation Problem

Use of the log-log model raises some issues in aggregation. The potential benefits from disaggregation arise from the use of extra information. If the regressors in the disaggregate equations were perfectly correlated, then aggregation would be exact and the forecast from the aggregate and disaggregate equations would be identical. Aggregate equations can sometimes forecast aggregates better than the aggregate forecast obtained as the sum of the forecasts from the disaggregated equations, but this usually indicates that aggregate variables should be included in the disaggregate equations. See, for example, Grunfeld and Griliches (1960), and Pesaran, Pierse and Kumar (1989). In the present study, the extra information in the disaggregate equations comes from the use of sector specific prices and heterogenous dynamics across the different sectors. The log-log specification causes a complication, in that the aggregate equation is the logarithm of the sum of sectoral energy demands, rather than the sum of the logarithms of energy demands, which is what aggregation of the sectoral equations would give. van Garderen, Lee, and Pesaran (1997) discuss this problem. Since our primary interest at this stage in the project is to examine the disaggregate equations for their own sake, rather than for forecasting the aggregate, these issues are of secondary importance and will not be pursued further.

CHAPTER 4

Dynamic Specifications

4.1 Introduction

In this chapter we discuss the econometric issues that arise in analysing energy demand within a single country. The next chapter deals with the problem of pooling of estimates across countries. All the various demand equations that we estimate can be written in the form of the following autoregressive distributed lag (ARDL) model of order 1:

$$\lambda(L) y_t = a + b_1(L) x_{1t} + b_2(L) x_{2t} + b_3(L) x_{3t} + u_t, \tag{4.1}$$

where y_t denotes the share of energy in total expenditures or logarithm of per-capita energy consumption (depending on the particular functional form used in the energy demand analysis), x_{1t}, x_{2t}, x_{3t} are the logarithms of energy and non-energy prices and real output,

$$\lambda(L) = 1 - \lambda L, \tag{4.2}$$
$$b_i(L) = b_{0i} + b_{1i}L, \quad i = 1, 2, 3,$$

L is the one-period lag operator $(Lw_{1t} = w_{1,t-1})$, and u_t is a serially uncorrelated error term. Higher order ARDL models can also be considered, but given the limited time-series observations available on energy consumption in Asian developing economies we shall confine our analysis to at most the first-order model. This model is still general enough for our purposes and yields the various dynamic formulations of energy demand equations discussed in Chapter 3 as special cases (see Section 3.3.1 for details). In this chapter we shall consider the econometric issues involved in the order selection and estimation of ARDL models and their associated error correction forms, when it is not known whether the price and income variables are trend or first-difference stationary. This is an important consideration particularly in the context of the present application where we have only 18 time series observations for each country and the use of the familiar cointegration techniques that assume *a priori* knowledge of the order of the integration of the underlying regressors may not be justified.

4.2   Error Correction Forms of the ARDL Model

In the context of the ARDL model (4.1), the parameters of interest are the long-run coefficients,

$$\theta_j = (b_{j0} + b_{j1})/(1 - \lambda), \quad j = 1, 2, 3, \tag{4.3}$$
$$\psi = a/(1 - \lambda), \tag{4.4}$$

and the speed of adjustment coefficient which is defined by $\varphi = 1 - \lambda$. In terms of these parameters, (4.1) can be written in the form of an Error Correction (EC) model:

$$\Delta y_t = -\varphi EC_{t-1} + \sum_{j=1}^{3} b_{j0} \Delta x_{jt}, \quad t = 1, 2, \ldots, T,$$

where the error correction term is the deviation from the long-run relationship

$$EC_t = y_t - \sum_{j=1}^{3} \theta_j x_{jt} - \psi. \tag{4.5}$$

The remaining parameters, b_{j0}, $j = 1, 2, 3$ represent the impact effects of the price and income changes on energy consumption. As it is shown in Section 3.3.1, a number of important dynamic models are nested within the above general ARDL(1, 1, 1, 1) specification. For example, the simple partial adjustment model (3.27 or 3.28) is obtained by setting $b_{j1} = 0$, $j = 1, 2, 3$. The simple error correction model is obtained by restricting the impact effects to be zero, namely $b_{j0} = 0$, $j = 1, 2, 3$.

4.3   ARDL Modelling and Unit Root Regressors

Historically ARDL models have played an important role in estimation of dynamic economic models, and were used extensively in the applied literature before cointegration techniques were introduced into econometrics by Granger (1986), Engle and Granger (1987) and others.[1] This latter literature which is concerned with the analysis of the long-run relations between integrated variables assumes, at least implicitly, that the traditional ARDL methodology is no longer applicable when it is known or suspected that the underlying regressors have unit roots (or are integrated of order 1). However, as shown recently by Pesaran and Shin (1997a), the traditional ARDL estimation technique is in fact valid both when the variables are integrated of order zero, $I(0)$, and when some or all of the variables are $I(1)$ and there is a single cointegrating relationship between the set of $I(1)$ variables. In contrast the application of cointegration

---

[1] For a review of the early literature on estimation of ARDL models see Hendry, Pagan and Sargan (1984), and Wickens and Breusch (1988).

techniques to the analysis of long-run relations will be valid only if it is known with certainty that all the variables under investigation are $I(1)$. This requirement invariably involves the pre-testing of the variables for unit roots, which could be particularly problematic when T, the number of time periods, is small. In the case of our investigation $T = 18$, and there seems little point in testing the series from individual countries for unit roots and cointegration, although we do report tests when we use a cointegrating VAR to analyse fuel shares. For most of this study, we shall rely on traditional ARDL techniques and estimate (4.1) by least squares and then compute the long-run coefficients, θ_i, using the relations in (4.3). As shown in Pesaran and Shin (1997a), the Ordinary Least Squares (OLS) estimators of the coefficients in the dynamic regression of y_t on x_{1t}, x_{2t}, and x_{3t} are $\sqrt{T}$-consistent irrespective of whether x_{it}'s are $I(1)$ or $I(0)$, so long as $|\lambda| < 1$. The estimates of the long-run coefficients, θ_i, computed using the ARDL estimates will also be $\sqrt{T}$-consistent when the x_{it}'s are $I(0)$, but will be super-consistent (or T-consistent), when the regressors are $I(1)$. Pesaran and Shin (1997a) further show that valid inferences on the long-run parameters can be made using standard normal asymptotic theory.

4.4 Order Selection Using AIC and SBC Criteria

One important consideration in the application of the ARDL methodology is the choice of the orders of the lags in the model. Economic theory is generally silent on the choice of the lag orders but in practice the choice is made using statistical tests and/or model selection criteria such as the Akaike Information Criteria (*AIC*, Akaike (1973, 1974)) or the Schwarz Bayesian Criteria (*SBC*, Schwarz (1978)).[2] In our analysis we set the maximum lag orders at unity and consider the partial adjustment model as well as models selected using Akaike and Schwartz criteria. In fixing the maximum lag order at unity we have been constrained by the fact that our sample covers the period 1973–1992, and we will only have $T = 17$ observations for estimating 8 unknown parameters contained in the first-order ARDL model (4.1).

Both the Akaike and Schwarz criteria are only concerned with the issue of "statistical fit" and provide different approaches to trading-off "fit" and "parsimony" of a given econometric model. The "fit" of a given model is measured by its maximized value of the log-likelihood function, and the complexity (or lack of parsimony) of the model is measured using different penalty functions. In the case of a general ARDL(p, q_1, q_2, ..., q_k) model with an intercept the

---

[2]Model selection in econometric analysis involves both statistical and non-statistical considerations. It depends on the objective(s) of the analysis, the nature and the extent of economic theory used, and the statistical adequacy of the model under consideration compared with other econometric models. For a general discussion see Pesaran and Smith (1995).

Akaike and Schwarz criteria are defined by

$$AIC(T, s) = LL_T - s \quad \text{and} \quad SBC(T, s) = LL_T - (s/2) \log T, \tag{4.6}$$

where LL_T is the maximized value of the log-likelihood function of the *ARDL* model and

$$s = 1 + p + \sum_{j=1}^{k} q_j.$$

Using the AIC criteria, for example, the lag orders that maximize the value of $AIC(T, s)$ are then selected. Between these two model selection criteria, the *SBC* selects the most parsimonious model (a model with the least number of freely estimated parameters) if $T \geq 8$, and *AIC* selects the least parsimonious model. Useful discussion of these and other model selection criteria can be found in Amemiya (1980), Judge *et al.* (1985, Chapter 21), and Lütkepohl (1991, Section 4.3). Under certain regularity conditions it can be shown that *SBC* is consistent, in the sense that for large enough samples its use leads to the correct model choice, assuming of course that the "true" model does in fact belong to the set of models over which one is searching. The same is not true of the *AIC* criteria. This does not, however, mean that the *SBC* is necessarily preferable to the *AIC*, bearing in mind that it is rarely the case that one is sure that the "true" model is one of the models under consideration.

CHAPTER 5

Econometric Methods for Pooling

5.1 Introduction

In this chapter, we discuss the methodological issues that arise in pooling of energy demand functions across countries, paying particular attention to problems of heterogeneity across countries and common technological trends. These issues are likely to arise in most examinations of panel data of this sort. We will argue that, contrary to the usual practice with panels, the starting point should be a relatively unrestricted model estimated separately for each country.

5.2 The Basic Model

The base-line country-specific model that we shall use is the autoregressive distributed lag (ARDL) and its error correction representations discussed in the previous chapter. For sake of expositional simplicity we shall focus our attention to the following first-order ARDL model

$$y_{it} = a_i + \lambda_i y_{i,t-1} + \mathbf{b}'_i(L)\mathbf{x}_{it} + u_{it}, \quad t = 1, 2, \ldots, T, \quad i = 1, 2, \ldots, N, \quad (5.1)$$

where y_{it} is the share or logarithm of energy consumption in country i at time t, $\mathbf{x}_{it}$ is a $k \times 1$ vector of explanatory variables for country i, $\mathbf{b}_i(L)$ is the distributed lag function on these explanatory variables given by

$$\mathbf{b}_i(L) = \mathbf{b}_{i0} + \mathbf{b}_{i1} L, \quad i = 1, 2, \ldots, N. \quad (5.2)$$

This model provides a useful initial framework for investigating the consequences of pooling and can be readily generalized to higher order ARDL specifications. The error correction forms of this model can be written in terms of the lagged error:

$$\Delta y_{it} = a_i - \varphi_i(y_{i,t-1} - {}'_i\mathbf{x}_{i,t-1}) + \mathbf{b}'_{i0}\Delta\mathbf{x}_{it} + u_{it}, \quad (5.3)$$

or as a partial adjustment type error correction plus changes:

$$\Delta y_{it} = a_i - \varphi_i(y_{i,t-1} - {}'_i\mathbf{x}_{it}) - \mathbf{b}'_{i1}\Delta\mathbf{x}_{it} + u_{it}, \quad (5.4)$$

where the adjustment coefficient, $\varphi_i = 1 - \lambda_i$, and the long-run response of y_{it} to a unit change in $\mathbf{x}_{it}$ is given by the $k \times 1$ vector ${}_i = (\mathbf{b}_{i0} + \mathbf{b}_{i1})/(1 - \lambda_i)$.

The dynamics of the adjustment towards equilibrium in the present simple model are governed by φ_i and $\mathbf{b}_{i0}$ (or $\mathbf{b}_{i1}$). The disturbance terms u_{it} will be assumed to be independently normally distributed both across time and across countries with expected value zero and variances σ_i^2, $i = 1, 2, \ldots, N$. The case where the errors may be correlated across countries will be addressed in Section 5.5 on "demeaning".

Both of the above error correction formulations assume that $\varphi_i \neq 0$, namely that there exists a long-run relationship between y_{it} and $\mathbf{x}_{it}$ for all i. This assumption can however be tested using cointegration techniques if it is known *a priori* that $\mathbf{x}_{it}$'s are integrated of order 1 (or $I(1)$), or one could apply the bounds test recently developed by Pesaran, Shin and Smith (1997) when it is *not* known with certainty whether $\mathbf{x}_{it}$'s are $I(1)$ or $I(0)$.[1] But in the case of the present study where the time series observations on individual countries are available only over a relatively short period (1973–1992), there seems little point in applying unit root and cointegration tests to the energy demand equations of the individual countries.[2] An alternative approach would be to focus on averages across i of the long-run elasticities, $_i$, and the adjustment coefficients, φ_i, namely

$$\bar{}_N = N^{-1} \sum_{i=1}^{N} {}_i \quad \text{and} \quad \bar{\varphi}_N = N^{-1} \sum_{i=1}^{N} \varphi_i.$$

Although we have specified a balanced panel here for notational convenience, this is not required. Samples could differ, so that $t = 1, 2, \ldots, T_i$ for country i. We discuss the treatment of unbalanced panels data in Chapter 9.

In the context of this model, we are interested in investigating the consequences of particular assumptions about homogeneity across countries of the error variances, σ_i^2, the intercepts, a_i, the short-run coefficients, $\varphi_i, \mathbf{b}_{i0}, \mathbf{b}_{i1}$, and the long-run parameters $_i$.

5.3   Alternative Panel Data Models and Estimators

The primary difference between the various panel data estimators is the degree to which they impose homogeneity across groups with respect to variances, short or long-run regression slope coefficients and intercepts. Homogeneity need not be an all or nothing choice. Some parameters may be common and some different. In particular, it might be supposed that the long-run parameters were more likely to be homogeneous than the short-run dynamic adjustment coefficients or variances.

---

[1] A variable is said to be $I(1)$ if it *must* be first-differenced to become stationary.

[2] The low power of these tests in small samples is well established in the literature.

The least restrictive procedure is the Mean Group estimator. This imposes no homogeneity and is calculated as the mean across countries of the individual country estimates of the long-run and adjustment coefficients. The standard error of the Mean Group estimate is calculated in exactly the same way as the standard error of the mean as the standard deviation of the individual coefficients divided by the square root of N (see Pesaran, Smith and Im (1996)). Define $\hat{\theta}_i$ as the vector of long-run coefficients, $(\hat{\theta}_{yi}, \hat{\theta}_{pi})$, where the Mean Group estimator is: $\hat{\theta}_{MG} = N^{-1} \sum_{i=1}^{N} \hat{\beta}_i / (1 - \hat{\lambda}_i)$, then the variance of the Mean Group estimator is consistently estimated by

$$\hat{V}(\hat{\theta}_{MG}) = (N(N-1))^{-1} \sum_{i=1}^{N} (\hat{\theta}_i - \hat{\theta}_{MG})(\hat{\theta}_i - \hat{\theta}_{MG})'. \qquad (5.5)$$

There is another Mean Group estimator, the Random Coefficient Model (RCM) estimator, which uses weighted averages of the individual short-run coefficients calculated using the Generalized Least Squares method of Swamy (1971). The long-run coefficients are then calculated from the average short-run coefficients, rather than as averages of the long-run coefficients. We do not report the RCM estimates, but experimented with this estimator. In general, the two MG estimators give very similar results, the exception being rare cases where estimates of the coefficient of the lagged dependent variable were greater than unity. Because the RCM forms an average of the lagged dependent variable before calculating the long-run coefficient, it is less sensitive to this problem. It should be noted that under the assumption that the short-run coefficients are normally distributed, the distribution of the long-run coefficients, the ratio of two normally distributed variables, will have no moments. Essentially the problem arises because the denominator, one minus the coefficient of the lagged dependent variable, can be zero. In principle, this problem could be avoided by using an estimation method which constrains the coefficient of the lagged dependent variable to lie within the unit circle, as is done in Lee, Pesaran and Smith (1997) for instance, but this approach has not been investigated here. In small samples the lack of moments means that the distribution is likely to have thick tails and this is a feature of our results; estimates which are large outliers are not uncommon. These occur more commonly in relatively unrestricted dynamic models, where degrees of freedom are small and in more disaggregated data where measurement errors are proportionately larger and using demeaned data.

The next least restrictive estimator is the Pooled Mean Group (PMG) estimator, which imposes equality of one or both of the long-run coefficients, θ_y and θ_p but allows dynamics and error variances to differ across countries. Maximum Likelihood estimation under these conditions is discussed in Pesaran, Shin and Smith (1997). Imposing equality restrictions, if they are valid, will increase the efficiency and reduce the standard errors of the estimates. The Pooled Mean

Group estimator is also less likely to be sensitive to outlying individual estimates than the Mean Group Estimator.

The most common panel estimator for relatively large T cases such as this is the Fixed Effect (FE) estimator (also known as the Within estimator, Least Squares Dummy Variables estimator, and the Analysis of Covariance estimator). This imposes equality of all slope coefficients and equality of error variances. In general, the evidence is that the variances differ significantly across countries. As a result, even if slope coefficients were homogeneous, the FE estimator would be inefficient and the estimated standard errors would be biased and inconsistent. Heteroskedasticity consistent standard errors can, of course, be calculated by the method of White (1980). We have not used them, but it would be fairly easy to relax the assumption of constant variances in the FE estimator. This could be done either by a two step feasible Generalized Least Squares FE estimator which used estimates of the variance from the first stage individual regressions or a full maximum likelihood FE estimator which allowed variances to differ across groups.

The various panel data models advanced in the literature, such as fixed and random effects models, can be viewed as restricted forms of the general specification in (5.1). The fixed effect model imposes the slope and error variance homogeneity

$$\lambda_i = \lambda, \quad \mathbf{b}_i = \mathbf{b}, \quad \sigma_i^2 = \sigma^2, \quad \text{for } i = 1, 2, \ldots, N, \tag{5.6}$$

but allows the intercepts a_i to differ *freely* across the groups. In terms of the error correction formulations (5.3) and (5.4) the fixed effect model imposes homogeneity on the long-run as well as on the short-run coefficients

$$\varphi_i = \varphi, \quad i = , \quad \mathbf{b}_{i0} = \mathbf{b}_0,$$

or

$$\varphi_i = \varphi, \quad i = , \quad \mathbf{b}_{i1} = \mathbf{b}_0.$$

The random effects model (or the error component model) further assumes that the intercepts a_i are random draws from a distribution with a zero mean and a constant variance, distributed independently of u_{it} and $\mathbf{x}_{it}$ over time and across groups

$$a_i \sim iid\left(0, \sigma_a^2\right). \tag{5.7}$$

It is, however, easily seen that in the context of the panel error correction model (5.3) the intercepts a_i will not be distributed independently of $y_{i,t-1}$ (or the error correction term $y_{i,t-1} - \,'\mathbf{x}_{it}$) for finite T (the number of available time periods). The same difficulty also applies to the fixed effects model.[3] In such

---

[3]Excellent reviews of the fixed and random effects models can be found in Hsiao (1986), Baltagi (1995) and Matyas and Sevestre (1996).

cases the dynamic model is often first-differenced to eliminate the troublesome intercepts and the following slope-homogenous model in first-differences

$$\Delta^2 y_{it} = -\varphi(\Delta y_{i,t-1} - {'}\Delta \mathbf{x}_{i,t-1}) + \mathbf{b}_0'\Delta^2 \mathbf{x}_{it} + \Delta u_{it}, \qquad (5.8)$$

is then considered for estimation. Note that $\Delta^2 y_{it}$ stands for second differences of y_{it}, namely $\Delta^2 y_{it} = \Delta y_{it} - \Delta y_{i,t-1}$. The use of the above first-differenced formulation poses two difficulties: the errors Δu_{it} are now correlated with $\Delta y_{i,t-1}$ (and hence with the error correction term, $y_{i,t-1} - {'}\mathbf{x}_{i,t-1}$) and are themselves serially correlated. A number of instrumental variables (IV) estimators have been proposed in the literature to deal with these difficulties in the case of small T and large N panels. These include the estimators proposed by Anderson and Hsiao (1981, 1982), Arellano and Bond (1991), Arellano and Bover (1993), Keane and Runkle (1992), and Ahn and Schmidt (1995), and reviewed in Baltagi (1995, Chapter 8). The performance of these estimators crucially depends on the choice of the instruments, and whether it is possible to find instruments that are uncorrelated with Δu_{it}, while at the same time exhibit a reasonable degree of correlation with the included regressors, namely $(\Delta y_{i,t-1} - {'}\Delta \mathbf{x}_{i,t-1})$ and $\Delta^2 \mathbf{x}_{it}$. For example in the case where $\mathbf{x}_{it}$'s are pure random walks their first differences, by construction, will be uncorrelated with any variable that could be used as an instrument.

5.4 Heterogeneity of Slopes and Error Variances

Tests of the homogeneity of error variances and/or the equality of short- or long-run slope coefficients across countries can be easily carried out using Likelihood Ratio or other classical statistical procedures, since the Pooled Mean Group and Fixed Effects estimators are obtained using restricted versions of the set of individual country equations. The unrestricted model, the set of individual country equations in the first order ARDL (5.1), has $N(2k+3)$ parameters: each equation has $2k$ coefficients on the exogenous regressors, an intercept, a coefficient for the lagged dependent variable and a variance. The Pooled Mean Group Estimator imposes $(N-1)k$ restrictions on the unrestricted model, since there is a single long-run coefficient for each of the k exogenous regressors. The Fixed Effects Estimator, which imposes common slopes and common variances imposes $(N-1)(2k+2)$ restrictions on the unrestricted model, leaving only N intercepts, $2k$ coefficients corresponding to the exogenous regressors, a lagged dependent variable coefficient and a common variance to be estimated. The Likelihood Ratio test will have its familiar desirable properties for N fixed and T large. However, in our case where T is small, the Likelihood Ratio test is almost certain to reject. In addition, for reasons that are discussed below, equality of all the parameters across countries is too stringent a requirement and a more reasonable criteria for homogeneity is that the pooled estimator provides an acceptable estimate of the mean of the parameter distribution. We consider Hausman tests for this hypothesis below after we have discussed the nature of the heterogeneity.

When model (5.1) is estimated, Likelihood Ratio tests usually reject homogeneity of variances or slopes, long-run and short-run, at conventional significance levels. It is not obvious how this statistically significant heterogeneity across countries should be interpreted. There are a number of possible interpretations.

Firstly, it is possible that these countries are significantly different and that these differences are economically important, i.e. there is little or no commonality. However, the pattern of coefficients across the countries, does not correlate particularly closely with known structural characteristics. In addition, as discussed above, outliers occur particularly in more disaggregated data, in demeaned data and in ARDL$(1, 1, 1)$ specifications. Thus in a number of cases, the country-specific estimates appear completely implausible.

Secondly, it is possible that there is substantial commonality, and that the dispersion is induced by specification error or small sample biases. This would be the case if there were country-specific omitted variables or particular shocks which were correlated with the regressors. As T became large one would expect such biases to decline, but in this case T is only 17. If such biases cancelled out over the sample, the average may provide a more reasonable estimate of the true coefficient than any of the individual country estimates. However, with N only 10 the average, the Mean Group Estimator, may still be sensitive to outliers and pooling may provide more accurate estimates. If there were such specification errors, the estimated standard errors for the individual countries would underestimate the true uncertainty attached to the coefficients.

Thirdly, one could regard the differences as statistically significant, but not large enough to be economically important, particularly given the Likelihood Ratio test's tendency to over-reject in small samples. Therefore assuming a common structure may be acceptable. A further instrumental justification for this approach is that it is well known that more parsimonious models forecast better, thus it may be appropriate to penalize over-parameterized models more strongly than conventional hypothesis tests do. At large sample sizes the *SBC* gives a much higher penalty to over-parameterization, though whether this is the right penalty is less clear. On the first interpretation, one would just use the individual country estimates; the second and third interpretations would support imposing a degree of homogeneity across countries despite rejection of the equality hypothesis.

When homogeneity is wrongly imposed it can lead to heterogeneity biases in the pooled estimators. Consider the simple case of heterogeneous coefficients and an ARDL$(1, 0)$ model:

$$y_{it} = \alpha_i + \beta_i x_{it} + \lambda_i y_{i, t-1} + u_{it}; \quad i = 1, \ldots, N; \quad t = 1, 2, \ldots, T, \quad (5.9)$$

where homogeneity is wrongly imposed, so that the estimated equation is:

$$y_{it} = \alpha_i + \beta x_{it} + \lambda y_{i,t-1} + v_{it}, \tag{5.10}$$

where

$$v_{it} = (\beta_i - \beta)x_{it} + (\lambda_i - \lambda)y_{i,t-1} + u_{it}.$$

The composite error term in (5.10) will be serially correlated causing the estimates to be inconsistent even for both N and T large. If the regressor, x_{it} is positively serially correlated, this will cause the estimate of λ to be biased upwards and the estimate of β to be biased down. For large T as the coefficient of serial correlation for x_{it} goes to unity, the fixed-effects estimators of λ and β go to unity and zero, irrespective of their true values. The estimated long-run coefficient $\theta = \beta/(1-\lambda)$ will be biased upward, but the biases in the numerator and denominator offset to some extent, so the bias in the long-run coefficient is likely to be smaller than in the short-run coefficients.

In the simple ARDL$(1, 1)$ case, where the model is:

$$y_{it} = \alpha_i + \beta_{1i}x_{it} + \beta_{2i}x_{i,t-1} + \lambda_i y_{i,t-1} + u_{it},$$

and the estimated model is:

$$y_{it} = \alpha_i + \beta_0 x_{it} + \beta_1 x_{i,t-1} + \lambda y_{i,t-1} + v_{it}.$$

For large T, as the coefficient of serial correlation for x_{it} goes to unity, the estimate of λ again goes to unity, but the estimate of β_0 is consistent. However, the estimate of β_1 goes to $-\beta_0$ again irrespective of its true value, see Pesaran, Smith and Im (1996). Again the estimate of the long-run coefficient, $\theta = (\beta_0 + \beta_1)/(1 - \lambda)$ is biased, but the bias is likely to be smaller than in the short-run coefficients.

In principle, it is straightforward to determine whether the biases in the pooled estimates are serious. Consistent estimates of the mean of the long-run coefficients can easily be obtained from the Mean Group estimator. These however, will be inefficient if slope homogeneity holds. If slope homogeneity holds, the fixed effect estimator is consistent and efficient. Therefore, the effect of heterogeneity on the means of the parameters can be determined by a Hausman test between the Mean Group and Fixed Effect, or Pooled Mean Group estimates. The details of these tests are discussed in Pesaran, Smith and Im (1996). Call the Mean Group estimator of the vector of long-run coefficients $\hat{\theta}_M$ and the pooled estimator $\hat{\theta}_P$ with Variance–Covariance matrices $V(\hat{\theta}_M)$ given by (5.5) and $V(\hat{\theta}_P)$. The Variance–Covariance Matrix of the difference is then: $V(\hat{\theta}_M - \hat{\theta}_P) = V(\hat{\theta}_M) - V(\hat{\theta}_P)$ and the Hausman test statistic is

$$h = (\hat{\theta}_M - \hat{\theta}_P)'(\hat{V}(\hat{\theta}_M) - \hat{V}(\hat{\theta}_P))^{-1}(\hat{\theta}_M - \hat{\theta}_P),$$

where $\hat{V}(\hat{\theta}_M)$ and $\hat{V}(\hat{\theta}_P)$ are consistent estimators of $V(\hat{\theta}_M)$ and $V(\hat{\theta}_P)$, respectively. Under the slope homogeneity hypothesis the Hausman's statistic is asymptotically distributed as a χ^2 with degrees of freedom equal to the dimension of θ.

There is no guarantee that $\hat{V}(\hat{\theta}_M) - \hat{V}(\hat{\theta}_P)$ will be positive definite, this was not often a problem in the applications and we report the cases where it arose.

Although the Mean Group estimator is consistent, when T is small there is the traditional lagged dependent variable bias, which biases the estimate of λ downwards. Large N does not help with this problem, since all the estimates are biased in the same direction. Given that $T = 18$ in our case, this will be a problem. Pesaran and Zhao (1997) propose a bias corrected Mean Group estimator, which adjusts the long-run coefficient by an estimate of its bias. We have not used this bias correction here, but we hope to investigate its effects. In the case of the pooled estimators, the downward lagged dependent variable bias, which they also suffer, may offset the upward heterogeneity bias to some extent, but it is difficult to judge the relative effects of the two biases in our sample.

5.5   Unobservable Components and Demeaning

Pooling examines whether there is commonality across countries in parameters: long-run coefficients, short-run coefficients or variances, but otherwise treats the countries as independent. In this section, we investigate another source of commonality: common shocks hitting each country. The most obvious source of common shocks is in the development of energy technology and one of the criticisms of the econometric approach, mentioned in the introduction, was that it could not deal with energy saving technical change. However, the panel structure of the data may, in certain circumstances, allow us to estimate unobserved technical efficiency changes. Suppose that there is some measure of technical efficiency, η_t, that influences all countries identically and that the slope coefficients are homogeneous across countries. The model can be written:

$$y_{it} = a_i + \mathbf{b}'\mathbf{x}_{it} + \lambda y_{i,t-1} + \eta_t + u_{it},$$

where $\mathbf{x}_{it}$ is a vector containing the exogenous regressors and (possibly) their lagged values, and $y_{i,t-1}$ contains lagged values of the dependent variable. This can be estimated by the familiar two way fixed effect model, which involves applying least squares to deviations from group and year means:

$$y_{it} - \bar{y}_t = a_i + \mathbf{b}'(\mathbf{x}_{it} - \bar{\mathbf{x}}_t) + \lambda'(y_{i,t-1} - \bar{y}_{t-1}) + (u_{it} - \bar{u}_t), \qquad (5.11)$$

where $\bar{y}_t$, $\bar{\mathbf{x}}_t$ and $\bar{u}_t$ are respectively the means of y_{it}, $\mathbf{x}_{it}$, and u_{it} over i for year t (namely $\bar{y}_t = N^{-1}\sum_i y_{it}$, etc.), such that

$$\bar{y}_t = a + \mathbf{b}'\bar{\mathbf{x}}_t + \lambda'\bar{y}_{t-1} + \eta_t + \bar{u}_t. \qquad (5.12)$$

where $a = N^{-1} \sum_i a_i$. The above demeaning procedure removes the common unobservable time-varying shocks, η_t, from the demeaned panel data model (5.11). Also, if N is sufficiently large, $\bar{u}_t$ will converge to zero and the aggregate equation (5.12) can be used to provide an estimate of η_t. This estimate will have mean zero over the sample, but is otherwise unrestricted: it could be trended, correlated with $\mathbf{x}_{it}$, etc.

If there were no lagged dependent variables and one were also willing to assume a random effects model for the intercepts (namely, $a_i = a + v_i$, $v_i \sim iid(0, \sigma_v^2)$), then the sequence of cross-section regressions:

$$y_{it} = a_t + \mathbf{b}'_t \mathbf{x}_{it} + u_{it} + v_i,$$

where $a_t = a + \eta_t$, would allow the investigation of both changes in technical efficiencies and the extent of time variation in the slope coefficients, $\mathbf{b}_t$. Pesaran and Smith (1995) discuss the circumstances under which the cross-section will provide estimates of the long-run relationship. However, if the coefficients are changing every year, there will be no well-defined long-run relationship.

When the slope coefficients are constant over time but differ across countries, the model becomes

$$y_{it} = a_i + \mathbf{b}'_i \mathbf{x}_{it} + \lambda_i y_{i,t-1} + u_{it} + \eta_t.$$

This seems to be the appropriate basic model, because all the evidence seems to indicate a significant degree of slope heterogeneity across countries. When the common shocks η_t are distributed independently of the regressors with a constant mean and are also serially uncorrelated, we can obtain consistent estimates of a_i, $\mathbf{b}_i$ and λ_i from the individual country regressions and estimate η_t from the mean of their residuals for each year. This estimate could then be used in a two step GLS estimator to improve the efficiency of the estimates of the individual country regressions, by adding the average residual to the equation. Full Maximum Likelihood estimation is also possible. This Heterogeneous Random Effects Model is a natural generalization of the traditional Random Effects model for time effects. It is also related to the familiar Zellner (1962) Seemingly Unrelated Regression Equation (SURE) approach, which is equivalent to including the residuals from each of the other equations in each equation. In our application where N is 10, the SURE estimator has the disadvantage that it requires the estimation of an error covariance matrix which is large relative to the sample size available. With $N = 10$ and $T = 17$ we need to estimate a total of $10(2k + 3) + 10 \times 11/2 = 85 + 20k$ unknown parameters with only 170 observations, where k is the number of regressors. This is likely to introduce additional small sample biases into the analysis. More importantly, since one would expect technical efficiency to be correlated with incomes and prices, it seems very unlikely that the common component of the shocks would be uncorrelated with the regressors, which is required for the SURE or the Random effects procedure. If η_t is correlated with any of the elements of $\mathbf{x}_{it}$

the individual country estimates will be inconsistent and the year means of the estimated residuals would not provide reliable estimates of η_t.

The different assumptions concerning slopes and common shocks and appropriate estimation strategies (for large N and T) can be summarized in the following table:

	Homogeneous slopes	Heterogeneous slopes
$\eta_t = 0$, Fixed a_i's	Fixed effects estimates	Individual country regressions
$\eta_t \neq 0$, Random a_i's	Random effects estimates on demeaned data	Heterogeneous REM/SURE
$\eta_t \neq 0$, Fixed a_i's	Fixed effects estimates on demeaned data	N/A

The question mark arises in the bottom right hand corner, because although one can still remove η_t by taking deviations from year means, in the case of heterogeneous slope coefficients this has other consequences, which we now consider. To examine these consequences, assume that the slope coefficients are distributed randomly and independently of $\mathbf{x}_{it}$:

$$\mathbf{b}_i = \mathbf{b} + {}_{bi}, \qquad \lambda_i = \lambda + \xi_{\lambda i},$$

with $E(\xi_{ji}) = 0$, $Var(\xi_{ji}) = \Omega_j$, $j = b, \lambda$.

When the model is averaged over groups to get year means it now becomes:

$$\bar{y}_t = \bar{a} + \mathbf{b}'\bar{\mathbf{x}}_t + \lambda\bar{y}_{t-1} + \bar{u}_t + \eta_t + N^{-1}\sum_{j=1}^{N}{}'_{bj}\mathbf{x}_{jt} + N^{-1}\sum_{j=1}^{N}\xi_{\lambda j}y_{j,t-1}.$$

Define the deviations from the year means as $\nabla y_{it} = y_{it} - \bar{y}_t$, $\nabla \mathbf{x}_{it} = \mathbf{x}_{it} - \bar{\mathbf{x}}_t$ then subtracting and noting that

$$\mathbf{b}'_i\mathbf{x}_{it} - \mathbf{b}'\bar{\mathbf{x}}_t = \mathbf{b}'_i\nabla\mathbf{x}_{it} + {}'_{bj}\bar{\mathbf{x}}_t,$$

$$\nabla y_{it} = (a_i - \bar{a}) + \mathbf{b}'_i\nabla\mathbf{x}_{it} + \lambda_i\nabla y_{i,t-1} + \nabla u_{it} + e_{it},$$

where

$$e_{it} = \left\{ {}'_{bi}\bar{\mathbf{x}}_t - N^{-1}\sum_{j=1}^{N}{}'_{bj}\mathbf{x}_{jt} \right\} + \left\{ \xi_{\lambda i}\bar{y}_{t-1} - N^{-1}\sum_{j=1}^{N}\xi_{\lambda j}y_{j,t-1} \right\}.$$

Notice that the process of demeaning has removed the common time-varying component, η_t, but has added new terms reflecting the neglected slope heterogeneity effects. The term e_{it} can be written:

$$e_{it} = \sum_j (\mathbf{b}_i - \mathbf{b})' \mathbf{x}_{jt}/N - \sum_j (\mathbf{b}_j - \mathbf{b})' \mathbf{x}_{jt}/N$$

$$+ \sum_j (\lambda_i - \lambda) y_{j,t-1}/N - \sum_j (\lambda_j - \lambda) y_{j,t-1}/N,$$

or

$$e_{it} = N^{-1} \sum_j (\mathbf{b}_i - \mathbf{b}_j)' \mathbf{x}_{jt} + N^{-1} \sum_j (\lambda_i - \lambda_j) y_{j,t-1}.$$

For $j = i$, the terms are zero and for $j \neq i$ they will be uncorrelated with the regressors in the ith equation as long as the slopes are distributed independently of the regressors and the regressors are uncorrelated across groups. If these assumptions are satisfied, we will be able to obtain consistent estimates of the parameters, using the Mean Group approach even when the individual country energy demands are subject to an observed common (technological) trend. However, the demeaning will increase the size of the error variances and could result in a substantial loss of efficiency. In this case the benefit of demeaning can be judged from the relative fit of the regressions on the demeaned and undemeaned data. The demeaned will fit better if the improvement from removing the common technological trend outweighs the loss from the added dispersion term.

In the light of this discussion, a comparison of the demeaned and undemeaned estimates may be regarded as a misspecification test, for the importance of the omission of a common technological trend and spillover effects. Demeaning the data has substantial advantages because it enables us to exploit the panel structure of the data to take out general technological or other trends of any form which influence all the countries and allow for spillovers. However, even if the demeaned equations are regarded as better, for forecasting it is also necessary to forecast the means over the sample. One way that this could be done is to construct a model of the averages, namely the aggregate time series regression:

$$\bar{y}_t = \bar{a} + \mathbf{b}' \bar{\mathbf{x}}_t + \lambda \bar{y}_{t-1} + \bar{u}_t.$$

As is discussed in Pesaran and Smith (1995), equations of this sort estimated on averages will be subject to a range of biases. There are various possible alternatives. One would be to include averages for the regressors and the lagged dependent variable in the equations directly, not constraining their effects to work through deviations from the mean. Pesaran, Pierse and Kumar (1989) and Binder and Pesaran (1997) use year averages of the regressors across groups to model the macro-effects on group-specific decisions.

An alternative approach would be to model η_t using the macro error correction term $\bar{y}_{t-1} - '\bar{x}_{t-1}$, under the assumption that the long-run coefficients are homogeneous. In this case we have

$$\Delta y_{it} = a_i - \varphi_i(y_{i,t-1} - 'x_{i,t-1}) - \delta_i(\bar{y}_{t-1} - '\bar{x}_{t-1}) + b'_i \Delta x_{it} + u_{it},$$

where changes in Δy_{it} are driven by both country-specific and global error correction terms. Although this approach seems worth investigating, in the case of Asian energy demand the year averages seem to add little to the explanatory power of the country-specific energy demand equations, perhaps because of the heterogeneity of the sample. Thus we have decided not to pursue this approach in the present study.

Part III

Empirical Results

CHAPTER 6

Aggregate Demand for Energy

In this chapter we will apply the methodology described in the previous chapters to the aggregate data for energy demand in Asian developing countries. We begin by considering the estimates for the individual countries, first choosing functional form and then examining their sensitivity to dynamic specification and to the use of demeaned data. Then we examine alternative pooled estimates and the cross-section estimates.

6.1 Individual Country Estimates

6.1.1 Choice of Functional Form

The starting point of an empirical analysis is the error correction model (ECM) for the share of energy derived in Section 3.3.1 in Chapter 3 (3.32). This makes the equilibrium share of energy in total expenditure a linear function of the logarithms of income and prices, but allows flexible first-order adjustment towards this equilibrium. The equation is:

$$M_w: \quad \Delta w_{it} = \varphi_i \alpha_i - \varphi_i(w_{i,t-1} - \beta_{1i}\ln(P_{it}) - \beta_{2i}\ln(CPI_{it}) - \delta_i\ln(y_{it}))$$
$$+ \kappa_{1i}\Delta\ln(P_{it}) + \kappa_{2i}\Delta\ln(CPI_{it}) + \kappa_{3i}\Delta\ln(y_{it}) + v_{it}, \qquad (6.1)$$

for $i = 1, 2, \ldots, N$ and $t = 1, 2, \ldots, T$, where $w_{it} = (P_{it} \times e_{it})/(CPI_{it} \times y_{it})$, e_{it} is the per-capita total energy consumption, measured in TOE per person in country i in year t, y_{it} is real per-capita GDP in international prices, taken from the PWT database in country i in year t, P_{it} is the price of energy and CPI is the consumer price index (CPI). The disturbance v_{it} is assumed to be independently normally distributed with expected value zero and variance σ_i^2.

This equation will be estimated as an ARDL(1, 1, 1, 1) model of the form discussed in Chapter 4:

$$\lambda_i(L)w_{it} = a_i + b_{1i}(L)\ln(P_{it}) + b_{2i}(L)\ln(CPI_{it}) + b_{3i}(L)\ln(y_{it}) + v_{it}, \qquad (6.2)$$

where

$$\lambda_i(L) = 1 - \lambda_i L, \qquad b_{ji}(L) = b_{j0i} + b_{j1i}L, \qquad (6.3)$$
$$j = 1, 2, 3, \quad i = 1, 2, \ldots, N \qquad (6.4)$$

79

and the parameters of the ECM in (6.1) can be derived from the parameters of the above ARDL model as:

$$\varphi_i = (1 - \lambda_i), \quad \beta_{1i} = (b_{10i} + b_{11i})/(1 - \lambda_i), \quad \text{etc.}$$

This model contains 8 unknown coefficients to be estimated from 17 observations, which leaves very few degrees of freedom. This is likely to be a severe problem, particularly given the presence of badly measured data and the danger of small sample biases. Therefore it is important to try and develop restricted versions of (6.1) that are data-acceptable. The restrictions we examine are the long-run price homogeneity hypothesis:

$$H_{lh}: \quad \beta_{1i} + \beta_{2i} = 0, \tag{6.5}$$

against

$$\beta_{1i} + \beta_{2i} \neq 0.$$

The long-run and short-run price homogeneity hypothesis:

$$H_h: \quad \beta_{1i} + \beta_{2i} = 0 \text{ and } \kappa_{1i} + \kappa_{2i} = 0, \tag{6.6}$$

against

$$\beta_{1i} + \beta_{2i} \neq 0 \quad \text{and/or} \quad \kappa_{1i} + \kappa_{2i} \neq 0.$$

The partial adjustment hypothesis:

$$H_{pa}: \quad \kappa_{1i} = \kappa_{2i} = \kappa_{3i} = 0, \tag{6.7}$$

against

$$\kappa_{1i} \neq 0, \qquad \kappa_{2i} \neq 0, \qquad \kappa_{3i} \neq 0.$$

And finally the partial adjustment hypothesis conditional on price homogeneity:

$$H_{pa|h}: \quad \kappa_{1i} = \kappa_{2i} = \kappa_{3i} = 0, \quad \text{and } \beta_{1i} + \beta_{2i} = 0, \tag{6.8}$$

against

$$H_{lh}: \quad \beta_{1i} + \beta_{2i} = 0, \quad \kappa_{1i} \neq 0, \quad \kappa_{2i} \neq 0, \quad \kappa_{3i} \neq 0.$$

The general first-order error correction model (6.1) was estimated for each country subject to the four sets of restrictions. Table 6.1 presents the F statistics for testing these restrictions.

It is clear that the above restrictions are generally accepted. Long-run homogeneity is only rejected at the 5 per cent level in Korea. The joint hypothesis of long-run and short-run homogeneity is rejected in Korea and Taiwan. The partial adjustment hypothesis (without imposing the homogeneity) is rejected only in the case of Taiwan, but when it is tested relative to the model which imposes homogeneity, the partial adjustment hypothesis is rejected in the case of Bangladesh and Malaysia. Overall, the results tend to support a simple partial adjustment model subject to the homogeneity hypothesis. This in turn suggests an ARDL$(1, 0, 0)$ model in the energy share, w_{it}, logarithm of real output, $\ln(y_{it})$, and logarithm of real energy prices $\ln(P_{it}/CPI_{it})$.

Table 6.1:   *F*-statistics for testing restrictions on the shares equation (6.1).

Country	H_{lh}	H_h	H_{pa}	$H_{pa|h}$
Bangladesh	0.82	1.50	3.48	**5.03**
India	0.12	0.09	0.44	0.90
Indonesia	1.68	1.37	1.28	0.89
Korea	**18.11**	**10.54**	0.65	2.09
Malaysia	2.22	2.60	2.24	**4.52**
Pakistan	4.42	2.41	1.19	0.94
Philippines	0.38	0.52	1.48	2.92
Sri Lanka	2.42	3.74	3.50	1.84
Taiwan	0.16	**6.69**	**5.81**	1.02
Thailand	0.28	0.37	1.84	2.72
D of F	$F(1, 9)$	$F(2, 9)$	$F(3, 9)$	$F(2, 11)$
5 per cent CV	5.12	4.26	3.86	3.98

H_{lh}: Long-run price homogeneity hypothesis, see (6.5).
H_h: Short-run and long-run homogeneity hypothesis, see (6.6).
H_{pa}: Partial adjustment restrictions, see (6.7).
$H_{pa|h}$: Partial adjustment restrictions conditional on the price homogeneity restrictions, see (6.8).

Table 6.2 presents estimates and diagnostic statistics for the partial adjustment version of the model subject to the price homogeneity hypothesis, i.e. under the $H_{pa|h}$ defined by (6.8). The table gives the estimates of φ_i, $\beta_i = \beta_{1i} = \beta_{i2}$, and δ_i. It is noticeable that $\lambda_i = 1 - \varphi_i$ is only significantly different from zero in only one of the ten countries, namely Malaysia, and in four countries it is negative. If $\varphi_i = 1$, adjustment is instantaneous and long-run and short-run coefficients are the same.

Based on the parameter estimates in Table 6.2 the long-run elasticities evaluated at sample means of the data are given in Table 6.3. These estimates are based on holding real income constant, since changes in a country's prices do not change GDP measured at international prices. A different elasticity measure is used below when measuring inter-fuel substitution and this is discussed in an appendix. The long-run income elasticities are significantly different from unity in Bangladesh, where it is substantially higher; Thailand, where it is very close to unity; Taiwan, where it is slightly below unity; and Sri Lanka where it is negative. Long-run price elasticities are significantly negative in four countries, insignificantly negative in one, insignificantly positive in four, and significantly positive in Korea.

The diagnostic statistics in Table 6.2 are for the error correction equation (6.1), so the $\bar{R}^2$ gives the proportion of the change in energy shares (Δw_{it}) explained, and the functional form and heteroskedasticity tests are based on auxiliary regressions on the fitted values of the change in the dependent variable (namely Δw_{it}). The Malaysian equation fits particularly poorly. At the 5 per cent level, the equation fails the test for residual serial correlation in

Table 6.2a: Country-specific estimates of the long-run coefficients of the total energy share equation (6.1) under (6.8).

Country	Parameter estimates[1]					
	$\hat{\varphi}$	$\hat{\delta}$	$\hat{\beta}$	$\hat{\sigma}$	$\bar{R}^2$	LL
Bangladesh	−0.936	0.182	0.192	0.017	0.69	46.98
	(0.156)	(0.045)	(0.024)			
India	−1.097	0.041	0.389	0.015	0.79	49.04
	(0.150)	(0.045)	(0.035)			
Indonesia	−0.998	4.820	22.526	1.401	0.86	−27.58
	(0.103)	(3.396)	(2.074)			
Korea	−1.144	−7.220	99.957	4.763	0.91	−48.38
	(0.102)	(3.752)	(4.216)			
Malaysia	−0.361	−0.069	0.229	0.009	0.50	58.47
	(0.120)	(0.081)	(0.087)			
Pakistan	−0.887	0.075	0.475	0.015	0.91	49.39
	(0.084)	(0.070)	(0.053)			
Philippines	−1.118	−0.331	0.929	0.087	0.88	19.61
	(0.106)	(0.273)	(0.085)			
Sri Lanka	−0.949	−0.844	0.862	0.053	0.85	28.13
	(0.111)	(0.185)	(0.079)			
Taiwan	−0.718	−0.714	3.912	0.174	0.70	7.93
	(0.155)	(0.278)	(0.385)			
Thailand	−1.083	0.082	0.819	0.026	0.95	40.22
	(0.065)	(0.030)	(0.034)			

[1] All the regressions are estimated over the period 1974–1990 inclusive ($T = 17$). The figures in brackets are standard errors, $\hat{\sigma}$ is the estimated standard error of the regression, $\bar{R}^2$ is the adjusted squared multiple correlation coefficient of the error correction model, $\hat{\varphi}$ is the coefficient of the error correction term which is imposed to be equal to −1 in case of models without lagged dependent variables. *LL* is the maximized value of the log-likelihood of the estimated equation.

Table 6.2b: Diagnostic statistics for the results in Table 6.2a.

Country	Diagnostic statistics[1]			
	$\chi^2_{SC}(1)$	$\chi^2_{FF}(1)$	$\chi^2_N(2)$	$\chi^2_H(1)$
Bangladesh	0.02	0.26	2.61	0.56
India	0.33	0.55	0.10	0.19
Indonesia	2.24	3.34	1.22	0.02
Korea	**9.14**	0.32	0.87	0.06
Malaysia	0.27	2.09	0.52	0.01
Pakistan	0.15	**7.25**	0.55	**4.64**
Philippines	**3.82**	0.88	1.60	0.08
Sri Lanka	0.64	**4.34**	0.79	0.07
Taiwan	3.48	5.91	0.20	**7.08**
Thailand	0.42	1.13	1.18	0.28

[1] $\chi^2_{SC}(1)$, $\chi^2_{FF}(1)$, $\chi^2_N(2)$, $\chi^2_H(1)$, are Lagrange multiplier statistics for tests of residual serial correlation, functional form mis-specification, non-normal errors, and heteroskedasticity.

Table 6.3: Long-run income and price elasticities, using the estimates of energy share equations in Table 6.2.

Country	Income[1]			Price[2]		
	Elasticity	*Standard error*	*t-ratio*[3]	*Elasticity*	*Standard error*	*t-ratio*[4]
Bangladesh	1.86	0.21	4.04	−0.10	0.11	−0.90
India	1.09	0.10	0.91	−0.18	0.07	−2.50
Indonesia	1.17	0.12	1.42	−0.21	0.07	−2.82
Korea	0.92	0.04	−1.92	0.11	0.05	2.44
Malaysia	0.55	0.52	−0.86	0.48	0.56	0.85
Pakistan	1.17	0.16	1.06	0.08	0.12	0.65
Philippines	0.75	0.20	−1.21	−0.31	0.06	−4.88
Sri Lanka	−0.05	0.23	−4.55	0.07	0.10	0.75
Taiwan	0.80	0.08	−2.57	0.08	0.11	0.77
Thailand	1.07	0.03	2.75	−0.29	0.03	−9.62
Average	0.93			−0.03		

[1] Calculated as the long-run income coefficient, divided by the average share +1.
[2] Calculated as the long-run price coefficient, divided by the average share −1.
[3] *t*-ratio for testing unit long-run income elasticity.
[4] *t*-ratio for testing zero long-run price elasticity.

Korea, the test for functional form in Pakistan, Sri Lanka and Taiwan and the test for heteroskedasticity in the cases of Pakistan and Taiwan.

If the fitted values w_{it} are used instead of the fitted values of the changes, Δw_{it}, the share equations would have failed the functional form test at the 5 per cent level in six out of the ten countries. This suggests that it may be worthwhile considering alternative functional forms for the energy demand equations.

A natural alternative to the share equation would be to use logarithms of the energy shares, i.e.

$$M_{lw}: \quad \Delta \ln(w_{it}) = \varphi_i^L \alpha_i^L - \varphi_i^L \left(\ln(w_{i,t-1}) - \beta_{1i}^L \ln(P_{it}) \right.$$

$$\left. - \beta_{2i}^L \ln(CPI_{it}) - \delta_i^L \ln(y_{it}) \right) + \kappa_{1i}^L \Delta \ln(P_{it})$$

$$+ \kappa_{2i}^L \Delta \ln(CPI_{it}) + \kappa_{3i}^L \Delta \ln(y_{it}) + v_{it}^L. \quad (6.9)$$

In theoretical terms, M_w is preferrable to M_{lw}, since it is consistent with the budget constraint and satisfies the adding up restrictions. However, in statistical terms, M_{lw} may fit better. This raises the difficult question of how one trades off theoretical consistency and statistical adequacy discussed in Pesaran and Smith (1985). If M_{lw} fits a little better, then one still may prefer to use M_w because of its theoretical advantage. However, if M_{lw} fits a great deal better than M_w, one may be unwilling to sacrifice fit for theoretical consistency.

Table 6.4 gives the test results for comparing simple versions of the specifications M_w and M_{lw}, using three non-nested tests (the Pesaran and Pesaran (1995) simulated Cox test statistic, S_c; the Bera and McAleer (1989) test, *BM*; and the Davidson and MacKinnon (1984) Double Length regression test, *DL*) and the

Table 6.4: Non-nested tests of share versus logarithmic share models.

Country	S_c test		BM test		DL test		Sargan criterion
	M_w versus M_{lw}	M_w versus M_{lw}	M_w versus M_{lw}	M_w versus M_{lw}	M_w versus M_{lw}	M_w versus M_{lw}	
Bangladesh	6.71	0.76	4.73	−0.66	3.64	1.19	−13.61
India	−3.46	1.75	1.73	−1.00	1.96	1.38	−1.26
Indonesia	−4.06	0.47	1.38	−0.39	2.28	1.14	−2.91
Korea	−8.56	1.98	4.52	−1.98	3.64	1.66	−8.02
Malaysia	−2.05	−0.32	1.88	−0.54	1.65	1.25	−0.73
Pakistan	−6.09	1.54	2.68	−0.67	2.96	1.23	−5.41
Philippines	−4.13	1.57	2.59	−2.78	3.22	1.48	−3.03
Sri Lanka	−3.96	−0.04	2.94	−0.57	2.00	1.14	−2.21
Taiwan	−3.45	1.49	3.33	−2.40	2.50	1.62	−2.08
Thailand	−1.76	−0.18	2.18	−0.98	1.47	1.18	−0.47

Sargan relative likelihood criterion. These tests are described in Pesaran and Pesaran (1997, Section 18.8). The results are clear cut. The linear share model, M_w, is rejected at the 5 per cent level against the logarithmic alternative in nine countries by the S_c test, seven countries by the BM test and eight countries by the BL test. The logarithmic model is rejected at the 5 per cent level by the linear alternative in one country by the S_c test, in three countries by the BM test and in no countries by the DL test. The Sargan criterion chooses the logarithmic model in every case. This is strong evidence in favour of the logarithmic model and suggests sacrificing theoretical consistency for statistical adequacy.

Using the following identity for the logarithm of the energy shares

$$\ln(w_{it}) = \ln(e_{it}) + \ln(P_{it}) - \ln(CPI_{it}) - \ln(y_{it}),$$

the logarithmic formulation of the energy shares model in (6.9) can also be written as

$$\Delta \ln(e_{it}) = a_i - \varphi_i \left(\ln(e_{i,t-1}) - \theta_{1i} \ln(P_{it}) - \theta_{2i} \ln(CPI_{it}) - \theta_{yi} \ln(y_{it}) \right)$$
$$+ \gamma_{1i} \Delta \ln(P_{it}) + \gamma_{2i} \Delta \ln(CPI_{it}) + \gamma_{3i} \Delta \ln(y_{it}) + u_{it}, \qquad (6.10)$$

where $a_i, \varphi_i, \theta_{1i}, \theta_{2i}, \theta_{yi}, b_{1i}$, etc. are related to the parameters of the log-share equation:

$$a_i = \varphi_i^L \alpha_i^L, \quad \varphi_i = \varphi_i^L, \quad \theta_{1i} = (\beta_{1i}^L - 1), \quad \theta_{2i} = (\beta_{2i}^L + 1), \quad \theta_{yi} = (\delta_i^L + 1),$$
$$\gamma_{1i} = (\kappa_{1i}^L - 1), \quad \gamma_{2i} = (\kappa_{2i}^L + 1), \quad \gamma_{3i} = (\kappa_{3i}^L + 1), \quad u_{it} = v_{it}^L.$$

The equation (6.10) is an error correction version of the traditional log-log form of demand function and is the form that we shall use below. This version has the advantage that the coefficients are the parameters of interest, the elasticities, and for forecasting it is more convenient to work with the logarithm of the quantity of energy demanded than the share of energy in output. In addition, it seems more likely that the long-run elasticities will be the same across countries than the coefficients of the share equation, which are sensitive to the scaling problem discussed in Section 2.4. Notice that for the log-log equation to be interpreted as a logarithmic share equation, the regressors must have a common lag length.

For comparison, the earlier set of tests were repeated on the logarithmic model. In the context of the log-log specification (6.10), the hypotheses that we examine are the long-run price homogeneity ($\theta_{1i} + \theta_{2i} = 0$), the long-run and short-run price homogeneity ($\theta_{1i} + \theta_{2i} = 0$ and $\gamma_{1i} + \gamma_{2i} = 0$), the partial adjustment hypothesis ($\gamma_{1i} = \gamma_{2i} = \gamma_{3i} = 0$), and the partial adjustment hypothesis conditional on price homogeneity ($\gamma_{1i} = \gamma_{2i} = \gamma_{3i} = 0$, conditional on $\theta_{1i} + \theta_{2i} = 0$). The tests were applied to the logarithmic energy equation rather than the log-share equation. Although these two specifications are equivalent when they are based on an ARDL(1, 1, 1, 1) equation of the form given above, they are not equivalent when the lag lengths on different variables in the ARDL model are not the same, as in the partial adjustment model with the ARDL(1, 0, 0, 0) specification. When both versions were estimated the partial adjustment form for log per-capita energy demand fitted better than a partial adjustment model in the log share of energy, in all but two of the countries (India and Taiwan). The lagged values of the logarithm of energy shares were significant only in the case of three countries: Indonesia, where it had the wrong sign, Malaysia and Taiwan; whereas lagged values of the logarithm of energy variable was significant in all but India, Sri Lanka and Taiwan. Since our prior view is that long-run and short-run responses should differ, this suggests choosing the log energy model rather than log energy share model.

The log energy share equation was estimated for each country under the four hypotheses H_{lh}, H_h, H_{pa}, and $H_{pa|h}$. Table 6.5 presents F statistics for testing these four hypotheses. The long-run price homogeneity hypothesis is now rejected in the case of Indonesia, Korea and Pakistan, although the joint hypothesis of the short-run and long-run homogeneity is rejected only in the case of Taiwan. This apparent contradiction simply reflects the relatively low power of the joint test. The partial adjustment hypothesis is rejected only in the case of Taiwan, irrespective of whether it is tested imposing the price homogeneity hypothesis or not. These test results point to an ARDL(1, 0, 0) model in the logarithm of energy consumption, ln (e_{it}), logarithm of real per-capita output, ln(y_{it}), and logarithm of real energy prices, ln (P_{it}/CPI_{it}), as the preferred specification for the analysis of energy demand in the case of the majority of the Asian economies under consideration.

The estimates of the ARDL(1, 0, 0) model for each of the ten countries are summarized in Table 6.6. The long-run income and price elasticity estimates for Malaysia and Sri Lanka are clearly implausible. The same also applies to the estimates obtained for Bangladesh and could be due to data inadequacies and the high level of aggregation used in the analysis. But it is interesting that if one excludes these three countries from the sample, the remaining estimates are largely reasonable. The estimates of the long-run income elasticity range from

Table 6.5:   *F*-Statistics for testing price homogeneity and partial adjustment restrictions on the logarithmic model, (6.10).

Country	H_{lh}	H_h	H_{pa}	$H_{pa|h}$
Bangladesh	0.003	0.011	0.034	0.057
India	0.002	0.021	0.43	1.00
Indonesia	**6.16**	3.45	1.29	0.074
Korea	**7.38**	3.76	1.56	0.10
Malaysia	2.13	2.00	1.20	0.30
Pakistan	**6.12**	3.15	1.01	1.14
Philippines	2.93	2.39	1.92	0.59
Sri Lanka	3.67	3.64	3.68	2.28
Taiwan	0.002	**5.28**	**11.39**	**6.63**
Thailand	0.002	0.20	0.35	0.42
D of F	$F(1,9)$	$F(2,9)$	$F(3,9)$	$F(2,11)$
5 per cent CV	5.12	4.26	3.86	3.98

H_{lh}: Long-run price homogeneity hypothesis ($\theta_{1i} + \theta_{2i} = 0$).
H_h: Short-run and long-run price homogeniety hypothesis ($\theta_{1i} + \theta_{2i} = 0$, $\gamma_{1i} + \gamma_{2i} = 0$).
H_{pa}: Partial adjustment restrictions ($\gamma_{1i} = \gamma_{2i} = \gamma_{3i} = 0$).
$H_{pa|h}$: Partial adjustment restrictions conditional on the price homogeneity hypothesis ($\gamma_{1i} = \gamma_{2i} = \gamma_{3i} = 0$ conditional on $\theta_{1i} + \theta_{2i} = 0$).

0.835 (Philippines) to 1.564 (Indonesia) with an average estimate of 1.12, and the long-run price elasticities range from 0.05 (Pakistan) to −0.488 (Indonesia) with an average estimate of −0.22. As noted above adjustment is much slower and more plausible in the log energy than in the log energy shares or shares models. All the estimates of the adjustment coefficient, φ_i, are negative and fall in the range (−0.132 to − 0.825).

The long-run income elasticity is significantly different from unity in three countries, Bangladesh, Indonesia and Thailand, and as with the shares model, in Thailand the estimated long-run income elasticity is close to unity. The estimates of the long-run price elasticities are much more plausible than those obtained using the shares model; only three are positive (Bangladesh, Pakistan and Sri Lanka) and none of them significantly so. There are three significantly negative price elasticities. Long-run income elasticities range from 2.22 (Malaysia) to 0.22 (Sri Lanka), and long-run price elasticities from 0.06 (Sri Lanka) to −1.16 (Malaysia).

The $\bar{R}^2$, which measures the proportion of the change in the logarithm of per-capita energy demand explained corrected for degrees of freedom, is substantially lower than for the shares equation and is very low for Malaysia and Pakistan. The better fit of the shares equation reflects the fact that when price elasticities are low, as they are here, price movements will explain a lot of the variation in the value shares and relatively little of the variation in quantity. The standard error of the regression can be interpreted as a proportionate error and varies from 1.7 per cent in the case of Thailand to 6.3 per cent in

Table 6.6a: Country-specific estimates of the long-run income and price elasticities based on ARDL(1, 0, 0) specifications.

Country	Parameter estimates[1]					
	$\hat{\varphi}$	$\hat{\theta}_y$	$\hat{\theta}_p$	$\hat{\sigma}$	$\bar{R}^2$	*LL*
Bangladesh	−0.597	1.979	0.035	0.036	0.68	34.50
	(0.126)	(0.177)	(0.095)			
India	−0.811	1.006	−0.068	0.027	0.38	39.44
	(0.243)	(0.102)	(0.080)			
Indonesia	−0.374	1.564	−0.488	0.034	0.52	35.52
	(0.171)	(0.234)	(0.195)			
Korea	−0.318	1.074	−0.136	0.031	0.54	37.17
	(0.147)	(0.125)	(0.189)			
Malaysia	−0.132	2.218	−1.159	0.042	0.02	31.94
	(0.117)	(1.228)	(1.182)			
Pakistan	−0.483	1.320	0.047	0.031	0.08	36.94
	(0.232)	(0.226)	(0.169)			
Philippines	−0.525	0.835	−0.431	0.044	0.56	31.35
	(0.132)	(0.290)	(0.110)			
Sri Lanka	−0.825	0.217	0.061	0.063	0.36	25.20
	(0.273)	(0.254)	(0.108)			
Taiwan	−0.458	0.897	−0.132	0.054	0.12	27.84
	(0.298)	(0.102)	(0.273)			
Thailand	−0.721	1.172	−0.341	0.017	0.91	47.12
	(0.097)	(0.047)	(0.042)			

[1] All the regressions are estimated over the period 1974–1990 inclusive ($T = 17$). The figures in brackets are standard errors, $\hat{\sigma}$ is the estimated standard error of the regression, $\bar{R}^2$ is the adjusted squared multiple correlation coefficient of the error correction model, $\hat{\varphi}$ is the coefficient of the error correction term. *LL* is the maximized value of the log-likelihood of the estimated equation.

Table 6.6b: Diagnostic statistics for the results in Table 6.6a.

Country	Diagnostic statistics[1]			
	$\chi^2_{SC}(1)$	$\chi^2_{FF}(1)$	$\chi^2_N(2)$	$\chi^2_H(1)$
Bangladesh	4.31	0.03	0.64	0.06
India	1.66	2.43	0.35	1.21
Indonesia	0.04	0.00	0.80	2.00
Korea	1.61	1.24	0.32	0.02
Malaysia	0.08	1.99	2.44	0.01
Pakistan	0.69	0.51	0.62	0.92
Philippines	0.07	1.34	0.91	0.57
Sri Lanka	2.44	0.00	0.54	0.69
Taiwan	1.00	0.00	9.16	0.08
Thailand	0.18	0.00	0.62	0.14

[1] $\chi^2_{SC}(1)$, $\chi^2_{FF}(1)$, $\chi^2_N(2)$, $\chi^2_H(1)$, are Lagrange multiplier statistics for tests of residual serial correlation, functional form mis-specification, non-normal errors, and heteroskedasticity.

the case of Sri Lanka. It is clear that the assumption that the error variances are equal across countries is not appropriate.

The diagnostic statistics are much better for the log energy than the share equation: one failure for serial correlation and one for normality. When the fitted value for the level rather than the change is used in the functional form test, it is failed at the 5 per cent level in four countries, and suggests that it may be possible to improve on the log-linear specification.

Before conducting a more detailed analysis of dynamic specification of the log-energy equations, we examined the sensitivity of the results to the alternative price measures. The partial adjustment, ARDL(1, 0, 0) log energy equation was used for comparison. Four measures of real energy prices (all in logarithms) were used: the aggregate real energy price series from the databank (AERP), the unit energy values deflated by CPI, the Stone real price index calculated using current weights, and the moving Stone real price index using the average of the two previous years shares as weights.[1] Non-nested tests indicated that there is relatively little to choose between the different price measures, and no one measure seems to dominate. This is not surprising, since they are all very highly correlated. It makes little difference to the aggregate results which is used. Therefore, we will continue to use the AERP series from the databank.

6.1.2   Sensitivity to Dynamic Specification

Although the partial adjustment model, ARDL(1, 0, 0), is rejected only in the case of Taiwan, it is of interest to examine the sensitivity of the results to the order of the ARDL model. Table 6.7 summarizes the country-specific estimates for the most general model we consider, the ARDL(1, 1, 1) model. This involves estimating six parameters from 17 observations, which could render the individual country estimates unreliable. The estimates of the adjustment coefficients fall outside the the the $(0, -1)$ range in the case of three countries: India, Sri Lanka and Taiwan, where it is very close to zero. An adjustment coefficient close to zero also sheds doubt on the validity of the implied estimates of the long-run coefficients. In particular, in Taiwan the adjustment is unstable with the error correction coefficient, φ, estimated to be very close to zero. This produces a very large estimate of the long-run income elasticity and a large positive price elasticity for Taiwan, though in both cases the standard errors are very large.

The long-run income effect has the correct sign because the two income coefficients sum to less than zero, so the two effects counteract. Conversely, the long-run price effect has the wrong sign, because the two price coefficients sum to less than zero as they should, but with φ estimated to be negative the overall price effect is positive! In India, short-run effects are greater than long-run

---

[1]For details of the construction of these price measures see Section 2.4.3.

Table 6.7a: Country-specific estimates of the long-run income and price elasticities based on ARDL(1, 1, 1) specifications.

Country	Parameter estimates[1]					
	$\hat{\varphi}$	$\hat{\theta}_y$	$\hat{\theta}_p$	$\hat{\sigma}$	$\bar{R}^2$	LL
Bangladesh	−0.596	1.994	0.034	0.039	0.63	34.59
	(0.190)	(0.198)	(0.121)			
India	−1.088	1.024	−0.075	0.027	0.38	40.86
	(0.320)	(0.082)	(0.062)			
Indonesia	−0.450	1.528	−0.433	0.037	0.44	35.63
	(0.330)	(0.228)	(0.198)			
Korea	−0.368	1.049	−0.111	0.033	0.46	37.33
	(0.241)	(0.118)	(0.196)			
Malaysia	−0.163	1.726	−0.664	0.045	−0.10	32.39
	(0.152)	(0.994)	(1.011)			
Pakistan	−0.672	1.197	0.142	0.031	0.10	38.54
	(0.263)	(0.189)	(0.138)			
Philippines	−0.432	0.876	−0.527	0.045	0.53	32.21
	(0.209)	(0.384)	(0.195)			
Sri Lanka	−1.051	0.279	0.051	0.057	0.46	28.15
	(0.321)	(0.194)	(0.080)			
Taiwan	0.035	2.952	2.084	0.039	0.53	34.56
	(0.30)	(17.48)	(16.27)			
Thailand	−0.899	1.168	−0.350	0.018	0.90	47.83
	(0.233)	(0.042)	(0.038)			

[1] All the regressions are estimated over the period 1974–1990 inclusive ($T = 17$). The figures in brackets are standard errors, $\hat{\sigma}$ is the estimated standard error of the regression, $\bar{R}^2$ is the adjusted squared multiple correlation coefficient of the error correction model, $\hat{\varphi}$ is the coefficient of the error correction term. LL is the maximized value of the log-likelihood of the estimated equation.

Table 6.7b: Diagnostic statistics for the results in Table 6.7a.

Country	Diagnostic statistics[1]			
	$\chi^2_{SC}(1)$	$\chi^2_{FF}(1)$	$\chi^2_{N}(2)$	$\chi^2_{H}(1)$
Bangladesh	6.72	0.24	0.70	0.02
India	0.66	1.49	0.12	2.37
Indonesia	0.20	0.03	0.80	1.69
Korea	1.34	0.48	0.31	0.16
Malaysia	0.02	5.71	3.46	0.01
Pakistan	0.12	0.43	0.97	0.40
Philippines	0.23	3.74	0.17	0.27
Sri Lanka	0.39	0.26	0.39	0.36
Taiwan	1.87	0.27	0.11	1.26
Thailand	0.53	0.09	0.12	0.25

[1] See the notes to Table 6.2b.

effects ($\varphi < -1$), which is implausible. There are four positive long-run price elasticities, none significant and four significantly negative price elasticities. In general, the estimates of the price and income elasticities are similar to the estimates based on the ARDL(1, 0, 0) model, the exceptions are Taiwan and Malaysia, where the faster speed of adjustment produces lower and more plausible long-run elasticities. Adding lagged prices and income does little for the fit and the $\bar{R}^2$ for Malaysia is now negative and the equation fails the functional form test. The only other failure is the residual serial correlation test in the case of Bangladesh.

Table 6.8 gives the estimates when the order of each lag in the ARDL model is chosen by the SBC for each country. A static model is chosen for India and Sri Lanka, the ARDL(1, 0, 0) specification is chosen in the case of seven countries, and for the remaining country, namely Taiwan the ARDL(1, 0, 1) model is selected, but it is unstable.

Table 6.8a: Country-specific estimates of the long-run coefficients based on ARDL specifications selected using the Schwarz criterion.

Country	Parameter estimates[1]					
	$\hat{\varphi}$	$\hat{\theta}_y$	$\hat{\theta}_p$	$\hat{\sigma}$	$\bar{R}^2$	LL
Bangladesh	−0.596	1.979	0.035	0.036	0.68	34.50
(1,0,0)	(0.126)	(0.177)	(0.095)			
India	−1.000	1.022	−0.072	0.025	0.47	40.80
(0,1,0)	NA	(0.077)	(0.060)			
Indonesia	−0.374	1.564	−0.488	0.034	0.52	35.52
(1,0,0)	(0.171)	(0.234)	(0.195)			
Korea	−0.318	1.074	−0.136	0.031	0.54	37.17
(1,0,0)	(0.147)	(0.125)	(0.189)			
Malaysia	−0.132	2.2318	−1.159	0.042	0.02	31.94
(1,0,0)	(0.117)	(1.228)	(1.182)			
Pakistan	−0.483	1.320	0.047	0.031	0.08	36.94
(1,0,0)	(0.232)	(0.226)	(0.169)			
Philippines	−0.525	0.835	−0.431	0.044	0.56	31.35
(1,0,0)	(0.132)	(0.290)	(0.110)			
SriLanka	−1.000	0.185	0.081	0.055	0.50	27.34
(0,1,0)	NA	(0.162)	(0.072)			
Taiwan	0.133	1.396	0.863	0.039	0.54	34.03
(1,0,1)	(0.271)	(1.023)	(1.539)			
Thailand	−0.721	1.172	−0.341	0.017	0.91	47.21
(1,0,0)	(0.097)	(0.047)	(0.042)			

[1] All the regressions are estimated over the period 1974–1990 inclusive ($T = 17$). The figures in brackets are standard errors, $\hat{\sigma}$ is the estimated standard error of the regression, $\bar{R}^2$ is the adjusted squared multiple correlation coefficient of the error correction model, $\hat{\varphi}$ is the coefficient of the error correction term which is imposed to be equal to −1 in case of models without lagged dependent variables. LL is the maximized value of the log-likelihood of the estimated equation. The three integers under the country names give the order of the ARDL model selected by the Schwarz criterion.

Table 6.8b: Diagnostic statistics for the results in Table 6.8a.

Country	Diagnostic statistics[1]			
	$\chi^2_{SC}(1)$	$\chi^2_{FF}(1)$	$\chi^2_N(2)$	$\chi^2_H(1)$
Bangladesh (1,0,0)	4.31	0.03	0.64	0.06
India (0,1,0)	0.73	2.92	0.44	2.43
Indonesia (1,0,0)	0.04	0.00	0.80	2.00
Korea (1,0,0)	1.61	1.24	0.32	0.02
Malaysia (1,0,0)	0.08	1.99	2.44	0.01
Pakistan (1,0,0)	0.69	0.51	0.62	0.92
Philippines (1,0,0)	0.07	1.34	0.91	0.57
SriLanka (0,1,0)	0.01	0.09	0.24	0.09
Taiwan (1,0,1)	1.29	0.19	0.07	0.87
Thailand (1,0,0)	0.18	0.00	0.62	0.14

[1] See the notes to Table 6.2b.

6.1.3 The Effect of Foreign Prices

The one remaining issue is the role of foreign prices, discussed in Chapter 2. Suppose that the choice is among three goods, energy, domestic goods and foreign goods with prices: P_{it}, CPI_{it} and $P^*_{it} = ER_{it} \times USCPI_t$, respectively where foreign prices, P^*_{it}, is the product of the exchange rate (local currency per dollar) and the US CPI. The equilibrium equation for the logarithmic form would then be:

$$\ln(e_{it}) = a_i + \theta_{1i} \ln(P_{it}) + \theta_{2i} \ln(P^*_{it}) + \theta_{3i} \ln(CPI_{it}) + \theta_y \ln(y_{it}),$$

and the price homogeneity in the long run requires that $\theta_{1i} + \theta_{2i} + \theta_{3i} = 0$. Imposing this restriction yields:

$$\ln(e_{it}) = a_i + \theta_{pi} \ln(P_{it}/CPI_{it}) + \theta_{xi} \ln(P^*_{it}/CPI_{it}) + \theta_y \ln(y_{it}),$$

which relates logarithm of per-capita energy consumption to the logarithm of the real exchange rate, $\ln(P^*_{it}/CPI_{it})$, as well as real energy prices and real per-capita output. In general one would expect $\theta_{xi} > 0$. The estimates for the ARDL(1, 0, 0, 0) version of the above long-run equation are given in Table 6.9. The long-run real exchange rate coefficient has the expected positive sign in eight of the ten countries, though it is significant only in the case of Malaysia and Sri Lanka. It is negative and insignificant in Pakistan and negative but significant in Korea. Including the real exchange rate makes the mean of the long-run price elasticity slightly larger, with a smaller dispersion. There is now only one positive price elasticity, Korea, though Sri Lanka shows a negative income elasticity. Sri Lanka also fails the residual serial correlation and the functional form tests. India fails the heteroskedasticity test. In terms of the individual countries the effect of including the real exchange rate is marginal, but the importance of this effect for analysis of energy demand will be examined further on the pooled data.

Table 6.9a: Country-specific estimates of the long-run income, price and real exchange rate elasticities, based on ARDL(1, 0, 0, 0) specifications.

Country	Parameter estimates[1]						
	$\hat{\varphi}$	$\hat{\theta}_y$	$\hat{\theta}_p$	$\hat{\theta}_x$	$\hat{\sigma}$	$\bar{R}^2$	LL
Bangladesh	−0.605	1.917	−0.026	0.204	0.037	0.67	34.87
	(0.129)	(0.191)	(0.132)	(0.279)			
India	−0.881	0.785	−0.104	0.597	0.025	0.48	41.53
	(0.227)	(0.145)	(0.071)	(0.337)			
Indonesia	−0.223	1.429	−0.818	0.775	0.034	0.53	36.31
	(0.219)	(0.420)	(0.742)	(1.335)			
Korea	−0.601	0.977	0.114	−0.880	0.026	0.67	40.70
	(0.169)	(0.047)	(0.072)	(0.262)			
Malaysia	−0.564	0.618	−0.199	2.035	0.041	0.08	33.19
	(0.333)	(0.339)	(0.241)	(0.534)			
Pakistan	−0.350	2.039	−0.061	−1.000	0.030	0.16	38.40
	(0.239)	(0.874)	(0.259)	(1.119)			
Philippines	−0.347	1.329	−0.716	1.112	0.042	0.59	32.63
	(0.180)	(0.701)	(0.390)	(1.271)			
Sri Lanka	−0.743	−0.191	−0.007	0.702	0.048	0.63	30.53
	(0.209)	(0.234)	(0.104)	(0.311)			
Taiwan	−0.386	1.189	−0.672	2.829	0.048	0.29	30.38
	(0.269)	(0.303)	(0.695)	(2.56)			
Thailand	−0.721	1.152	−0.339	0.127	0.018	0.90	47.46
	(0.100)	(0.058)	(0.043)	(0.215)			

[1] All the regressions are estimated over the period 1974–1990 inclusive ($T = 17$). The figures in brackets are standard errors, $\hat{\sigma}$ is the estimated standard error of the regression, $\bar{R}^2$ is the adjusted squared multiple correlation coefficient of the error correction model, $\hat{\varphi}$ is the coefficient of the error correction term. LL is the maximized value of the log-likelihood of the estimated equation.

Table 6.9b: Diagnostic statistics for the results in Table 6.9a.

Country	Diagnostic statistics[1]			
	$\chi^2_{SC}(1)$	$\chi^2_{FF}(1)$	$\chi^2_N(2)$	$\chi^2_H(1)$
Bangladesh	2.88	0.07	0.53	1.68
India	1.95	1.49	0.16	7.74
Indonesia	0.17	0.48	1.14	2.44
Korea	0.44	1.28	0.40	0.53
Malaysia	1.11	1.86	5.64	0.00
Pakistan	1.65	0.36	0.36	0.19
Philippines	1.86	0.20	0.43	0.95
Sri Lanka	7.67	4.09	0.18	0.04
Taiwan	0.01	3.30	3.35	0.86
Thailand	0.30	0.22	0.78	0.02

[1] See the notes to Table 6.2b.

6.1.4 Sensitivity to Demeaning the Data

In this section we investigate the effect of the presence of common shocks across countries on the elasticity estimates. As described in Chapter 5, we do this by repeating the analysis using as observations not the original data, namely $\ln(e_{it})$, $\ln(y_{it})$, etc., but their deviations from the means for each year calculated over all ten countries in the sample:

$$\nabla \ln(e_{it}) = \ln(e_{it}) - \overline{\ln e_t}, \qquad \nabla \ln(y_{it}) = \ln(y_{it}) - \overline{\ln y_t}, \quad \text{etc.}$$

where

$$\overline{\ln e_t} = N^{-1} \sum_{i=1}^{N} \ln(e_{it}), \qquad \overline{\ln y_t} = N^{-1} \sum_{i=1}^{N} \ln(y_{it}), \quad \text{etc.}$$

The individual country results are given in Table 6.10 for the ARDL$(1, 0, 0, 0)$ case, i.e. including the logarithm of the real exchange rate. In Bangladesh, demeaning results in an estimate for the error correction coefficient, φ_i, close to zero, thus giving rise to very large estimates of the long-run income and

Table 6.10a: Country-specific estimates of the long-run income, price and real exchange rate elasticities of aggregate energy demand based on demeaned ARDL$(1, 0, 0, 0)$ regressions.

Country							
	$\hat{\varphi}$	$\hat{\theta}_y$	$\hat{\theta}_p$	$\hat{\theta}_x$	$\hat{\sigma}$	$\bar{R}^2$	LL
Bangladesh	−0.008	49.9	−38.2	35.0	0.054	0.32	28.57
	(0.319)	(2072.0)	(1564.0)	(1441.0)			
India	−0.679	1.242	−0.319	0.360	0.030	0.49	38.55
	(0.302)	(0.222)	(0.271)	(0.476)			
Indonesia	−0.290	0.504	−0.515	0.732	0.029	0.60	38.74
	(0.137)	(0.649)	(0.276)	(0.559)			
Korea	−0.533	0.763	0.250	−0.744	0.39	0.027	40.41
	(0.170)	(0.188)	(0.190)	(0.354)			
Malaysia	−0.774	−0.081	−0.737	0.376	0.040	0.31	33.38
	(0.246)	(0.215)	(0.208)	(0.574)			
Pakistan	−0.258	0.800	−0.876	0.314	0.035	0.09	35.73
	(0.199)	(0.923)	(0.670)	(1.369)			
Philippines	−0.291	1.285	−1.054	3.149	0.039	0.50	34.10
	(0.193)	(0.181)	(1.021)	(2.042)			
Sri Lanka	−0.206	0.370	−1.207	2.072	0.054	0.37	28.55
	(0.127)	(1.435)	(0.711)	(1.700)			
Taiwan	−0.316	−0.476	−1.753	0.705	0.042	0.18	32.83
	(0.368)	(3.900)	(2.656)	(2.542)			
Thailand	−0.778	1.522	−0.323	1.201	0.026	0.69	41.01
	(0.230)	(0.233)	(0.128)	(0.305)			

[1] All the regressions are estimated over the period 1974–1990 inclusive ($T = 17$). The figures in brackets are standard errors, $\hat{\sigma}$ is the estimated standard error of the regression, $\bar{R}^2$ is the adjusted squared multiple correlation coefficients of the error correction model, $\hat{\varphi}$ is the coefficient of the error correction term. LL is the maximized value of the log-likelihood of the estimated equation.

Table 6.10b: Diagnostic statistics for the results in Table 6.10a.

Country	Diagnostic statistics[1]			
	$\chi^2_{SC}(1)$	$\chi^2_{FF}(1)$	$\chi^2_N(2)$	$\chi^2_H(1)$
Bangladesh	3.75	2.94	1.30	0.13
India	2.93	1.69	0.18	0.19
Indonesia	0.37	0.00	0.26	0.60
Korea	0.31	1.50	0.86	0.79
Malaysia	0.01	1.11	0.17	1.44
Pakistan	1.85	1.95	8.02	0.64
Philippines	0.48	4.48	0.57	1.29
Sri Lanka	5.37	0.31	0.44	1.21
Taiwan	1.21	0.16	1.52	0.43
Thailand	1.22	3.26	0.46	0.29

[1] See the notes to Table 6.2b.

price elasticities. Malaysia and Taiwan have negative income elasticities, though Malaysia is the only country with an income elasticity that is significantly different from unity. The price elasticities tend to be somewhat larger in absolute value (as compared to the estimates obtained using undemeaned observations), and the estimate for Korea remains the only positive one.

As the theoretical discussion in Chapter 5 indicated, demeaning will not only remove the technological trend from the disturbances, but also add another term which will depend on the dispersion of parameter estimates across countries. The $\bar{R}^2$ measures are not comparable between the original and the demeaned data, because the dependent variable is different, however the standard error of regression can be compared. On this basis the regressions on the demeaned data fit better in five countries using the ARDL(1, 0, 0, 0) specification.

6.2 Alternative Pooled Estimators

6.2.1 Sensitivity to Dynamic Specification

In this section we examine the effects of pooling the data on the estimates of the long-run elasticities using different pooling procedures and dynamic specifications. We confine our attention to the logarithmic model since this model fitted so much better than the shares or log-shares models. The results are summarized in Tables 6.11–6.14. Each table presents estimates of the long-run GDP and price elasticities and the adjustment coefficient, together with the maximized log-likelihood, the number of observations and the number of parameters estimated. Note that the number of parameters estimated includes the error variances. These statistics are given for four estimators, discussed in

Table 6.11: Alternative pooled estimators of the long-run output and price elasticities of aggregate energy demand in Asian developing economies (based on ARDL(1, 0, 0) specifications).

	Mean group estimators	Pooled mean group estimators	Dynamic fixed effects estimators	Static fixed effects estimators
Output	1.228	1.184	1.301	1.009
elasticity $(\hat{\theta}_y)$	(0.183)	(0.039)	(0.109)	(0.037)
Price	−0.261	−0.339	−0.365	−0.067
elasticity $(\hat{\theta}_p)$	(0.118)	(0.033)	(0.097)	(0.030)
Error correction	−0.524	−0.298	−0.235	−1
coefficient $(\hat{\varphi})$	(0.070)	(0.063)	(0.040)	(N/A)
Log-likelihood	347.12	322.79	288.36	186.95
(LL)				
$N \times T$	170	170	170	170
No. of est. parameters	50	32	14	13

Table 6.12: Alternative pooled estimators of the long-run output and price elasticities of aggregate energy demand in Asian developing economies (based on ARDL(1, 1, 1) specifications).

	Mean group estimators	Pooled mean group estimators	Dynamic fixed effects estimators
Output	1.279	1.171	1.181
elasticity $(\hat{\theta}_y)$	(0.230)	(0.034)	(0.147)
Price	0.015	−0.346	−0.324
elasticity $(\hat{\theta}_p)$	(0.245)	(0.029)	(0.137)
Error correction	−0.568	−0.245	−0.153
coefficient $(\hat{\varphi})$	(0.117)	(0.084)	(0.042)
Log-likelihood	362.09	335.33	300.27
(LL)			
$N \times T$	170	170	170
No. of est. parameters	70	52	16

Chapter 5. The Mean Group (MG) estimator does not impose any restrictions and pools the different elasticity estimates as the unweighted mean of the estimates from individual countries. It will tend to be sensitive to the outliers discussed in the previous section. The Pooled Mean Group (PMG) estimator, imposes equality of long-run coefficients, but allows short-run coefficients, including the adjustment coefficient, and error variances to differ across countries. The estimate of the adjustment coefficient given in the tables for the PMG estimator is the mean of the individual country estimates. The Dynamic Fixed Effect Estimator imposes equality of all slope coefficients and error variances, and allows only the intercepts to differ across countries. The Static Fixed Effect model is given for comparison since it is widely used, but we would not expect it to be dynamically well specified. In each case Likelihood Ratio tests

Table 6.13:   Alternative pooled estimators of the long-run output and price elasticities of aggregate energy demand in Asian developing economies (based on ARDL SBC specifications).

	Mean group estimators	Pooled mean group estimators	Dynamic fixed effects estimators
Output	1.277	1.171	1.301
elasticity ($\hat{\theta}_y$)	(0.182)	(0.036)	(0.109)
Price	−0.160	−0.301	−0.365
elasticity ($\hat{\theta}_p$)	(0.164)	(0.028)	(0.097)
Error correction	−0.502	−0.417	−0.235
coefficient ($\hat{\varphi}$)	(0.113)	(0.121)	(0.040)
Log-likelihood	356.81	315.41	288.36
(LL)			
$N \times T$	170	170	170
No. of est.	51	33	14
parameters			

Table 6.14:   Alternative pooled estimators of the long-run output and price elasticities of aggregate energy demand in Asian developing economies (based on ARDL(1, 0, 0, 0) specifications containing the real exchange rate variable).

	Mean group estimators	Pooled mean group estimators	Dynamic fixed effects estimators	Static fixed effects estimators
Output	1.124	1.149	1.215	0.989
elasticity ($\hat{\theta}_y$)	(0.204)	(0.043)	(0.094)	(0.037)
Price	−0.283	−0.365	−0.638	−0.134
elasticity ($\hat{\theta}_p$)	(0.106)	(0.038)	(0.133)	(0.038)
Real exchange	0.650	0.363	1.156	0.280
rate elasticity ($\hat{\theta}_x$)	(0.372)	(0.117)	(0.284)	(0.099)
Error correction	−0.542	−0.320	−0.236	−1.0
coefficient ($\hat{\varphi}$)	(0.066)	(0.057)	(0.037)	(N/A)
Log-likelihood	366.00	326.95	302.26	191.13
(LL)				
$N \times T$	170	170	170	170
No. of est.	60	33	15	14
parameters				

were conducted for parameter equality and in nearly all cases the hypothesis of equality was rejected. In addition, Hausman tests of the equality of the PMG and MG estimates were conducted, and in nearly all cases equality could not be rejected. This apparent contradiction is largely due to the MG estimates often having very large standard errors, which causes the Hausman test to have low power. These test results suggest that the hypothesis that the elasticities are the same across countries is rejected. But if the focus of the analysis is on average (across countries) income and price elasticities, then the PMG estimates are probably preferable to the MG estimates on the grounds of their better precision and the fact that they are less sensitive to outlier estimates. In this context the Hausman test can be seen as providing formal statistical evidence that we are not in gross violation of the data by relying on PMG estimates rather than the MG estimates.

Table 6.11 presents results for the ARDL(1, 0, 0) specification. These suggest an estimate of the long-run income elasticity of 1.2 and of the price elasticity of −0.3. The PMG estimates are close to the MG estimates, and the DFE estimates are rather larger. The dynamics clearly matter and the static fixed effects estimator has an insignificant price effect. The standard errors of both the PMG and the DFE are very much smaller than those of the MG; pooling sharpens the estimates considerably. Pooling also leads to a much smaller estimated speed of adjustment; the MG estimates suggest speeds of convergence to equilibrium of around 50 per cent a year, the PMG 30 per cent, the DFE about 20 per cent.

Table 6.12 gives alternative pooled estimators for the ARDL(1, 1, 1) specification. The PMG estimates of the long-run price and income elasticities hardly change, the DFE estimates of these elasticities are now very close to the PMG estimates and the pattern on adjustment coefficients remains. The striking shifts are in the MG estimates, influenced by the outliers discussed above. The MG long-run price elasticity is now positive and the much larger standard errors indicate the increased dispersion of the coefficients for the individual countries.

Table 6.13 gives MG and PMG estimates when the order of the specification in the individual countries is chosen by the SBC. This procedure cannot be used with the fixed effect estimator. Again the PMG estimates of the long-run price and income elasticities hardly change, though the estimated speed of adjustment is rather higher, partly because the SBC chooses the static model, with instantaneous adjustment, in some countries. Using the SBC gives a substantial improvement in the Maximized Log-Likelihood (MLL) for the MG estimator, (at 357 it is close to the ARDL(1, 1, 1) MLL of 362, with far fewer parameters) but less for the PMG, where the SBC MLL is worse than the ARDL(1, 0, 0) MLL. It is clear that homogeneity restrictions and dynamic specification interact in a complex way. What might be the optimal order for the country-specific estimates, may not be the optimal order when cross-country homogeneity restrictions are imposed.

Table 6.14 gives the estimates for the ARDL(1, 0, 0, 0) specification, which includes the logarithm of the real exchange rate. The PMG estimates of the long-run price and income elasticities change very little, a slightly smaller income effect and a slightly larger price effect and the real exchange rate has a significant positive effect, which is in line with theory's prediction. As would be expected from the individual country results, the long-run real exchange rate elasticity based on the MG estimates, is not statistically significant. The DFE estimator produces a much larger price elasticity and a much larger real exchange rate elasticity than the PMG procedure.

6.2.2   Sensitivity to Demeaning the Data

Table 6.15 gives the alternative pooled estimators for the ARDL(1,0,0,0) specification based on demeaned observations. As compared to the results based on
undemeaned data, the demeaned data rejects slope homogeneity of long-run
coefficients less clearly. The log-likelihood ratio statistic for testing the equality
of long-run coefficients is 40.33 with 27 degrees of freedom, compared to a
5 per cent critical value of 40.11, so the homogeneity of long-run coefficients
only just fails at the 5 per cent level. This suggests either that once one removes
any technological trend, there is more evidence for homogeneity of long-run
responses across countries, or that the larger dispersion of the demeaned coefficients is reducing the power of the tests.

The PMG estimate of income elasticity is rather lower than the previous
estimates, just below unity, but not significantly different from unity; and the
price effect substantially larger, almost -0.8. The strong covariance between
price and income elasticities is a common feature of the pooled estimates.
The real exchange rate effect is substantially larger using the demeaned data,
and is estimated to be around 1.2 rather than 0.4, obtained when the original
observations were used. The DFE and PMG estimates are rather similar. The
MG estimators are very sensitive to the outliers produced by demeaning and
yield rather implausible estimates.

The main effect of demeaning is to lower the income elasticity and raise
the price elasticity. To consider whether this effect is consistent with the interpretation of demeaning as removing the effect of technological progress,
suppose that the underlying model relating log energy demand to log income,

Table 6.15: Alternative pooled estimators of the long-run output and price elasticities of aggregate energy demand in Asian developing economies (based on ARDL$(1, 0, 0, 0)$ demeaned
specifications).

	Mean group estimators	Pooled mean group estimators	Dynamic fixed effects estimators	Static fixed effects estimators
Output elasticity ($\hat{\theta}_y$)	5.585 (4.930)	0.968 (0.115)	1.005 (0.130)	0.917 (0.064)
Price elasticity ($\hat{\theta}_p$)	−4.473 (3.751)	−0.789 (0.135)	−0.962 (0.181)	−0.239 (0.060)
Real exchange rate elasticity ($\hat{\theta}_x$)	4.318 (3.428)	1.175 (0.225)	1.397 (0.320)	0.375 (0.0127)
Error correction coefficient ($\hat{\varphi}$)	−0.413 (0.083)	−0.246 (0.070)	−0.242 (0.034)	−1.000 (N/A)
Log-likelihood (LL)	351.88	331.72	319.64	198.22
$N \times T$	170	170	170	170
No. of est. parameters	60	32	15	14

log prices and technology, τ_t is

$$\ln e_t = \alpha + \theta_y \ln y_t + \theta_p \ln p_t + \psi \tau_t + u_t,$$

and there are auxiliary regressions describing the relationship between technology and income and prices of the form:

$$\tau_t = a_0 + a_1 \ln y_t + a_2 \ln p_t + v_t,$$

then the equation which omits technology will be estimated as:

$$\ln e_t = \alpha + \delta a_0 + (\theta_y + \psi a_1) \ln y_t + (\theta_p + \psi a_2) \ln p_t + u_t + \psi v_t.$$

It is likely that $\psi < 0$, since improved technology reduces energy demand and a_1 is positive, the level of technology is related to income. Therefore this suggests that omitting technology should lead to a lower estimate of the income elasticity, rather than a higher one. With respect to prices, a_2 should be positive, higher energy prices should lead to improvements in energy efficiency, again this suggests that omitting technology should lead to a lower (larger absolute price elasticity) contrary to these results. This argument can only be tentative, since the technology is international and the correlation with the particular countries' prices and incomes may not be positive. However, it does raise a question about the interpretation of demeaning as removing a technological trend.

6.3   Cross-Section Patterns

It is argued in Pesaran and Smith (1995) that under certain assumptions, the cross-section regressions based on long averages may provide good estimates of the long-run effects. In this case, the sample of countries under consideration is small and heterogeneous, and there are difficulties, discussed in Section 2, of obtaining comparable measures of real energy price across countries. In a cross-section regression of the average values of the sample of the logarithm of per-capita energy demand, $\ln(e_{it})$ on the logarithm of per-capita GDP, $\ln(y_{it})$, and the logarithm of relative price $\ln(p_{it})$ using 1985 exchange rates, the results were:

$$\overline{\ln(e_i)} = -12.17 + 1.897 \overline{\ln(y_i)} - 0.562 \overline{\ln(p_i)},$$
$$(3.58) \quad (0.35) \quad\quad (0.56)$$

$$\sigma = 0.56, \quad\quad \bar{R}^2 = 0.78,$$

where

$$\overline{\ln(e_i)} = T^{-1} \sum_{t=1}^{T} \ln(e_{it}),$$

$$\overline{\ln(y_i)} = T^{-1} \sum_{t=1}^{T} \ln(y_{it}), \quad \text{etc.}$$

The fit is very poor. Although the income elasticity is substantially greater than unity and the price elasticity much larger than most of the pooled estimates, the hypothesis of a unit income elasticity would only just be rejected, while the hypothesis of a zero price elasticity would not. However, with a small sample, the results are sensitive to the inclusion of particular observations and the treatment of the exchange rate. If average rather than 1985 exchange rates are used, the results are similar though with larger income and price effects. The significance is unchanged with the price effect still not significantly different from zero, and the income elasticity significantly greater than unity.

$$\overline{\ln(e_i)} = -10.08 + 2.161 \, \overline{\ln(y_i)} - 0.792 \, \overline{\ln(p_i)},$$
$$(5.49) \quad (0.47) \qquad\qquad (0.75)$$
$$\hat{\sigma} = 0.55, \qquad \bar{R}^2 = 0.77.$$

The equation does not fail standard tests for normality, functional form or heteroskedasticity. The scatter diagram of the logarithm of energy intensity against the logarithm of per-capita income shows a fairly tight positive relationship, with three low income countries – India, Pakistan and Indonesia – which have higher energy intensities than the relationship with income would suggest. If the cross-section relationship reflected substitution away from traditional biomass fuels towards modern fuels, this might account for the higher elasticity. But this substitution has also occurred over time in many of these countries and thus should be reflected in the time series and pooled estimates. The general conclusion must be that in this case N, the number of observations, is too small to put much faith in cross-section estimates.

6.4   Conclusions

Although the theory suggests an equation determining the value share of energy, the data strongly prefer a traditional equation explaining the logarithm of energy demand, though this may reflect deficiencies in the measure of the share used. Although the log-log model shows less functional form misspecification than the share equation, some non-linearity remains and there is some indication that the income elasticity may fall with income.

There is substantial heterogeneity in the individual country estimates, and LR tests reject pooling though it is not clear how this heterogeneity should be interpreted. The averages across countries for the long-run elasticities are sensible and very similar to the pooled estimates; Hausman tests do not reject equality of the Mean Group and Pooled Mean Group estimators. Pooling substantially increases the precision of the estimates, though the small estimated standard errors may exaggerate the precision given the parameter heterogeneity. The Fixed Effect estimator gives very misleading estimates of the speed of adjustment. Allowing for dynamics increases the estimated size of both the price and income elasticities. The static model suggests an income elasticity around unity and a price elasticity of -0.07. The dynamic models suggest an income elasticity around 1.2 and a price elasticity around -0.3. Demeaning the data increases the evidence for homogeneity of the long-run coefficients, though except for the ARDL$(1, 0, 0)$ case it would still be rejected at the 1 per cent level. The estimates from the demeaned data are broadly similar to those from the original data, but demeaning does not produce a clear improvement in fit. This indicates that the benefit of removing a common technological trend is offset by the addition of dispersion terms to the disturbance. It is clear from the results that demeaning, dynamic specification and homogeneity restrictions interact in quite complex ways and that the estimates are sensitive to the specification. The cross-section estimates indicate much higher price and income elasticities, but given the small and heterogenous sample, it is difficult to give these much weight.

CHAPTER 7

Sectoral Energy Demand

7.1 Introduction

The aggregate equations presented in the previous chapter illustrate the application of the methods. However, a number of interesting issues about energy demand concern estimates of income and price elasticities at disaggregated levels: sectors, industries and fuel types. This raises such questions as whether demand is more homogeneous across countries at a disaggregate level than at an aggregate level and whether there are systematic differences across sectors and fuels. As a first stage in disaggregation, consider final consumption by the main sectors of the economy: industry, transport, residential and commercial. The commercial sector also includes agriculture and public energy use and was not further disaggregated, because there were no data on energy consumption in the agriculture sector for a number of countries. It will be remembered from the discussion of the data in Chapter 2, that there were large differences across countries in the share of energy used by each of these sectors.

Given the poor performance of the energy share equation at the aggregate level, we will confine our attention to the logarithmic equation. The form of the energy demand equations that we shall consider in this chapter, will thus be an ARDL(p, q_1, q_2, q_3), p, q_1, q_2, $q_3 \leq 1$ regression of the logarithm of per-capita energy demand on the logarithms of per-capita GDP, the real energy price and the real exchange rate. More specifically we will report individual country and pooled estimates based on ARDL(1, 0, 0), ARDL(1, 1, 1), the order chosen by the Schwarz criterion and the ARDL(1, 0, 0, 0) including the log of the real exchange rate. The results from the analysis of the aggregate data suggested that we could not estimate complicated dynamic models from the 17 time series observations available. Therefore we would not expect the ARDL(1, 1, 1) model to perform well.

We do not report results based on demeaned data, partly because demeaning did not suggest an unambiguous improvement in fit at the aggregate level and partly because it is rather more difficult to interpret the demeaned data as removing some common technological trend at a sectoral level. Sectoral estimates using demeaned data also showed very large numbers of outliers.

Per-capita GDP is not the relevant activity measure for modelling disaggregated energy demands, and we use it primarily for comparability, since it is interesting to compare the disaggregate energy GDP elasticities with those for the aggregate. The energy data-bank contains indices of industrial production and value added measures, which are more appropriate measures of activity. But they are often of doubtful quality and are not comparable across countries, while the GDP series that we are using are not subject to the latter limitation. The estimated elasticity of sectoral energy demand to GDP, θ_{ys}, will be the product of the elasticity of energy demand to sectoral transactions and the elasticity of sectoral transactions to GDP.

The price index used is the Stone Index, weighted by the current value shares for the relevant sector as discussed in Chapter 2. Since price homogeneity was so widely accepted by the aggregate data and because there are strong theoretical reasons for imposing it, we impose homogeneity and the Stone Indices are deflated by the CPI. The real exchange rate measure is exactly the same as in Chapter 6.

The potential benefits from disaggregation arise from the use of extra information. In our case, the extra information in the disaggregate equations comes from the use of sector specific prices and lagged dependent variable. The log-log specification causes a complication, in that the aggregate equation is the logarithm of the sum of sectoral energy demands, rather than the sum of the logarithms of energy demands, which is what aggregation of the sectoral equations would give. The potential disadvantage of disaggregation is that the available detailed data may be less reliable. While the total amount of energy used by an economy may be reasonably well estimated from supply sources, there may be a lack of information about which sector actually uses the fuel (see, for example, Aigner and Goldfeld (1974) and Pesaran, Pierse and Kumar (1989)).

We follow the same structure as with the aggregate data, first discussing the individual country results for each sector, then discussing the pooled results for each sector.

7.2 Individual Country Estimates

7.2.1 Industrial Sector

Table C.1 reports the individual country estimates of long-run income and price elasticities for the industrial sector based on the ARDL(1, 0, 0) model.[1] The long-run income elasticities range from 1.96 (0.235) in Bangladesh to −0.008 (2.435) in Sri Lanka (standard errors are in brackets). Only the Bangladesh estimate is significantly different from unity. The average income

---

[1] The tables for this chapter are collected in Appendix C.

elasticity over the ten countries is estimated to be 1.123 which is slightly lower than the aggregate, with a similar degree of dispersion. The long-run price elasticities range from 0.012 (0.108) in Bangladesh (the only positive elasticity) to -1.009 (0.529) in the Philippines. Only in Thailand is the price elasticity significantly negative. The average price elasticity is rather higher than the average for the aggregate ARDL(1, 0, 0), -0.43 as compared to -0.26, with rather less dispersion. As a result the mean price elasticity is significantly different from zero. The fit varies substantially across countries and the $\bar{R}^2$ (which measures the proportion of the variance of the change in log per-capita energy consumption explained by the regression) is negative in Malaysia.[2] The standard error of regression varies substantially from 3.6 per cent in Korea to 15.3 per cent in Sri Lanka. In all countries the standard error of regression is larger for the industrial sector than for the aggregate, though in two countries the $\bar{R}^2$ is larger for the disaggregate regressions as compared to the aggregate estimates. Comparison of both measures with the aggregate are informative, since the standard error may be small because there is little variation in the dependent variable. With the exception of India all the adjustment coefficients lie in the $(-1, 0)$ range. The Indian adjustment coefficient, which is a little greater than unity suggests that a static model may be better. None of the diagnostic statistics suggest misspecification (see Table C.1b).

Table C.2 gives the estimates for the ARDL(1, 1, 1) specification. As with the aggregate this specification produces some implausible estimates. The estimated adjustment coefficient is outside the zero minus one interval for India and Taiwan, the latter being unstable as was the case with the aggregate model. The long-run income elasticity is negative in Indonesia, Pakistan and Sri Lanka and the mean is only 0.72. The price elasticity is positive in five countries and the mean is positive. The $\bar{R}^2$ of changes in log per-capita energy consumption is negative in Malaysia and Sri Lanka. The Philippines equation fails the serial correlation and heteroskedasticity tests. As with the aggregate regression, low degrees of freedom cause a very large dispersion in the estimates. Little reliance can be placed on these estimates.

Table C.3 gives the estimates where the lag order is selected by the Schwarz criterion. In Bangladesh and India the static model is chosen; in Pakistan and Taiwan ARDL(1, 0, 1), in Philippines ARDL(1, 1, 0), in Thailand ARDL(0, 1, 1) and in the other four countries, the partial adjustment model ARDL(1, 0, 0). Again Taiwan is unstable and Malaysia has a negative $\bar{R}^2$. Pakistan and Sri Lanka have negative income elasticities while Bangladesh, Pakistan and Taiwan have

---

[2] The $\bar{R}^2$ usually reported for the ARDL regressions refers to the proportion of the variance of the level of the dependent variable (in the present application the log per-capita energy consumption) explained by the regression line and is not appropriate for trended variables. Typically, it will be around 0.90 even if there is no significant long-run relationship between the variables in the model. In contrast the $\bar{R}^2$ of the changes in the dependent variable is valid for variables with linear trends and is not subject to the spurious correlation problem.

positive price elasticities. In terms of plausibility, the ARDL(1, 0, 0) does rather better than when the lag order is determined by the data.

Table C.4 gives the estimates with the addition of the logarithm of the real exchange rate, the ARDL(1, 0, 0, 0). The Indian adjustment coefficient again suggests a static model. The income elasticity is again negative in Sri Lanka and the price elasticity positive in Korea. The real exchange rate is negative and significant in Korea, positive and significant in Malaysia. As compared to the ARDL(1, 0, 0), the price elasticity is somewhat larger, and although the dispersion is larger, it is still significant. The mean coefficient for the real exchange rate is positive though not significantly different from zero. The fit as measured by $\bar{R}^2$ improves in five countries relative to the ARDL(1, 0, 0), though India fails on the heteroskedasticity and Malaysia on the functional form diagnostic tests.

In most respects the industrial estimates are rather similar to the aggregate results. Income elasticities are close to unity, with the exception of Bangladesh, which is significantly larger, and price effects are negative. The price elasticity is rather larger for industry than the aggregate. As with the aggregate individual country results the ARDL(1, 1, 1) produces implausible estimates and there is not strong support for a significant real exchange rate effect.

7.2.2 Transport Sector

Table C.5 gives the ARDL(1, 0, 0) estimates of energy demand for the transportation sector. Income elasticities range from 3.3 in Malaysia to 0.4 in India. Bangladesh, Korea and Thailand have income elasticities significantly greater than unity, India and Sri Lanka significantly less than unity. The average long-run income elasticity is 1.375. The long-run price elasticity is almost exactly zero in Bangladesh and positive though not significant in Pakistan and Sri Lanka. The average is −0.375, similar to the aggregate. The Standard Error of Regression is better for transport than the aggregate in India and Indonesia (though the $\bar{R}^2$ is worse), Malaysia has a better fit by both criteria. $\bar{R}^2$ is negative in Pakistan. There is much more evidence of misspecification in the transport equation than the aggregate or industry. Taiwan fails on serial correlation, Indonesia, Philippines and Taiwan on functional form, and the Philippines on normality and heteroskedasticity. It is likely that GDP is a poor proxy for activity in transport.

Table C.6 gives the ARDL(1, 1, 1) transport estimates. Three countries have adjustment coefficients greater than unity, Bangladesh, India and Taiwan. The long-run income elasticity is significantly greater than unity in Bangladesh, Korea and Thailand and significantly less than unity in India. The long-run price elasticity is positive in Bangladesh, Pakistan, Sri Lanka and Taiwan. There are now eight failures of diagnostic tests as compared to six for the

ARDL(1, 0, 0), and the Philippines now fails all the four tests. Again the ARDL(1, 1, 1) estimates seem unreliable.

Table C.7 gives the estimates when the lag order is chosen by the Schwarz criterion. The static model is chosen in Sri Lanka and Taiwan, ARDL(0, 1, 0) in Bangladesh and ARDL(0, 0, 1) in India. The partial adjustment ARDL(1, 0, 0) equation already discussed is chosen in the other six countries. Imposing instantaneous adjustment and allowing for lagged income in Bangladesh makes the income elasticity larger at 1.74. Imposing instantaneous adjustment and allowing for lagged price in India hardly changes the results from the ARDL(1, 0, 0). The static estimates for Sri Lanka and Thailand are very similar to the ARDL(1, 0, 0). This tends to confirm the fact that ARDL(1, 0, 0) is the sensible common specification.

Table C.8 gives the estimates for transport demand for the ARDL(1, 0, 0, 0) equation including the log of the real exchange rate. The most noticeable effect of adding the real exchange rate is on Pakistan. Pakistan had negative $\bar{R}^2$ for transport for all three of the previous specifications, but with the real exchange rate (which is negative and significant), its $\bar{R}^2$ rises to 0.4. The income elasticity at 2.3 is now significantly greater than unity. The real exchange rate is positive and significant in Sri Lanka and Thailand. The mean effect of the real exchange rate at 0.5 is similar to industry and bigger than the aggregate. Income and price elasticities are somewhat higher when the real exchange rate is included. The diagnostic statistics continue to indicate widespread misspecification.

Like the industry results, the results for the transport sector are generally similar to the aggregate, but with higher long-run income elasticity estimates. The dispersion is rather greater and there is more evidence of misspecification. This may be because GDP is a poor proxy for the relevant activity measure for transport.

7.2.3　Residential Sector

Table C.9 gives the ARDL(1, 0, 0) estimates of energy demand for the residential sector. The adjustment coefficient in the Philippines suggests immediate adjustment. Income elasticities range from 2.9 in Pakistan to 0.4 in Sri Lanka. India, Pakistan and Thailand have income elasticities significantly greater than unity, Korea significantly less than unity. The average long-run income elasticity is 1.312. The long-run price elasticity is significantly positive in Korea and the Philippines and significantly negative in Indonesia and Sri Lanka. The average price elasticity of −0.135 is rather lower than the aggregate of the other sectors. The standard errors of the residential regressions are smaller than the aggregate in the case of Indonesia and Taiwan and in both cases the $\bar{R}^2$ is larger in the case of residential as compared to the aggregate equation. The diagnostic statistics for residential regressions are better than transport, but worse than industrial or the aggregate. The functional form test is failed in Bangladesh, Pakistan and the Philippines.

Table C.10 gives the estimates for the ARDL(1, 1, 1) model of residential energy demand. Overall the pattern is similar to those obtained using the ARDL(1, 0, 0) model and the estimates of the elasticities averaged across countries remain largely unaffected as we move from ARDL(1, 0, 0) to ARDL(1, 1, 1). But more countries have long-run income elasticities significantly different from unity. India and Pakistan are significantly greater and Korea, Sri Lanka and Taiwan are significantly less. The positive price elasticity in the Philippines is no longer significant, but that in Korea remains. There are only two failures for the functional form test.

Table C.11 presents the estimates for residential demand when the lag order is chosen by the Schwarz criterion. There is a much greater variety of lag orders than for industry or transport regressions, five of the eight possible forms of the equation were chosen. Static in Korea and Thailand, partial adjustment in India and Pakistan, ARDL(0, 0, 1) in the Philippines and ARDL(0, 1, 1) in Sri Lanka and the most popular was ARDL(1, 0, 1) chosen in the case of the remaining four countries. The long-run price elasticity is positive in Taiwan and significantly positive again in Korea and the Philippines. However, the average long-run income and price elasticities are very similar to those of the ARDL(1, 0, 0) model. There are four failures of functional form test, with the Philippines test statistic being very large.

Table C.12 presents the estimates based on the ARDL(1, 0, 0, 0) specification including the logarithm of the real exchange rate. As with the ARDL(1, 0, 0) and ARDL(1, 1, 1) the adjustment coefficient in the Philippines is greater than unity. The income elasticity is negative and significantly less than unity in Sri Lanka, significantly less than unity in Korea and significantly greater than unity in Pakistan and the Philippines. The price elasticity is again significantly positive in Korea and the Philippines. The real exchange rate is significantly positive in Taiwan and Thailand, and negative only in Bangladesh and Korea. The mean effect is similar to the aggregate at 0.25 and is significant. Functional form remains a problem.

The dispersion in the estimates for residential demand is rather greater, so any general conclusions drawn from these results must be tentative, although the estimates averaged across countries are not that different from those obtained using the aggregate specifications.

7.2.4   Commercial Sector

Table C.13 gives the estimates for the ARDL(1, 0, 0) model of commercial energy demand. It will be remembered that the commercial sector also includes public and agricultural use of energy and thus is a rather heterogeneous aggregate. Adjustment coefficients are greater than unity in Pakistan, Taiwan and Thailand. The estimate for Taiwan, 1.5, is almost significantly greater than unity and implies massive over-reaction. There is a very wide range of estimates for long-run income elasticity, with three estimates larger than 2.5, Bangladesh equal to almost 4 and Pakistan at -0.62. The price elasticities are positive though not statistically significant in Pakistan and Thailand and negative and significant with a coefficient of -1.9 in Indonesia. Standard errors of regression are usually much larger than the aggregate regression. The largest is Indonesia which has a standard error of regression of 24.7 per cent in the commercial sector compared with 3.4 per cent in the aggregate. However, the variance of the dependent variable is also substantially greater, so the $\bar{R}^2$ is better in the commercial sector. In Sri Lanka and Taiwan, the standard error of the commercial sector is smaller than the aggregate. In Malaysia the $\bar{R}^2$ is very close to zero. The diagnostic tests statistics indicate misspecification: failure on functional form in Bangladesh and Indonesia, on normality in the Philippines and Taiwan and on heteroskedasticity in Indonesia.

Table C.14 presents the ARDL$(1, 1, 1)$ estimates. The adjustment coefficient is greater than unity in the same three countries as the ARDL$(1, 0, 0)$. Pakistan still has a negative income elasticity, and there is one less positive price elasticity, Bangladesh is now just negative. In Malaysia the $\bar{R}^2$ is now negative and the number of diagnostic failures has increased from five to ten, five of those on functional form. Although the mean price and income elasticities have not changed very much relative to the ARDL$(1, 0, 0)$, the pattern of poor performance by the ARDL$(1, 1, 1)$ model persists.

Table C.15 presents the estimates where the order of the ARDL is chosen by the Schwarz criterion. Again there are a variety of orders: three static and three partial adjustment, with $(1, 1, 1)$ $(0, 1, 1)$ $(0, 1, 0)$ and $(0, 0, 1)$ each being chosen by one country. The mean estimates are very similar and failure on the diagnostic tests is worse than the ARDL$(1, 0, 0)$ but not as bad as the ARDL$(1, 1, 1)$. The wide dispersion in income elasticities persists.

Table C.16 presents the estimates for the ARDL$(1, 0, 0, 0)$ including the log of the real exchange rate, which is significant and negative in Thailand and negative and insignificant in Bangladesh, Philippines and Sri Lanka. There are now three negative income elasticities, though Bangladesh is now over 4. There are three positive price elasticities.

Like residential, commercial demand shows a much greater dispersion. This may reflect both the lack of an appropriate activity measure and the greater heterogeneity of this sector across countries.

7.2.5   Comparison of the Individual Estimates

Overall, the sectoral results are similar to the aggregate estimates though there is rather more dispersion at the sectoral levels. The lack of clear sectoral differences, at least as far as the long-run income and price elasticities are concerned, makes it useful to look at all 40 estimates together. In most cases there is more noise in the disaggregate data. In three-quarters of the 40 cases, the standard deviation of the logarithm of per-capita energy demand is larger in the sectoral demand than in the aggregate and in the large majority of the individual country regressions the standard error of the regression is larger for the sectors than for the aggregate. Figure 7.1 plots the estimates of the long-run income and price elasticities based on the ARDL$(1, 0, 0)$ model. Across countries and sectors, there is a negative correlation between estimates of price and income elasticities, a higher income elasticity is associated with a higher (absolute) price elasticity. To a large extent this correlation is a product of outliers, four or five cases where there are very large income and price elasticities, and if these are removed there is less association between the estimates of income and price effects.

Figures 7.2 and 7.3 indicate the sensitivity of the estimates to lag order. Figure 7.2 plots the estimates for the long-run income elasticity from the ARDL$(1, 0, 0)$ specifications against the estimates from the ARDL$(1, 1, 1)$ specifications. In the large majority of the cases, the estimates are quite close, but there are a number of outliers. It is clear that there are far more negative estimates in the case of ARDL$(1, 1, 1)$ as compared to the ARDL$(1, 0, 0)$ model. Figure 7.3 provides the same graph for the estimates of the long-run price elasticities, and shows a similar pattern. The outliers, with positive price elasticities from the ARDL$(1, 1, 1)$ and negative ones from the ARDL$(1, 0, 0)$ all come from the industry sector in four cases where the estimates of the price elasticity

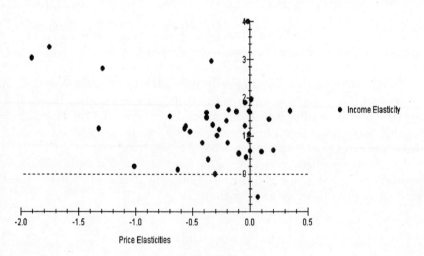

Figure 7.1: Long-run income and price elasticities of sectoral energy demand – ARDL$(1, 0, 0)$ specification.

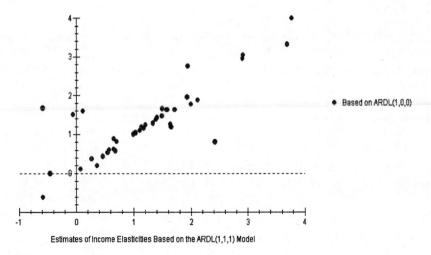

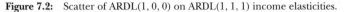

Estimates of Income Elasticities Based on the ARDL(1,1,1) Model

Figure 7.2: Scatter of ARDL(1, 0, 0) on ARDL(1, 1, 1) income elasticities.

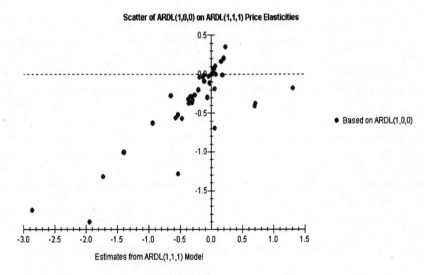

Figure 7.3: Scatter of ARDL(1, 0, 0) on ARDL(1, 1, 1) price elasticities.

are quite sensitive to lag order. The broad conclusion is that in most cases, the long-run estimates are not very sensitive to dynamic specification, but that the effects are quite extreme in the minority of cases where it matters. Overall, the ARDL(1, 0, 0) estimates are probably more reliable, though they are not necessarily the ones that would be chosen by the data. When lag order is chosen by the SBC, there is a wide variety of orders chosen. The most common is the ARDL(1, 0, 0) with 15 out of the 40 cases, followed by the static (0, 0, 0) with 9, the (1, 1, 0) with 6, the (0, 0, 1) and the (0, 1, 1) with 3 each, the (0, 1, 0) with 2 and the (1, 1, 0) and (1, 1, 1) with 1 each. There is no obvious pattern across sectors. As with the aggregate, allowing for dynamics tends to increase the size of the price and income responses, as is to be expected.

The figures indicate a very wide range of estimates for both income and price elasticities. There is some indication that the sectors are more price sensitive than the aggregate. This is a common result: disaggregation tends to lead to larger estimates of the price elasticities. However, the dispersion of the estimates is such that this conclusion cannot be drawn with great confidence.

7.3   Pooled Estimates

7.3.1   Industrial Sector

Table C.17 gives the alternative pooled estimates for the ARDL(1, 0, 0) model for the industry sector: the Mean Group (MG), Pooled Mean Group (PMG) which imposes homogeneity of long-run coefficients only, the Dynamic Fixed Effect (DFE) which imposes homogeneity of all slope coefficients and error variances, and the Static Fixed Effect (SFE).[3] As we would expect, the MG estimator suggests faster adjustment than the PMG, which suggests faster adjustment than the DFE. In the SFE instantaneous adjustment is imposed. This pattern of adjustment coefficients is what we would expect given the theoretical discussion in Chapter 5 and below we only note the cases where this does not hold. It should be remembered that the MG and PMG estimates of the adjustment coefficient are averages over individual country estimates and thus may be sensitive to outliers. Pooled long-run income elasticities are very similar to the aggregate and long-run price elasticities substantially larger. The PMG estimate of the long-run income and price elasticities for the industrial sector are 1.238(0.081) and $-0.518(0.091)$, respectively, which are very similar to the DFE estimates. The pooled estimates based on the static specification are, however, usually smaller, particularly as far as the price elasticity is concerned. An unusual feature of these results is that while pooling increases the precision of the long-run output elasticity, as usual, it does not increase the precision of the long-run price elasticity, which is quite sharply estimated by

---

[3] The DFE model contains the same dynamics as the ARDL model specified for the individual country equations. Notice that there are no corresponding DFE estimators when the orders of the ARDL model for individual countries, are selected by the Schwarz criterion.

the MG estimator. The PMG has the same standard error, the DFE estimator a larger standard error than the MG. Imposing homogeneity of long-run elasticities does not cause a very large reduction in fit, whereas imposing complete slope homogeneity does.

Table C.18 gives the four sets of estimates for the ARDL(1, 1, 1) in the industry sector. This is the case where half of the individual country-specific estimates of long-run price elasticities were positive and three of the income elasticities were negative. The MG estimator reflects this, whereas the PMG, which gives less weight to the outliers remains relatively robust, the income and price elasticities changing little. This is also the case when the lag order is chosen by the Schwarz criterion, given in Table C.19. The big change in the PMG estimator is the increase in the estimated speed of adjustment, reflecting the cases where the Schwarz criterion chose a static model. The MG estimates based on the Schwarz criterion are very close to the ARDL(1, 0, 0). Table C.20 gives the estimates including the real exchange rate variable. Including this variable reduces the income elasticity somewhat, does not change the price elasticity very much for the MG and PMG, and increases both the estimate and its standard error for the DFE. The SFE also gives a larger estimate of the price elasticity; though it remains much smaller than those given by the dynamic models. The PMG estimate of the real exchange rate effect is very similar to that obtained for the aggregate specification.

These results are largely consistent with what one would expect from the performance of the estimators on the aggregate data and with the individual country results from the industrial sector. Estimates are similar to the pooled aggregate estimates reported in Section 6.2, but with a larger price elasticity. The PMG estimates also seem to be quite robust to the outliers. It is also worth noting that the pooling is justified as far as long-run elasticities are concerned. The MG, PMG and DFE estimators tend not to be significantly different from one another.

7.3.2   Transport Sector

Table C.21 gives the estimates from the alternative pooled estimators for the ARDL(1, 0, 0) model. Except for the adjustment coefficient, the estimates from the MG and the dynamic pooled estimators are close. The SFE underestimates both price and income elasticities. Both price and income elasticities are larger than those obtained using the aggregate observations. Table C.22 gives the estimates for the ARDL(1, 1, 1), which are broadly similar except for a sharp drop in the estimated long-run price elasticity in the case of the PMG estimator. In this case the normal ranking of the adjustment coefficients does not hold, the PMG shows very slightly slower adjustment than the DFE. It is not clear why this is happening, but the phenomenon remains when the lag length is chosen by the Schwarz criterion presented in Table C.23. The PMG still gives a low estimate of the price elasticity, as well as a low estimate of the income elasticity although it is not significantly different from unity. Adjustment is now much faster as one would expect, given the choice of a static model in a number of countries. The imposition of long-run homogeneity causes a substantial reduction in fit. The ARDL(1, 0, 0, 0) estimates containing the real exchange rate variable are more similar to the ARDL(1, 0, 0) model that excludes it (compare the estimates in Tables C.21 and C.24). The real exchange rate effect is slightly larger than the estimate obtained for the aggregate model (compare the estimates in Tables C.24 and 6.14).

Unlike the aggregate and industry estimates in the transport sector the PMG estimates seem sensitive to dynamic specification. But overall the results suggest a slightly larger income and price effect in the transportation sector than in the aggregate.

7.3.3   Residential Sector

Table C.25 presents the results for the alternative pooled estimates based on the ARDL(1, 0, 0) model. The SFE shows the same pattern as the aggregate; an income elasticity close to unity and a price elasticity close to zero. The DFE and PMG also give estimates of income elasticities close to unity, the MG gives a slightly larger estimate, but not significantly different from unity. The estimates of the long price elasticity are very different: the estimates based on the MG and SFE procedures are small and insignificant, the DFE gives a larger estimate but it is still not significantly different from zero. Only the PMG method yields a long-run price elasticity, namely -0.475 (0.005) which is statistically different from zero. The ARDL(1, 1, 1) estimates are presented in Table C.26. Price and income elasticities are lower than the ARDL(1, 0, 0) case for all three estimators, though not by much for the MG. When the lag order is chosen by the Schwarz criterion, the PMG and MG estimators are similar to the ARDL(1, 0, 0) with a large income elasticity and an insignificant price elasticity (see Table C.27). Table C.28 gives the estimates for the ARDL(1, 0, 0, 0) model including the real exchange rate variables. The real exchange rate is significant according to the MG, but not according to the pooled estimators. *A priori*, the residential sector seems least likley to be influenced by foreign prices.

The estimates for the residential sector seem to be sensitive to choice of dynamic specification and the pooling procedure estimator. Focusing on the ARDL(1, 0, 0) specification the DFE and PMG procedure suggest an income elasticity close to unity and quite a large price elasticity, although the price elasticity is significantly different from zero only in the case of the PMG. The estimates based on the MG lie in between the DFE and the PMG estimators.

7.3.4 Commercial Sector

It will be remembered that this sector also includes agriculture and public energy use and thus is very heterogeneous. Table C.29 gives results for the alternative estimators using the ARDL(1, 0, 0) specification. The MG and DFE procedures suggest high price and income elasticities; quite high for MG 1.5 and −0.4, and unbelievably high for two of the dynamic pooled estimators. The dynamic pooled estimators indicate much slower adjustment than the MG and this may be influencing the estimates of the long-run elasticities. In contrast the PMG procedure yields very low income and price elasticities. The large disparities across the pooled estimates are a clear indication of the significant heterogeneities that exist across the commercial energy demand equations. Table C.30 gives the ARDL(1, 1, 1) estimates. These are rather similar to the estimates obtained using the ARDL(1, 0, 0) specifications. When the order is chosen by the Schwarz criterion, the results are similar to the ARDL(1, 1, 1) as Table C.31 indicates. When the real exchange rate is added in the ARDL(1, 0, 0, 0) specification in Table C.32, the MG price and income elasticities are reduced, the PMG continues to have an income elasticity significantly less than unity and a price elasticity close to zero. The DFE continues to show large price and income effects. The effect of the real exchange rate is positive for the MG and DFE, but negative for the PMG. The PMG estimates are sensitive to the inclusion of Malaysia; if this is dropped, the long-run income elasticity is −1.9 rather than 0.6, there is a large negative price elasticity and a positive effect of the real exchange rate.

7.4 Conclusions

The results of this analysis are broadly in accord with the aggregate analysis. There is considerable heterogeneity, more at a sectoral level than at aggregate level. The MG estimators are thus potentially more sensitive to outliers, given that N is relatively small. Given the dispersion of the estimates and the sensitivity to dynamic specification, conclusions must be cautious. The equations for the industry and transport sectors worked rather well, in that there was agreement between estimators and little sensitivity to dynamic specification. The long-run GDP elasticity for the industrial sector seemed similar to the aggregate estimate, around 1.2, the estimate for the transport sector was a little higher, at around 1.4. Both sectors seemed more price sensitive than the aggregate. The long-run price elasticity of energy consumption in the industrial sector turned out to be around −0.5, while this estimate for the transport sector was around −0.35. The residential sector seemed to be less price sensitive than the aggregate. The income elasticity of the commercial sector seemed higher than the aggregate and it seemed to be more price sensitive than the aggregate.

7.5 Tables

Table 7.1: Aggregate and sectoral long-run income elasticities of energy demand in Asian developing economies (Based on ARDL(1, 0, 0) specifications).[1]

Country	Aggregate	Industry	Transport	Residential	Commercial
Bangladesh	1.979	1.960	1.625	1.252	3.994
	(0.177)	(0.235)	(0.256)	(0.494)	(0.624)
India	1.006	1.156	0.436	1.643	2.762
	(0.102)	(0.124)	(0.066)	(0.160)	(1.329)
Indonesia	1.564	1.508	1.286	1.187	3.042
	(0.234)	(1.154)	(0.158)	(0.161)	(0.380)
Korea	1.074	1.094	1.387	0.624	0.881
	(0.125)	(0.173)	(0.101)	(0.041)	(0.160)
Malaysia	2.218	1.597	3.318	1.004	1.777
	(1.228)	(1.612)	(2.459)	(0.238)	(0.840)
Pakistan	1.320	1.675	1.425	2.947	−0.620
	(0.226)	(0.898)	(0.235)	(0.296)	(0.311)
Philippines	0.835	0.194	1.187	1.654	0.108
	(0.290)	(1.020)	(1.579)	(0.381)	(1.110)
Sri Lanka	0.217	−0.008	0.578	0.376	1.880
	(0.254)	(2.435)	(0.184)	(0.411)	(0.408)
Taiwan	0.897	0.810	1.038	0.811	0.602
	(0.102)	(0.231)	(0.052)	(0.153)	(0.028)
Thailand	1.172	1.244	1.474	1.629	0.530
	(0.047)	(0.188)	(0.088)	(0.117)	(0.071)
Mean group estimates	1.228	1.123	1.375	1.312	1.495
	(0.183)	(0.201)	(0.248)	(0.229)	(0.459)
Pooled MG estimates	1.184	1.238	1.406	0.947	0.616
	(0.039)	(0.081)	(0.051)	(0.092)	(0.029)
Dynamic fixed effects	1.301	1.288	1.449	1.086	2.377
	(0.109)	(0.177)	(0.109)	(0.165)	(0.524)
Static fixed effects	1.009	1.027	1.191	0.976	1.360
	(0.037)	(0.061)	(0.050)	(0.070)	(0.125)

[1] The sectoral and pooled estimates are drawn from Tables C.1, C.5, C.9, C.13, and Tables C.17, C.21, C.25, and C.29, respectively. The aggregate estimates are drawn from Tables 6.6 and 6.11.

Table 7.2: Aggregate and sectoral long-run price elasticities of energy demand in Asian developing economies (based on ARDL(1, 0, 0) specifications).[1]

Country	Aggregate	Industry	Transport	Residential	Commercial
Bangladesh	0.035	0.012	0.000	−0.043	−0.015
	(0.095)	(0.108)	(0.123)	(0.235)	(0.369)
India	−0.068	−0.269	−0.033	−0.005	−1.290
	(0.080)	(0.185)	(0.070)	(0.219)	(1.241)
Indonesia	−0.488	−0.697	−0.324	−0.569	−1.903
	(0.195)	(0.939)	(0.120)	(0.115)	(0.468)
Korea	−0.136	−0.520	−0.203	0.203	−0.014
	(0.189)	(0.480)	(0.120)	(0.035)	(0.243)
Malaysia	−1.159	−0.376	−1.753	−0.286	−0.280
	(1.182)	(1.105)	(2.067)	(0.214)	(0.665)
Pakistan	0.047	−0.181	0.165	−0.334	0.069
	(0.169)	(0.560)	(0.160)	(0.195)	(0.161)
Philippines	−0.431	−1.009	−1.324	0.347	−0.629
	(0.110)	(0.529)	(0.651)	(0.089)	(0.458)
Sri Lanka	0.061	−0.302	0.101	−0.363	−0.040
	(0.108)	(0.993)	(0.086)	(0.160)	(0.146)
Taiwan	−0.132	−0.413	−0.005	−0.191	0.004
	(0.273)	(0.729)	(0.081)	(0.388)	(0.046)
Thailand	−0.341	−0.558	−0.375	−0.114	−0.095
	(0.042)	(0.158)	(0.075)	(0.118)	(0.066)
Mean group estimates	−0.261	−0.431	−0.375	−0.135	−0.419
	(0.118)	(0.090)	(0.204)	(0.087)	(0.211)
Pooled MGE estimates	−0.339	−0.518	−0.364	−0.475	−0.078
	(0.033)	(0.091)	(0.042)	(0.065)	(0.042)
Dynamic fixed effects	−0.365	−0.567	−0.439	−0.269	−1.269
	(0.097)	(0.170)	(0.095)	(0.126)	(0.487)
Static fixed effects	−0.067	−0.165	−0.138	−0.056	−0.123
	(0.030)	(0.051)	(0.039)	(0.050)	(0.097)

[1] The sectoral and pooled estimates are drawn from Tables C.1, C.5, C.9, C.13, and Tables C.17, C.21, C.25, and C.29, respectively. The aggregate estimates are drawn from Tables 6.6 and 6.11.

CHAPTER 8

Inter-Fuel Substitutions

8.1 Introduction

The structure of fuels used by a country reflects to a considerable extent its natural resources. Countries which have domestic supplies of coal, oil or natural gas will use their indigenous resources more intensively. To a certain extent access will be reflected in price and the indigenous fuels will be relatively cheaper. As was seen in Chapter 2, there is considerable cross-country and intertemporal variation in the use of particular fuels, though petroleum products generally take the largest share, with electricity the second largest. For some countries consumption of coal is small and for others consumption of natural gas is negligible. There are also problems with both the coal and the natural gas price data. Thus we will confine our attention to petroleum products, electricity and an aggregated category, other fuels, which is the sum of coal plus natural gas consumption. The price index for other fuels was constructed as the unit value:

$$P_{it}^{OF} = (P_{it}^{NG}E_{it}^{NG} + P_{it}^{CL}E_{it}^{CL})/(E_{it}^{NG} + E_{it}^{CL}).$$

Inter-fuel substitution has been the subject of considerable investigation. See, for example, Bacon (1992). Most of this work has been done within the context of translog models or other flexible functional forms, which model value shares for each fuel. We follow this approach in modelling the long-run fuel share equations, and adopt two different approaches for modelling the dynamics of adjustments. In Section 8.2, we discuss a vector partial adjustment model of fuel shares of the type discussed in Chapter 3. This model assumes that prices and total energy expenditure are exogenous, which may be a strong assumption in this particular case where the two fuels account for such a large proportion of the total. Therefore in Section 8.3, we treat all the variables as endogenous and estimate long-run structural relationships for fuel shares, using a cointegrating VAR approach subject to long-run theory restrictions (see Pesaran and Shin (1997b) and Pesaran (1997)). Section 8.4 summarizes the results.

8.2 A Vector Partial Adjustment Model of Fuel Shares

The initial theoretical model is the vector partial adjustment model given by equation (3.20) in Section 3.3.1. To apply it to fuel shares we replace real income, Y_t/P_t, by per capita total energy consumption, e_t, and the system of fuel share equations will then be:

$$\Delta \mathbf{w}_t = \Lambda \left\{ \mathbf{w}_{t-1} - \quad - \quad \ln(\mathbf{P}_t) - \quad \ln(e_t) \right\} + \varepsilon_t, \tag{8.1}$$

where in the present application $\mathbf{w}_t$ is an $m \times 1$ vector of fuel value shares, and   are $m \times 1$ vectors of unknown long-run coefficients, $\ln(\mathbf{P}_t) = (\ln(P_{1t}),$ $\ln(P_{2t}), \ldots, \ln(P_{mt}))'$, $= (\beta_{ij})$ is an $m \times m$ matrix of price coefficients, and $\Lambda = (\lambda_{ij})$ is an $m \times m$ matrix of adjustment coefficients. This system of equations can now be estimated subject to the short-term and long-term additivity conditions, namely $'\Lambda = \mathbf{0}$. This form of equation assumes separability or two stage budgeting, with total nominal expenditures on fuels and fuel prices as exogenous. The allocation of income between energy and other goods is first determined, given total income and the prices of energy and other goods, and then the allocation of energy demand between different fuels is determined given total energy demand and the prices of individual fuels. Notice that the usual real income measure is total expenditure deflated by some price index, i.e. Y/P. In the case of the fuel share equations we have a good measure of total energy consumption, namely the physical units of energy consumption measured in TOE, so we do not need to deflate nominal expenditures to obtain a quantity measure. Correspondingly, the implicit price index for total energy would be the unit value measure discussed in Chapter 2.

The system of equations in (8.1) can be written as:

$$\mathbf{w}_t = \mathbf{a} + \mathbf{B}\ln(\mathbf{P}_t) + \mathbf{C}\mathbf{w}_{t-1} + \mathbf{d}\ln(e_t) + \varepsilon_t, \tag{8.2}$$

where

$$\mathbf{a} = -\Lambda \quad , \quad \mathbf{B} = -\Lambda \quad , \quad \mathbf{C} = \mathbf{I} + \Lambda, \quad \mathbf{d} = -\Lambda . \tag{8.3}$$

We shall set $m = 3$, and consider three fuel value shares for the petroleum products, electricity and other fuels (comprising of coal and natural gas). Denoting the elements of $\mathbf{a}, \mathbf{B}, \mathbf{C}$ and $\mathbf{d}$ by a_i, b_{ij}, c_{ij} and d_i for $i, j = p, e$ and o, and imposing adding up by dropping the equation for other fuels, gives the following two share equations for each country:

$$w_{tp} = (a_p - c_{po}) + b_{pp}\ln\left(P_t^{PP}\right) + b_{pe}\ln\left(P_t^{EL}\right) + b_{po}\ln\left(P_t^{OF}\right)$$
$$+ (c_{pp} - c_{po})w_{t-1,p} + (c_{pe} - c_{po})w_{t-1,e} + d_p\ln(e_t) + \varepsilon_{tp}, \tag{8.4}$$

and

$$w_{te} = (a_e - c_{eo}) + b_{ep}\ln\left(P_t^{PP}\right) + b_{ee}\ln\left(P_t^{EL}\right) + b_{eo}\ln\left(P_t^{OF}\right)$$
$$+ (c_{ep} - c_{eo})w_{t-1,p} + (c_{ee} - c_{eo})w_{t-1,e} + d_e\ln(e_t) + \varepsilon_{te}. \tag{8.5}$$

The share of other fuels, w_{to}, can be obtained from the adding up restriction $w_{to} = 1 - (w_{tp} + w_{te})$, where

$$w_{tp} = P_t^{PP}E_t^{PP} / \left(P_t^{PP}E_t^{PP} + P_t^{EL}E_t^{EL} + P_t^{OF}E_t^{OF}\right), \tag{8.6}$$

and

$$w_{te} = P_t^{EL}E_t^{EL}/(P_t^{PP}E_t^{PP} + P_t^{EL}E_t^{EL} + P_t^{OF}E_t^{OF}). \tag{8.7}$$

Imposing price homogeneity implies that $b_{pp} + b_{pe} + b_{po} = b_{ep} + b_{ee} + b_{eo} = 0$. Subject to homogeneity, symmetry implies that $b_{ep} = b_{pe}$.

The coefficients in (8.4) and (8.5) are not elasticities, but elasticities can be derived from them. There are two types of elasticities that may be of interest. We could calculate the elasticities holding total (nominal) expenditure on energy constant, which is the traditional way given the way the budget constraint is defined, or holding total energy consumption constant, which would be appropriate if energy was in inelastic supply. Here we will use the former. The derivation of the elasticities is given in an appendix. In this case, the short-run elasticities with respect to total energy use are:

$$\left.\begin{array}{l} \varepsilon_p = 1 + d_p/w_p, \\ \varepsilon_e = 1 + d_e/w_e. \end{array}\right\} \tag{8.8}$$

The short-run elasticities with respect to energy prices are:

$$\left.\begin{array}{l} \varepsilon_{pp} = b_{pp}/w_p - d_p - 1, \\ \varepsilon_{ee} = b_{ee}/w_e - d_e - 1, \\ \varepsilon_{pe} = b_{pe}/w_p - d_p w_e/w_p, \\ \varepsilon_{ep} = b_{ep}/w_e - d_e w_p/w_e. \end{array}\right\} \tag{8.9}$$

Notice that in general ε_{pe} need not be equal to ε_{ep}.

The long-run elasticities with respect to total energy are computed by first solving the long-run steady state solution of the dynamic fuel share equations (8.4) and (8.5) and then applying the above formulae to the coefficients of these long-run equations. Designating these coefficients by an asterisk we first note that

$$\mathbf{B}^* = \begin{pmatrix} 1 - (c_{pp} - c_{po}) & -(c_{pe} - c_{po}) \\ -(c_{pe} - c_{po}) & 1 - (c_{ee} - c_{eo}) \end{pmatrix}^{-1} \begin{pmatrix} b_{pp} & b_{pe} & b_{po} \\ b_{ep} & b_{ee} & b_{eo} \end{pmatrix},$$

$$\mathbf{d}^* = \begin{pmatrix} 1 - (c_{pp} - c_{po}) & -(c_{pe} - c_{po}) \\ -(c_{pe} - c_{po}) & 1 - (c_{ee} - c_{eo}) \end{pmatrix}^{-1} \begin{pmatrix} d_p \\ d_e \end{pmatrix}.$$

The long-run price and expenditure elasticities can now be computed after replacing d_i by d_i^*, and b_{ij} by b_{ij}^* in (8.8) and (8.9).

For estimation, prices and energy use are expressed as index numbers having the value of unity in 1990. In this case, a_i^*, $i = p, e$, the two elements of $\mathbf{a}^*$ defined by

$$\mathbf{a}^* = \begin{pmatrix} 1 - (c_{pp} - c_{po}) & -(c_{pe} - c_{po}) \\ -(c_{pe} - c_{po}) & 1 - (c_{ee} - c_{eo}) \end{pmatrix}^{-1} \begin{pmatrix} a_p \\ a_e \end{pmatrix},$$

give the steady state shares of each fuel. The two equations and various restricted versions were estimated by SURE and the maximized log-likelihood for the system calculated. Except for the case where symmetry is imposed, SURE is identical to OLS, since the same explanatory variables appear in both equations, though the system log-likelihood is not equal to the sum of the individual equation log-likelihood values.

In order to see whether the model could be simplified, a series of restrictions were considered. The first was homogeneity: $b_{pp} + b_{pe} + b_{po} = b_{ep} + b_{ee} + b_{eo} = 0$. Homogeneity was not rejected at the 5 per cent level in Indonesia, Pakistan and the Philippines, but was rejected in all the others. As with the aggregate, many of the coefficients of the lagged dependent variables were not significantly different from zero. Value shares seem to adjust very fast because they respond instantaneously to price, and price is very significant because quantity shares hardly adjust, so there are significant effects of price on value shares. Therefore the second set of restrictions considered was immediate adjustment: $c_{pp} = c_{pe} = c_{ep} = c_{ee} = 0$. The static model is not rejected in Korea at the 5 per cent level and not rejected at the 1 per cent level in Bangladesh and Taiwan, but rejected in the others. Thus although many individual coefficients on the lagged dependent variables are not significant, jointly they are. The third restriction was unit income elasticity: $d_p = d_e = 0$, which was widely accepted at the aggregate level, though that was the elasticity with respect to GDP rather than to total energy expenditure as here. Unit income elasticities are not rejected in Indonesia, Malaysia, Pakistan and Sri Lanka at the 5 per cent level and Taiwan at the 1 per cent level. Even allowing for the tendency of the Likelihood Ratio tests to over-reject in small samples, there is little indication of a simplification of the model that can be applied to all countries. In particular the failure on homogeneity contrasts with the aggregate results, where it was generally accepted. Eight out of the twenty equations showed signs of misspecification. Failure of functional form in both petroleum and electricity in Bangladesh, serial correlation in both in Indonesia and Korea, serial correlation and heteroskedasticity in the electricity equation in Malaysia, heteroskedasticity in the petroleum equation and failure on functional form for the electricity equation in Pakistan. There are some real outliers at the individual country levels, the Philippines in particular. What causes the problem is large fluctuations in particular prices (oil products in the Philippines case) which in turn causes large fluctuations in the value shares and distorts the dynamics. The petroleum own price elasticity was positive in three countries and the electricity own price elasticity was positive in two countries. Even when negative, the own price elasticities were very small, and usually insignificant. Since the equation did not perform well, particularly with respect to the failure to accept homogeneity in most countries, we do not report the full results and instead investigate alternative specifications.

The form of equation estimated above has the undesirable property that asymptotically as total energy demand grows, one share will grow beyond unity and one decline to less than zero. Share equations of this sort are not bounded in the zero one interval and given a trended regressor will give predictions that lie outside the unit interval eventually. To deal with this problem we experimented with the reciprocal of per-capita energy demand instead of the logarithm. As growth continues this tends to zero and the shares tend to steady state values. The elasticity of electricity demand with respect to total energy demand is given by

$$\varepsilon_e = 1 - \delta_e/(e\,w_e),$$

and for petroleum product demand

$$\varepsilon_p = 1 - \delta_p/(e\,w_p),$$

where δ_i, $i = p$, e, are the coefficients of the reciprocal of e, per-capita energy-demand and w_i are the shares, $i =$ petroleum products and electricity. Thus asymptotically as e goes to zero, the expenditure elasticity goes to unity. The model was re-estimated using the reciprocal rather than the logarithm. In general there is very little difference between the fits of the two forms, the reciprocal fits better in five countries, the logarithm in five countries. The only case where the logarithmic did a lot better was in Korea where it had a system log-likelihood of 131 compared to 121 for the reciprocal. However, given the theoretical attractions of the reciprocal formulation this seems preferable.

The conclusion of this section is that the Vector Partial Adjustment model assuming exogenous prices and energy expenditure did not perform well, with evidence of misspecification and rejection of homogeneity. It is likely that the exogeneity assumptions are an explanation for the poor performance.

8.3 A Cointegrating VAR Model of Fuel Shares

The approach used above, follows the standard practice of assuming prices and total energy demand as exogenously given. This is unlikely to be true, when the two main shares, petroleum products and electricity account for so much of energy demand. Thus the situation is quite different from the aggregate and sectoral estimates where energy demand accounts for relatively little of the activity variable, per-capita GDP. The failure of the exogeneity assumption may be a reason for the relatively poor performance of the model.

There is an alternative approach, described in Pesaran and Shin (1997b) where it is applied to a complete demand system of this form. Using the reciprocal of energy demand as the expenditure measure, let $\mathbf{x}_t = \left(w_{pt}, w_{et}, \ln\left(p_{et}^{EL}\right), \ln\left(p_{pt}^{PP}\right), \ln\left(p_t^{OF}\right), 1/e_t\right)'$. For this set of variables, the first order VAR model can be written as:

$$\Delta \mathbf{x}_t = \mathbf{a} - \Pi \mathbf{x}_{t-1} + \varepsilon_t. \tag{8.10}$$

Given the number of observations available, it is not sensible to consider higher order VARs. If the elements of $\mathbf{x}_t$ are $I(1)$ and cointegrated, the rank of Π will be the number of cointegrating vectors. If there are two demand functions, as the model above suggests the rank of Π must at least be two. Given two cointegrating vectors, which is broadly consistent with the data, we can then write the model:

$$\Delta x_t = a - GH'x_{t-1} + \varepsilon_t, \tag{8.11}$$

where G is a 6×2 matrix of adjustment coefficients, and H is a 6×2 matrix, each column of which is a cointegrating vector. The long-run relations can be exactly identified by the restrictions that w_{pt} is the dependent variable in the first cointegrating vector and w_{et} in the second, and that w_{et} does not appear in the first vector, while w_{pt} does not appear in the second vector. Under these exactly identifying restrictions the columns of H in (8.11) are given by

$$H = \begin{pmatrix} 1 & 0 \\ 0 & 1 \\ \beta_{pp} & \beta_{ep} \\ \beta_{pe} & \beta_{ee} \\ \beta_{po} & \beta_{eo} \\ \delta_p & \delta_e \end{pmatrix}. \tag{8.12}$$

This allows the long-run structural estimates to be directly estimated from the VAR, without making any assumptions about exogeneity of energy use and energy prices. It should be noted that the estimates are based on the equations for all the six variables $\left(w_{pt}, w_{et}, \ln\left(p_{et}^{EL}\right), \ln\left(p_{pt}^{PP}\right), \ln\left(p_t^{OF}\right), 1/e_t\right)$, and not merely the two share equations as was the case with the vector partial adjustment model. All the cointegration results below are based on a cointegrating VAR(1) model with no linear trends and restricted intercepts (namely case II described in Pesaran, Shin and Smith (1997) and Pesaran and Pesaran (1997, Section 19.6)).

Within this structure homogeneity was tested, and Table 8.1 gives the estimates, standard errors and t ratios for $(\beta_{pp} + \beta_{pe} + \beta_{po})$ and $(\beta_{ep} + \beta_{ee} + \beta_{eo})$. Performance on the homogeneity test is very much better than with the vector partial adjustment form assuming exogenous prices and income. Homogeneity is accepted in all but five of the 20 cases. It is only rejected for the petroleum products share in India, and by both shares in Sri Lanka and Taiwan. This suggests that we can reformulate the system as a five equation VAR with x_t now defined as $\left(w_{pt}, w_{et}, \ln(P_t^{EL}/P_t^{OF}), \ln(P_t^{PP}/P_t^{OF}), 1/e_t\right)'$.

The five equation VAR(1) model was estimated and cointegration tests carried out again. Table 8.2 reports the number of cointegrating vectors identified by Johansen's maximum eigenvalue and trace tests at the 5 per cent and 10 per cent level. At the 10 per cent level, the maximum eigenvalue test identifies two cointegrating vectors in five countries, one in two countries, and none in two countries. Korea seems to have four cointegrating vectors. The trace identifies one cointegrating vector in two countries, two in five, three in

Table 8.1: Tests of price homogeneity hypothesis in cointegrating VAR(1) model of fuel shares with reciprocal of per-capita energy.

Country	Petroleum Products[1]			Electricity[1]		
	$\hat{\gamma}_p$	S.E. $(\hat{\gamma}_p)$	$t_{\hat{\gamma}p}$	$\hat{\gamma}_e$	S.E. $(\hat{\gamma}_e)$	$t_{\hat{\gamma}e}$
Bangladesh	0.007	0.199	0.035	−0.020	0.136	−0.147
India	−0.055	0.009	**−6.111**	0.004	0.013	0.308
Indonesia	0.037	0.594	0.062	0.252	0.699	0.361
Korea	1.395	5.546	0.252	−0.761	3.161	−0.241
Malaysia	−7.780	46.890	−0.166	−3.340	18.310	−0.182
Pakistan	−0.063	0.053	−1.189	−0.490	0.960	−0.510
Philippines	−0.113	0.337	−0.335	0.168	0.497	0.338
Sri Lanka	0.028	0.004	**7.000**	−0.026	0.004	**−6.500**
Taiwan	−0.081	0.271	−0.299	0.164	0.183	0.896
Thailand	0.077	0.006	**12.833**	−0.081	0.007	**−11.571**

[1] γ_p and γ_e are defined by $\gamma_p = \beta_{pp} + \beta_{pe} + \beta_{po}$ and $\gamma_e = \beta_{ep} + \beta_{ee} + \beta_{eo}$ where β_{ij}, $i, j = p, e, o$ are defined in (8.12).

Table 8.2: Number of cointegrating vectors implied by Johansen's Tests (at the 5 and 10 per cent level) in a VAR(1) model of fuel shares subject to price homogeneity using reciprocal of per-capita energy consumption (no trends, restricted intercepts).

Country	Maximum eigenvalue statistic		Trace statistic	
	5 per cent	10 per cent	5 per cent	10 per cent
Bangladesh	2	2	2	2
India	1	2	2	3
Indonesia	2	2	2	2
Korea	4	4	4	4
Malaysia	1	1	1	1
Pakistan	0	0	1	2
Philippines	0	0	2	2
Sri Lanka	1	1	1	1
Taiwan	2	2	2	2
Thailand	1	2	2	3

two and four in Korea again. Given the small sample size and the theoretical considerations, two seems a reasonable choice.

The interpretation of the number of cointegrating vectors depends on the order of integration of the original series. One might get two cointegrating vectors if two of the original series happened to be $I(0)$. However, the assumption that the variables are $I(1)$ is not rejected by the data. Table 8.3 gives ADF statistics for the value shares for petroleum products and electricity, the relative prices of petroleum products and electricity to other fuels and the reciprocal of energy demand. These are all ADF(1) statistics including an intercept, except for the reciprocal of energy demand which is ADF(1) with intercept and trend.

Table 8.3:   Augmented Dickey–Fuller unit-root test statistics.

Country	w_{pt}	w_{et}	$\ln(P_t^{EL}/P_t^{OF})$	$\ln(P_t^{PP}/P_t^{OF})_t$	$1/e_t$
Bangladesh	−1.12	−2.66	−2.62	−2.55	−2.91
India	−1.93	−1.99	−1.08	−0.94	−1.60
Indonesia	−1.10	0.65	−0.79	−1.32	−2.12
Korea	−2.02	−2.44	−1.63	−0.58	−3.09
Malaysia	−2.08	−2.19	−2.66	−2.35	−2.90
Pakistan	1.26	0.28	−1.81	−1.44	−1.51
Philippines	−1.54	−1.49	−3.00	−2.14	−2.33
Sri Lanka	−0.96	−0.99	−1.27	−1.59	−2.73
Taiwan	−1.17	−1.18	0.13	−1.70	−5.05
Thailand	−0.94	−1.05	−1.49	−1.42	−1.31
5 per cent critical values	−3.06	−3.06	−3.06	−3.06	−3.73

Notes
1. The test statistics are computed using ADF(1) regressions with intercept and no trends, except for $1/e_t$ where it is based on the ADF(1) regression with trend.
2. w_{pt} is share of petroleum products, w_{et} is share of electricity, $\ln(P_t^{EL}/P_t^{OF})$ is log of the ratio of petroleum to other prices, $\ln(P_t^{PP}/P_t^{OF})$ is log of the ratio of electricity to other prices, and $1/e_t$ is the inverse of the per-capita energy consumption.

In only one of the 50 cases is the null hypothesis of a unit root rejected. Of course, these tests have very low power, particularly given the small sample size.

Given homogeneity, symmetry was accepted in every country except the Philippines and Taiwan. In most cases, the test statistics were very small, symmetry seems to hold very well for most countries. The estimates of the long-run elasticities derived from the cointegrating VAR with symmetry and homogeneity, evaluated at 1990 shares, are presented in Table 8.4.

The elasticities and their standard errors were obtained directly from the estimates by reparameterizing the system in a way described in Appendix B. Those for the Philippines do not impose symmetry, since the estimates failed to converge when it was imposed. The estimates show the heterogeneity characteristic of individual country estimates, but seem broadly sensible. Thailand and Korea have very large standard errors. Own price elasticities for petroleum are negative in every country except Thailand. Own price elasticities for electricity are negative in every country but the Philippines and again Thailand. There are no significantly positive own price elasticities, six of the petroleum elasticities and two of the electricity elasticities are significantly negative. The cross-price elasticities are positive in Indonesia, Korea and Taiwan, in both equations; elsewhere they are negative. This suggests that in most countries both electricity and petroleum tend to substitute with other fuels (coal and natural gas) rather than directly with each other, but that in more industrialized countries they substitute with each other. However, such conclusions can only be tentative.

Inspection of the **G** matrix of the adjustment coefficients in (8.11) indicated that the feedbacks tended to be on all the variables which tends to support the

Table 8.4: Elasticity estimates from a cointegrating VAR in fuel shares subject to homogeneity and symmetry restrictions (specification contains the reciprocal of the per-capita energy consumption).

Country	Petroleum equations			Electricity equations		
	ε_{pp}[1]	ε_{pe}	ε_p	ε_{ep}	ε_{ee}	ε_e
Bangladesh	−0.333	−0.190	0.596	−1.320	−0.350	1.782
	(0.096)	(0.051)	(0.053)	(0.188)	(0.101)	(0.104)
India	−0.469	−0.429	1.101	−0.771	−0.405	1.064
	(0.069)	(0.065)	(0.121)	(0.111)	(0.891)	(0.245)
Indonesia	−0.925	0.376	0.543	0.110	−1.832	1.825
	(0.294)	(0.522)	(0.271)	(0.939)	(1.934)	(0.798)
Korea	−1.494	1.556	0.949	2.739	−7.699	0.600
	(4.015)	(9.161)	(0.939)	(17.746)	(40.535)	(4.132)
Malaysia	−0.239	−0.146	0.533	−0.878	−0.220	1.341
	(0.136)	(0.107)	(0.057)	(0.270)	(0.227)	(0.176)
Pakistan	−0.244	−0.384	0.724	−0.782	−0.408	1.303
	(0.094)	(0.101)	(0.030)	(0.160)	(0.174)	(0.048)
Philippines[2]	−0.851	−0.506	1.261	−0.140	0.042	0.244
	(0.161)	(0.053)	(0.142)	(0.303)	(0.100)	(0.267)
Sri Lanka	−0.521	−0.317	0.661	−2.259	−0.073	2.130
	(0.163)	(0.070)	(0.159)	(0.500)	(0.193)	(0.501)
Taiwan	−1.119	0.148	0.858	0.028	−0.950	1.195
	(0.670)	(0.521)	(0.147)	(0.659)	(0.513)	(0.144)
Thailand	1.267	−2.220	0.881	−4.677	3.617	1.230
	(10.478)	(11.3)	(0.624)	(21.803)	(23.519)	(1.299)

[1] ε_{pp} is the own-price elasticity of petroleum products. ε_{pe} is the cross-elasticity of petroleum products with respect to electricity prices. ε_p is the total expenditure elasticity of petroleum products, and so on. The figures in brackets are standard errors. All elasticities are computed using sample observations in 1990.
[2] The results for the Philippines do not impose the symmetry restrictions.

concern about the exogeneity assumption and indicates that there is information in the responses of prices and total expenditure as well as the shares.

For completeness, we also applied the cointegrating VAR to the model using the usual logarithm rather than the reciprocal of energy demand. The pattern on the cointegration tests was very similar to the VAR using the reciprocal, two cointegrating vectors was the most common result. At the 10 per cent level the trace suggested one cointegrating vector in Malaysia and Sri Lanka, two in Bangladesh, Indonesia, Philippines and Taiwan, three in India and Thailand, and four in Korea and Pakistan. In Pakistan, the eigenvalue test suggested no cointegrating vectors even at the 10 per cent level. The elasticities evaluated at 1990 shares are given in Table 8.5. Homogeneity and symmetry are imposed except in Taiwan, where the estimates did not converge when symmetry was imposed. The estimates of the price elasticities are quite similar to those from the reciprocal model. Symmetry is rejected in the same two countries, Philippines and Taiwan. Both the petroleum and electricity own price elasticities are now significantly negative and sensible in Korea. The Malaysian petrol own price elasticity has become insignificantly positive. The majority of the cross price

Table 8.5: Elasticity estimates from a cointegrating VAR in fuel shares subject to homogeneity and symmetry restriction specification containing the logarithm of per-capita energy consumption.

Country	Petroleum equations			Electricity equations		
	ε_{pp} [1]	ε_{pe}	ε_p	ε_{ep}	ε_{ee}	ε_e
Bangladesh	−0.312	0.526	0.525	−1.357	−0.412	1.914
	(0.139)	(0.075)	(0.086)	(0.268)	(0.144)	(0.167)
India	−0.527	−0.423	1.109	−0.794	−0.440	1.133
	(0.103)	(0.074)	(0.233)	(0.132)	(0.090)	(0.296)
Indonesia	−0.780	0.164	0.554	−0.412	−1.127	1.851
	(0.213)	(0.321)	(0.192)	(0.724)	(1.169)	(0.476)
Korea	−0.799	0.054	0.638	−0.434	−0.732	1.598
	(0.194)	(0.223)	(0.186)	(0.202)	(0.238)	(0.190)
Malaysia	0.018	−0.320	0.450	−1.272	0.256	1.205
	(0.176)	(0.168)	(0.056)	(0.382)	(0.388)	(0.137)
Pakistan	−0.300	−0.238	0.641	−0.654	−0.614	1.342
	(0.038)	(0.037)	(0.023)	(0.078)	(0.066)	(0.075)
Philippines	−1.348	−0.373	1.685	0.605	−0.149	−0.397
	(0.178)	(0.057)	(0.122)	(0.237)	(0.087)	(0.135)
Sri Lanka	−0.470	−0.301	0.601	−2.396	−0.115	2.322
	(0.171)	(0.069)	(0.183)	(0.501)	(0.202)	(0.579)
Taiwan[2]	−1.641	1.542	0.966	0.427	−2.151	1.128
	(1.328)	(2.064)	(0.211)	(1.165)	(1.810)	(0.185)
Thailand	0.913	−1.135	0.191	−3.887	1.331	2.642
	(3.055)	(2.169)	(1.025)	(6.291)	(4.464)	(2.110)

[1] See footnote 1 of Table 8.4.
[2] The results for Taiwan do not impose the symmetry restrictions.

elasticities remain negative. The expenditure elasticities change rather more, as one might expect. The electricity expenditure elasticity in the Philippines is now negative for the logarithmic case, though this is not strictly comparable since symmetry is imposed in the logarithmic case and not in the reciprocal case.

It is also straightforward to allow some of the elements of $\mathbf{x}_t$ to be exogenous (see Pesaran, Shin and Smith (1997)). Suppose $\mathbf{x}_t$ is partitioned into $\mathbf{z}_{1t}$, and $\mathbf{z}_{2t}$, where

$$\mathbf{z}_{1t} = (w_{pt}, w_{et}, \ln(e_t))' \quad \text{and} \quad \mathbf{z}_{2t} = \left(\ln \left(p_t^{EL}/p_t^{OF} \right), \ln \left(p_t^{PP}/p_t^{OF} \right) \right)',$$

then the corresponding VARX(1) model would be:

$$\Delta \mathbf{z}_{1t} = \mathbf{a}_1 - \Pi_{11}\mathbf{z}_{t-1} + \mathbf{A}_0 \Delta \mathbf{z}_{2t} + \varepsilon_{1t}.$$

Again there should be two cointegrating vectors, but in this case there is no feedback from the error correction terms to prices, and current prices can influence current shares and total energy demand. This is closer to the vector partial adjustment model of the previous section, but allows for feedbacks through total energy demand, and does not treat it as exogenous. Since prices are also likely to be endogenous, we did not investigate this route.

8.4 Summary

This chapter examined the demand for three fuels, petroleum products, electricity and other fuels (coal plus natural gas). The models used made the equilibrium value share of each fuel a function of the logarithms of fuel prices and a function of per-capita total energy demand. We investigated four models which differed in what function of total energy demand was used, the logarithm or reciprocal, and what exogeneity and adjustment assumptions were used.

We adopted two approaches to the adjustment to equilibrium. The first model treated total energy demand and prices as exogenous, used the logarithm of total energy demand and allowed for dynamics by a vector partial adjustment formulation, which made each share a function of the current exogenous variables and two lagged shares. This model did not work particularly well, homogeneity was widely rejected, there was evidence of misspecification, and adjustment tended to be implausibly fast, though instantaneous adjustment could be rejected. It also had the unfortunate property that as total energy demand grew, predicted shares would fall outside the unit interval. The second model used the reciprocal rather than the logarithm of total energy demand. This has the desirable property that as income grows expenditure elasticities tend to unity, constant shares conditional on price. This model had a very similar fit to the logarithmic, but there were the same problems with the vector partial adjustment formulation.

The second approach to adjustment that we examined, treated all the variables, the two shares, the prices and total energy demand, as endogenous and estimated a cointegrating VAR. The theory suggests that there should be two cointegrating vectors, one for each fuel share equation, and the cointegration tests broadly confirmed this. The third model used the cointegrating VAR and the reciprocal of energy demand. Homogeneity and symmetry were generally accepted, own price elasticities, while showing considerable dispersion across countries, were generally negative and of a reasonable size. The estimates from the fourth model, using the logarithm of energy demand were similar.

There are two main conclusions. Firstly, while reciprocal and logarithmic models have similar fit, the reciprocal model although not strictly consistent with the theory, is likely to have better long-run forecasting properties, tending as income grows to constant shares conditional on price, rather than trended shares which will eventually move outside the unit interval. Secondly, the cointegrating VAR adjustment mechanism, which allowed all the variables to be endogenous did substantially better than the vector partial adjustment model, which treated prices and total expenditure as exogenous. This better performance was reflected in the fact that homogeneity and symmetry tended to hold, and there was evidence of larger own price elasticities.

CHAPTER 9

Industrial Demand for Energy

9.1 Introduction

The analysis of energy demand in Chapter 7 showed a number of important differences in the sectoral estimates of output and (particularly) price elasticities. This naturally raises the issue of the heterogeneity of elasticity estimates across industries. Due to lack of reliable time series a comprehensive analysis of energy demand at the level of individual industries is not possible. But as it turns out the bulk of energy consumption in the industrial sector of the Asian economies in our sample over the period 1970–1992 is accounted for by four main industries: chemicals, iron and steel, non-metallic minerals, and paper, pulp and printing. Consequently, in this chapter we consider industrial energy demand only in the case of these four industries.

Examining individual industries allows us to use data on the index of industrial production for those industries, as well as industry specific price indices, which reflect the composition of fuels used by particular industries. As we move to a finer level of disaggregation, the data becomes more sparse and in some cases less reliable. In a number of countries, these industries either do not exist or are very small, while data are missing for a number of years in some cases. Often when particular industries are small, they are aggregated with the unspecified industry category and observations on energy consumptions of these industries are recorded only when they exceed a certain threshold. Data on prices and industrial production are also missing in some cases. This means that we have to work with an unbalanced panel of a sub-sample of countries. This does not change any of the econometric procedures, except that the Mean Group estimator requires there to be enough observations in each country to estimate an individual country regression. However, the variable quality of the data does raise the possibility of sample selection bias in the average estimates. As was seen with aggregate and sectoral results, pooled estimates and particularly mean group estimates can be very sensitive to individual country estimates which are outliers. Therefore, an important issue is how sensitive the estimates are to changes in the sample of countries included in the analysis.

The general procedure we followed was to consider a base-line model in which the largest available sample is used to estimate an ARDL(1, 0, 0) model of the logarithm of industrial energy demand on the logarithm of a Stone price index for that industry relative to the CPI and the logarithm of the index of industrial production for that industry. We then examined the sensitivity of the results to (a) letting the lag order, up to a maximum of one, be chosen by the Schwarz criterion; (b) using the logarithm of the aggregate energy price AERP; (c) dropping some countries from the sample. As before, equations are estimated for each country individually and the Mean Group (MG) estimator calculated; then the data are pooled and the Pooled Mean Group (PMG), Dynamic Fixed Effect (DFE) and Static Fixed Effect (SFE) estimators computed by the Maximum Likelihood (ML) procedure discussed in Chapter 5. We conducted Likelihood Ratio and Hausman type procedures to test the equality of long-run parameters using the MG and PMG estimates. As with the earlier results, the Likelihood Ratio test generally rejects equality of long-run slope coefficients, while the Hausman test does not. In a number of cases the ML procedure in the case of PMG estimators converged to a local maximum of the likelihood function; obtaining different estimates depending on whether the initial values were based on the MG or DFE estimates. We discuss the estimates that gave the highest log-likelihoods, but there is no guarantee that there may not be a higher maximum.

9.2   Chemicals

Over this period, there were large changes in the relative importance of the chemical industries of the ten countries in our sample. The index of industrial production cannot be used to compare the relative size of the chemical industries in different countries, but a reasonable indication of their relative importance is each country's share of the total energy used in all ten countries by chemical industries. In 1971 India accounted for 40 per cent of total energy used in the chemical industries in the region, but by 1992 this had fallen to 30 per cent, while Korea's share had increased from 11 to 34 per cent over the same period. The share of Taiwan was relatively stable around 20 per cent, though falling to 16 per cent at the end of the period. Pakistan fell from 10 to 5 per cent. The other countries accounted for a relatively small amount of total energy used in the chemical industries (see Figure 9.1).

Within countries, the importance of the chemical industry also differs, though there is a general trend for the industry to take an increasing proportion of total industrial energy consumption in almost all the countries under consideration. In Bangladesh, the proportion of total industrial energy use accounted for by the chemical industry fluctuated considerably over the period, rising from 36 to 60 per cent, accounting for about 30 per cent of the country's energy consumption by the end of the period. In Indonesia, the share of chemicals in total industrial energy use rose from 16 to 43 per cent, 15 per cent

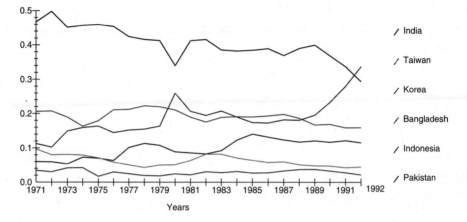

Figure 9.1:   Share of energy consumption in chemical industries of six major Asian economies.

of total energy use at the end of the period. In India, the share of chemicals in total industrial energy use rose from 11 to 21 per cent, 12 per cent of total energy use at the end of the period. In Korea energy used in chemical industries as the proportion of total industrial use rose from 11 to 40 per cent, or 20 per cent of total energy used in the economy as a whole at the end. Pakistan 20 to 30 per cent of industrial use, Thailand 1 to 9 per cent of industrial use, Taiwan 24 to 40 per cent of industrial use, 23 per cent of total use at the end.

Some electricity is used by all the chemical industries, plus differing amounts of petroleum products and natural gas, depending on availability of the latter. The data show some marked switches in fuel use. The Stone price indices use electricity and natural gas prices in Bangladesh, all four prices in India, all but natural gas in Indonesia and Taiwan, electricity and petroleum products in Korea, Philippines, Natural Gas and Petroleum products in Pakistan.

Sri Lanka and Malaysia are excluded from this analysis, since there were no energy consumption data, leaving eight countries. For each country we have 19 observations, except Taiwan which has 15 observations, data on industrial production being missing from 1971 to 1976 and Thailand, which has 17 observations. The individual country estimates, for the ARDL(1, 0, 0) using the Stone price indices are given in Table 9.1. Most of the elasticities with respect to the index of industrial production, the production elasticity, are close to unity. All fall in the range 0.7–1.3 except Indonesia −0.013 (0.489), Philippines 0.097 (0.304) and Thailand 2.083 (0.37). All the price elasticities except for India are negative and the Indian price elasticity is not significantly positive. The price elasticities show a large range, the largest being Thailand at −1.49 (0.47). The price elasticity is significantly negative in four countries, Bangladesh, Indonesia, Taiwan and Thailand. Four countries fail the functional form test: India, Korea, Pakistan and the Philippines and Korea also shows substantial

Table 9.1a: Country-specific estimates of the long-run production and price elasticities for the chemical industries based on ARDL(1, 0, 0) model.

Country	Parameter estimates[1]					
	$\hat{\varphi}$	$\hat{\theta}_y$	$\hat{\theta}_p$	$\hat{\sigma}$	$\bar{R}^2$	LL
Bangladesh	−0.748	1.003	−1.115	0.222	0.46	3.86
	(0.196)	(0.120)	(0.349)			
India	−0.660	0.801	0.177	0.071	0.43	25.67
	(0.178)	(0.073)	(0.480)			
Indonesia	−0.407	−0.013	−0.295	0.135	0.44	13.36
	(0.151)	(0.489)	(0.118)			
Korea	−0.279	0.983	−0.556	0.131	0.18	13.90
	(0.240)	(0.182)	(1.016)			
Pakistan	−1.124	1.124	−0.024	0.079	0.42	23.46
	(0.309)	(0.088)	(0.149)			
Philippines	−0.616	0.097	−0.856	0.163	0.40	9.73
	(0.205)	(0.304)	(0.657)			
Taiwan	−0.966	0.704	−0.268	0.036	0.73	30.85
	(0.156)	(0.028)	(0.060)			
Thailand	−0.826	2.083	−1.491	0.282	0.59	−0.32
	(0.195)	(0.370)	(0.470)			

[1] Figures in the brackets are the standard errors. $\hat{\sigma}$ is the estimated standard error of the regression. LL is the maximized value of the log-likelihood function. $\bar{R}$ is the adjusted multiple correlation coefficient. $\hat{\varphi}$ is the coefficient of the error correction term. $\hat{\theta}_y$ and $\hat{\theta}_y$ are the estimated long-run production and price elasticities.

Table 9.1b: Diagnostic statistic for the results in Table 9.1a.

Country	Diagnostic statistics[1]			
	$\chi^2_{SC}(1)$	$\chi^2_{FF}(1)$	$\chi^2_N(2)$	$\chi^2_H(1)$
Bangladesh	2.70	0.32	0.14	0.00
India	0.35	5.59	0.85	0.05
Indonesia	1.00	0.46	2.70	1.08
Korea	1.36	4.48	55.71	0.45
Pakistan	0.98	6.89	0.01	1.11
Philippines	0.31	12.91	4.84	2.90
Taiwan	0.06	0.61	1.08	0.15
Thailand	1.76	0.10	0.37	0.69

[1] See the footnote to Table 6.2b for the description of the diagnostic statistics.

non-normality. The fit of the regression varies substantially, with a standard error ranging from 7 per cent in India and Pakistan to 28 per cent in Thailand. Less than 50 per cent of the annual changes is explained in all countries other than Thailand and Taiwan.

The pooled estimates of the long-run production and price elasticities for the chemical industries are summarized in Tables 9.2–9.5. The results in Tables 9.2 and 9.3 are obtained using a weighted Stone energy price index, while those

Table 9.2: Alternative pooled estimators of the long-run production and price elasticities of energy demand for chemical industries in Asian developing economies (based on ARDL$(1, 0, 0)$ specifications and weighted Stone energy price indices).

	Mean group estimators	*Pooled mean group estimators*	*Dynamic fixed effects estimators*	*Static fixed effects estimators*
Production elasticity ($\hat{\theta}_y$)	0.848 (0.230)	0.741 (0.026)	0.679 (0.117)	0.762 (0.045)
Price elasticity ($\hat{\theta}_p$)	−0.554 (0.200)	−0.145 (0.029)	−0.169 (0.077)	−0.146 (0.030)
Error correction coefficient ($\hat{\phi}$)	−0.703 (0.098)	−0.411 (0.108)	−0.294 (0.068)	−1 (N/A)
Log-likelihood (*LL*)	120.52	87.03	25.20	−17.42
$\sum_{i=1}^{8} T_i$	146	146	146	146
No. of est. parameters	40	26	12	11

Table 9.3: Alternative pooled estimators of the long-run production and price elasticities of energy demand for chemical industries in Asian developing economies (based on ARDL-SBC specifications and weighted Stone energy price indices).

	Mean group estimators	*Pooled mean group estimators*	*Dynamic fixed effects estimators*	*Static fixed effects estimators*
Production elasticity ($\hat{\theta}_y$)	0.805 (0.241)	0.826 (0.023)	(N/A)	0.762 (0.045)
Price elasticity ($\hat{\theta}_p$)	−0.326 (0.164)	−0.095 (0.031)	(N/A)	−0.146 (0.030)
Error correction coefficient ($\hat{\phi}$)	−0.822 (0.092)	−0.795 (0.105)	(N/A)	−1 (N/A)
Log-likelihood (*LL*)	140.50	68.48	(N/A)	−17.42
$\sum_{i=1}^{8} T_i$	146	146	(N/A)	146
No. of est. parameters	39	25	(N/A)	11

in Tables 9.4 and 9.5 are based on the aggregate real energy price index. The MG estimate of the production elasticity is 0.85 (0.23), which is not significantly different from unity, and the MG estimate of the long-run price elasticity is −0.55 (0.20), which is just significantly different from zero. The DFE yields much smaller production 0.68 (0.12) and price −0.17 (0.08) elasticities. The PMG likelihood function shows multiple maxima. Using initial values from the DFE produces a larger maximum, 87, than using initial values from the MG, 82. The unrestricted log-likelihood is 121 and there may be another maximum higher than that generated by DFE initial values. The PMG estimates computed using the DFE estimates as initial values, are 0.74 (0.03) and −0.15 (0.03), similar to the DFE estimates. As is usual, the PMG estimate suggests slower

Table 9.4: Alternative pooled estimators of the long-run production and price elasticities of energy demand for chemical industries in Asian developing economies (based on ARDL(1, 0, 0) specifications and average real energy price indices).

	Mean group estimators	*Pooled mean group estimators*	*Dynamic fixed effects estimators*	*Static fixed effects estimators*
Production	0.850	0.830	0.709	0.803
elasticity $(\hat{\theta}_y)$	(0.215)	(0.035)	(0.142)	(0.048)
Price	−0.218	0.013	0.013	0.014
elasticity $(\hat{\theta}_p)$	(0.208)	(0.005)	(0.031)	(0.011)
Error correction	−0.671	−0.411	−0.245	−1
coefficient $(\hat{\phi})$	(0.101)	(0.088)	(0.064)	(N/A)
Log-likelihood (*LL*)	108.04	83.33	23.09	−28.20
$\sum_{i=1}^{8} T_i$	146	146	146	146
No. of est. parameters	40	26	12	11

Table 9.5: Alternative pooled estimators of the long-run production and price elasticities of energy demand for chemical industries in Asian developing economies (based on ARDL-SBC specifications and average real energy price indices).

	Mean group estimators	*Pooled mean group estimators*	*Dynamic fixed effects estimators*	*Static fixed effects estimators*
Production	0.778	0.864	(N/A)	0.803
elasticity $(\hat{\theta}_y)$	(0.217)	(0.022)		(0.048)
Price	0.077	0.013	(N/A)	0.014
elasticity $(\hat{\theta}_p)$	(0.193)	(0.003)		(0.011)
Error correction	−0.777	−0.686	(N/A)	−1
coefficient $(\hat{\phi})$	(0.117)	(0.159)		(N/A)
Log-likelihood (*LL*)	133.76	95.30	(N/A)	−28.20
$\sum_{i=1}^{8} T_i$	146	146	(N/A)	146
No. of est. parameters	41	27	(N/A)	11

adjustment than the MG, around 40 per cent a year as compared to 70 per cent a year for the MG.

When the lag order was chosen by the Schwarz criterion, using the Stone price index on the eight countries, a static model was chosen for three countries, and the unrestricted log-likelihood, the sum over the eight countries of the maximized log-likelihoods for the individual equations increased from 120 to 140. However, the restricted log-likelihood for the PMG estimator was lower using the SBC order than using a common ARDL(1, 0, 0) specification. This interaction of equality restrictions and lag order was noted in Chapter 6. The MG and PMG estimates of the production elasticity were similar to those for the ARDL(1, 0, 0) at 0.8, but the estimated PMG price elasticity was substantially smaller at −0.09 (0.03). This seems to confirm the conclusion from the aggregate results that the common ARDL(1, 0, 0) is a safer choice (see Table 9.3).

When the Stone price index was replaced by the aggregate real energy price for the eight country sample, the production elasticities hardly changed, still around 0.8, the MG estimate of the price elasticity fell to −0.22 and the PMG estimate became positive. One would expect the sector specific price index to be more appropriate, and the fit was better for the Stone price index (see Tables 9.4 and 9.5).

The analysis was repeated also excluding Indonesia, which had a positive price elasticity and a production elasticity close to the mean, and the Philippines, which had a very small production elasticity but quite a large price elasticity. Given the coefficients of the countries excluded, the MG production and price elasticity estimates, 1.11 (0.2) and −0.54 (0.26), do not change a lot. However, the PMG estimates do change, both the production elasticity 0.72 (0.02) and the price elasticity −0.27 (0.05) are lower.

The conclusion of the sensitivity analysis suggests that the ARDL(1, 0, 0) on the eight country sample using the Stone price index are to be preferred.

9.3   Iron and Steel

In terms of the total energy consumption by the iron and steel industry in all ten countries, India's share fell from 84 to 54 per cent, Korea's rose from 6 to 28 per cent and Taiwan's from 5 to 12 per cent. The other countries had very small shares (see Figure 9.2). The share of India's industrial energy use by the iron and steel industry fluctuated around 25 per cent, rising from 12 to 15 per cent of total energy use. In Korea iron and steel's share of total energy use rose from 3 to 10 per cent. The Philippines saw marked variations rising from 2 to 9 per cent of total energy use and then falling back to 1 per cent.

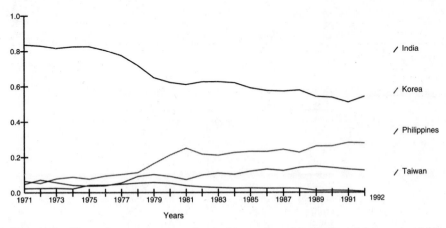

Figure 9.2: Share of energy consumption in iron and steel industries of four major Asian economies.

In Taiwan it also fluctuated substantially, rising from 5 to 11 per cent of total energy use. Differing mixtures of coal, electricity and petroleum products are used, with the large producers, India and Korea using large amounts of coal.

Bangladesh, Pakistan and Sri Lanka are excluded from the analysis, because of the poor quality of the data. There are 19 observations for India, Indonesia, and Korea; 18 for Malaysia and the Philippines, 16 for Thailand and 14 for Taiwan. The individual country estimates for the ARDL(1, 0, 0) model using the Stone price are given in Table 9.6. Production elasticities average just below unity, but there is considerable dispersion from −0.4 (1.06) for the Philippines to 1.53 (0.16) in Thailand. Price elasticities are negative except in Korea 0.06 (0.21) averaging about −0.5 and ranging up to −1.6 (1.9) in Indonesia. However, none of them are significantly negative. Again fit varies substantially between countries and again it is only in Thailand and Taiwan that over half the

Table 9.6a:　Country-specific estimates of the long-run production and price elasticities for the iron and steel industries based on ARDL(1, 0, 0) model using Stone price index.[1]

Country	Parameter estimates					
	$\hat{\varphi}$	$\hat{\theta}_y$	$\hat{\theta}_p$	$\hat{\sigma}$	$\bar{R}^2$	LL
India	−0.620	0.520	−0.263	0.076	0.44	24.31
	(0.196)	(0.140)	(0.159)			
Indonesia	−0.235	0.699	−1.585	0.372	−0.09	−5.91
	(0.197)	(0.584)	(1.897)			
Korea	−0.529	0.857	0.056	0.097	0.38	19.55
	(0.183)	(0.080)	(0.206)			
Malaysia	−0.649	1.391	−0.096	0.415	0.31	−7.44
	(0.237)	(0.516)	(0.094)			
Philippines	−0.308	−0.395	−1.385	0.280	0.16	−0.38
	(0.191)	(1.057)	(1.614)			
Taiwan	−0.943	1.141	−0.156	0.110	0.65	14.89
	(0.257)	(0.172)	(0.313)			
Thailand	−0.868	1.527	−0.287	0.145	0.62	9.57
	(0.192)	(0.155)	(0.332)			

[1] See notes to Table 9.1b.

Table 9.6b:　Diagnostic statistics for the results in Table 9.6a.

Country	Diagnostic statistics			
	$\chi^2_{SC}(1)$	$\chi^2_{FF}(1)$	$\chi^2_N(2)$	$\chi^2_H(1)$
India	1.67	0.14	0.30	0.91
Indonesia	3.80	2.35	3.32	0.03
Korea	8.96	0.01	3.09	0.00
Malaysia	0.96	1.33	2.71	0.93
Philippines	1.87	0.54	19.78	0.68
Taiwan	0.11	0.02	0.29	0.07
Thailand	1.11	0.46	0.37	0.97

variation in annual changes in logarithm of energy use is explained, and $\bar{R}^2$ is negative in the case of the estimates for Indonesia. There is less evidence of misspecification than for Chemicals: Korea fails the diagnostic tests for residual serial correlation, and Philippines the functional form.

The MG and PMG estimates of the production elasticity are almost identical at 0.82 and 0.84, respectively, with the PMG standard error of 0.06 being a quarter that of the MG. There is a marked contrast between the PMG estimate of the price elasticity, -0.07 (0.06) and the MG estimate, -0.5 (0.25), though the Hausman test is just below the margin of significance. The DFE has a lower production elasticity and a positive price elasticity (see Table 9.7).

When the lag order was chosen by the Schwarz criterion, the static model was chosen in two and the ARDL(1, 0, 0) in three of the seven countries and

Table 9.7: Alternative pooled estimators of the long-run production and price elasticities of energy demand for iron and steel industries in Asian developing economies (based on ARDL(1, 0, 0) specifications and weighted Stone energy price indices).

	Mean group estimators	*Pooled mean group estimators*	*Dynamic fixed effects estimators*	*Static fixed effects estimators*
Production	0.820	0.836	0.504	0.540
elasticity ($\hat{\theta}_y$)	(0.244)	(0.057)	(0.147)	(0.057)
Price	-0.531	-0.073	0.013	-0.085
elasticity ($\hat{\theta}_p$)	(0.251)	(0.058)	(0.126)	(0.047)
Error correction	-0.593	-0.421	-0.266	-1
coefficient ($\hat{\phi}$)	(0.099)	(0.085)	(0.065)	(N/A)
Log-likelihood	54.59	35.96	-9.83	-56.69
(*LL*)				
$\sum_{i=1}^{7} T_i$	123	123	123	123
No. of est. parameters	35	23	11	10

Table 9.8: Alternative pooled estimators of the long-run production and price elasticities of energy demand for iron and steel industries in Asian developing economies (based on ARDL-SBC specifications and weighted Stone energy price indices).

	Mean group estimators	*Pooled mean group estimators*	*Dynamic fixed effects estimators*	*Static fixed effects estimators*
Production	0.886	1.216	(N/A)	0.540
elasticity ($\hat{\theta}_y$)	(0.166)	(0.047)		(0.057)
Price	-0.427	-0.089	(N/A)	-0.085
elasticity ($\hat{\theta}_p$)	(0.232)	(0.044)		(0.047)
Error correction	-0.660	-0.473	(N/A)	-1
coefficient ($\hat{\phi}$)	(0.131)	(0.188)		(N/A)
Log-likelihood	59.67	41.17	(N/A)	-56.69
(*LL*)				
$\sum_{i=1}^{7} T_i$	123	123	(N/A)	123
No. of est. parameters	34	22	(N/A)	10

the results were very similar to those for the ARDL(1, 0, 0) specification. The MG estimates were 0.89 (0.17) and −0.43 (0.23), while the PMG estimates were 1.22 (0.05) and −0.09 (0.04) (see Table 9.8). Thus the low PMG price elasticity remains. The PMG Schwarz likelihood was higher than its ARDL(1, 0, 0) likelihood in contrast to the results obtained for the chemicals. When the aggregate rather than the Stone price was used, the results were again similar. The MG estimates were 0.64 (0.37) and −0.33 (0.45); while the PMG estimates were 0.85 (0.06) and −0.05 (0.06) (see Tables 9.9 and 9.10).

In the case of Iron and Steel, the sensitivity analysis broadly confirms the estimates from the ARDL(1, 0, 0) model using a Stone price index. The production elasticity seems to be around 0.8, but there is a conflict between the MG and the PMG about the price elasticity, with the MG suggesting an estimate around −0.53 (0.25) and the PMG around −0.07 (0.06).

Table 9.9:   Alternative pooled estimators of the long-run production and price elasticities of energy demand for iron and steel industries in Asian developing economies (based on ARDL(1, 0, 0) specifications and average real energy price indices).

	Mean group estimators	Pooled mean group estimators	Dynamic fixed effects estimators	Static fixed effects estimators
Production	0.639	0.854	0.493	0.533
elasticity ($\hat{\theta}_y$)	(0.366)	(0.057)	(0.144)	(0.056)
Price	−0.325	−0.053	0.0498	−0.030
elasticity ($\hat{\theta}_p$)	(0.447)	(0.061)	(0.125)	(0.048)
Error correction	−0.615	−0.420	−0.265	−1
coefficient ($\hat{\phi}$)	(0.119)	(0.086)	(0.062)	(N/A)
Log-likelihood	51.66	37.34	−8.55	−58.52
(LL)				
$\sum_{i=1}^{7} T_i$	126	126	126	126
No. of est.	35	23	11	10
parameters				

Table 9.10:   Alternative pooled estimators of the long-run production and price elasticities of energy demand for iron and steel industries in Asian developing economies (based on ARDL-SBC specifications and average real energy price indices).

	Mean group estimators	Pooled mean group estimators	Dynamic fixed effects estimators	Static fixed effects estimators
Production	0.745	0.976	(N/A)	0.533
elasticity ($\hat{\theta}_y$)	(0.218)	(0.037)		(0.056)
Price	−0.330	−0.090	(N/A)	−0.030
elasticity ($\hat{\theta}_p$)	(0.441)	(0.044)		(0.048)
Error correction	−0.712	−0.666	(N/A)	−1
coefficient ($\hat{\phi}$)	(0.143)	(0.164)		(N/A)
Log-likelihood	59.37	42.67	(N/A)	−58.52
(LL)				
$\sum_{i=1}^{7} T_i$	126	126	(N/A)	126
No. of est.	34	22	(N/A)	10
parameters				

9.4   Non-metallic Minerals

This is likely to be a very heterogeneous industry, with quite different types of products being made in different countries. India's share in the total energy use for this industry in the region falls from 54 to 30 per cent, being almost exactly matched by Korea's rise from 2 to 24 per cent. Pakistan's share falls, Indonesia's rises, and Taiwan's fluctuates markedly, rising from 19 to 30 per cent in 1980 and then falling back to 13 per cent (see Figure 9.3).

As a share of industrial energy use within each country, the share of this industry falls in Bangladesh, India, Pakistan and Taiwan, rises in Korea and fluctuates markedly in the Philippines. A mix of fuels are used in this industry. In Bangladesh only coal use is recorded, in Indonesia and Pakistan no electricity use is recorded.

Malaysia and Sri Lanka were excluded because there were no energy consumption data for this industry. The sample is 19 observations for all countries except Taiwan where it is 15. The individual country estimates for the ARDL(1, 0, 0) model using the Stone price are given in Table 9.11. The dispersion in production elasticities is much larger than in the previous two industries. The estimates for Bangladesh and Taiwan are negative, though not significantly different from zero. Indonesia and Korea have production elasticities greater than two, and both are significantly greater than unity. Price elasticities are positive, though not significantly so in Bangladesh, Korea and the Philippines, and significantly negative in India. Less than half the variation in annual changes is explained in every country. There is evidence of residual serial correlation in Pakistan and the Philippines and misspecified functional form in India and Taiwan.

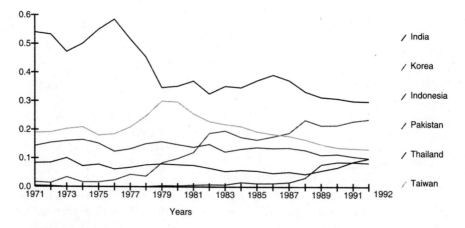

Figure 9.3:   Share of energy consumption of non-metallic minerals of major Asian economies.

Table 9.11a: Country-specific estimates of the long-run production and price elasticities for the non-metallic mineral industries based on ARDL(1, 0, 0) model using Stone price index.[1]

Country	Parameter estimates					
	$\hat{\varphi}$	$\hat{\theta}_y$	$\hat{\theta}_p$	$\hat{\sigma}$	$\bar{R}^2$	LL
Bangladesh	−0.575	−0.781	0.212	0.442	0.18	−9.20
	(0.239)	(0.925)	(0.635)			
India	−0.533	0.293	−0.722	0.114	0.32	16.52
	(0.175)	(0.167)	(0.256)			
Indonesia	−0.295	2.646	−0.072	0.545	0.08	−13.19
	(0.143)	(1.010)	(0.304)			
Korea	−0.371	2.117	0.524	0.268	0.30	0.28
	(0.156)	(0.309)	(0.289)			
Pakistan	−0.516	0.640	−0.014	0.056	0.21	30.18
	(0.197)	(0.080)	(0.008)			
Philippines	−0.557	1.174	0.106	0.426	0.13	−8.51
	(0.240)	(0.352)	(0.306)			
Taiwan	−0.169	−0.506	−1.952	0.056	0.43	24.34
	(0.215)	(2.519)	(3.110)			
Thailand	−0.240	1.343	−0.321	0.140	0.37	12.70
	(0.169)	(0.638)	(0.757)			

[1] See the notes to Table 9.1b.

Table 9.11b: Diagnostic statistics for the results in Table 9.11a.

Country	Diagnostic statistics			
	$\chi^2_{SC}(1)$	$\chi^2_{FF}(1)$	$\chi^2_N(2)$	$\chi^2_H(1)$
Bangladesh	0.47	2.63	2.48	0.06
India	0.54	4.51	0.70	0.61
Indonesia	0.51	3.26	0.32	0.34
Korea	0.17	1.42	0.84	0.33
Pakistan	4.31	2.41	0.60	0.90
Philippines	5.86	0.53	1.12	0.19
Taiwan	0.24	9.16	1.43	0.31
Thailand	0.46	0.02	0.27	0.42

The estimates from the MG and PMG are very different. The MG suggests a production elasticity of 0.9 (0.4) and a price elasticity of −0.3 (0.3); while the PMG estimates yield 0.25 (0.1) and −0.7 (0.2) for output and price elasticities respectively. Though large in economic terms, these differences are not quite significant by a Hausman test. The DFE procedure yields completely different estimates with a production elasticity of 1.63 (0.36) and a price elasticity of −0.04 (0.11) (see Tables 9.12).

When the lag order is chosen by the Schwarz criterion, the ARDL(1, 0, 0) is chosen in four of the eight countries and the ARDL(1, 0, 1) in three. The MG production elasticity hardly changes, 0.95 (0.38) and the price elasticity gets smaller −0.13 (0.14). The PMG production elasticity is now 0.65 (0.03)

Table 9.12: Alternative pooled estimators of the long-run production and price elasticities of energy demand for non-metallic mineral industries in Asian developing economies (based on ARDL(1, 0, 0) specifications and weighted Stone energy price indices) computed with mean group estimators as initial values.

	Mean group estimators	Pooled mean group estimators	Dynamic fixed effects estimators	Static fixed effects estimators
Production elasticity ($\hat{\theta}_y$)	0.866 (0.423)	0.250 (0.118)	1.629 (0.362)	1.442 (0.112)
Price elasticity ($\hat{\theta}_p$)	−0.280 (0.272)	−0.677 (0.168)	−0.038 (0.107)	−0.073 (0.034)
Error correction coefficient ($\hat{\phi}$)	−0.407 (0.056)	−0.213 (0.081)	−0.164 (0.043)	−1 (N/A)
Log-likelihood (LL)	53.12	32.69	-41.26	-138.68
$\sum_{i=1}^{8} T_i$	148	148	148	148
No. of est. parameters	40	26	12	11

Table 9.13: Alternative pooled estimators of the long-run production and price elasticities of energy demand for non-metallic mineral industries in Asian developing economies (based on ARDL-SBC specifications and weighted Stone energy price indices).

	Mean group estimators	Pooled mean group estimators	Dynamic fixed effects estimators	Static fixed effects estimators
Production elasticity ($\hat{\theta}_y$)	0.946 (0.380)	0.652 (0.028)	(N/A)	1.442 (0.112)
Price elasticity ($\hat{\theta}_p$)	−0.134 (0.142)	−0.014 (0.003)	(N/A)	−0.073 (0.034)
Error correction coefficient ($\hat{\phi}$)	−0.521 (0.079)	−0.4254 (0.112)	(N/A)	−1 (N/A)
Log-likelihood (LL)	63.22	42.67	(N/A)	−138.68
$\sum_{i=1}^{8} T_i$	148	148	(N/A)	148
No. of est. parameters	43	29	(N/A)	11

and the price elasticity has fallen to −0.14 (0.003) (see Table 9.13). When the average rather than the Stone price is used in the ARDL(1, 0, 0), both MG and PMG give an estimated production elasticity of almost exactly unity. Four of the eight individual price elasticities are positive and the MG estimate of the price elasticity is 0.113 (0.306). The PMG estimate gives less weight to these poorly determined positive elasticities and gives a price elasticity of −0.72 (see Tables 9.14 and 9.15).

Non-metallic products is a very heterogeneous industry and the estimates reflect this. However, looking across the results, it suggests a production elasticity rather less than unity and quite a high price elasticity.

Table 9.14: Alternative pooled estimators of the long-run production and price elasticities of energy demand for non-metallic mineral industries in Asian developing economies (based on ARDL(1, 0, 0) specifications and average real energy price indices).

	Mean group estimators	Pooled mean group estimators	Dynamic fixed effects estimators	Static fixed effects estimators
Production	1.005	1.052	1.321	1.217
elasticity ($\hat{\theta}_y$)	(0.418)	(0.121)	(0.229)	(0.088)
Price	0.113	−0.715	−0.496	−0.533
elasticity ($\hat{\theta}_p$)	(0.306)	(0.159)	(0.146)	(0.057)
Error correction	−0.460	−0.239	−0.249	−1
coefficient ($\hat{\phi}$)	(0.079)	(0.059)	(0.053)	(N/A)
Log-likelihood	57.55	36.19	−37.59	−104.48
(LL)				
$\sum_{i=1}^{8} T_i$	148	148	148	148
No. of est.	40	26	12	11
parameters				

Table 9.15: Alternative pooled estimators of the long-run production and price elasticities of energy demand for non-metallic mineral industries in Asian developing economies (based on ARDL-SBC specifications and average real energy price indices).

	Mean group estimators	Pooled mean group estimators	Dynamic fixed effects estimators	Static fixed effects estimators
Production	1.071	0.730	(N/A)	1.217
elasticity ($\hat{\theta}_y$)	(0.400)	(0.047)		(0.088)
Price	0.212	−0.023	(N/A)	−0.533
elasticity ($\hat{\theta}_p$)	(0.274)	(0.064)		(0.057)
Error correction	-0.577	-0.507	(N/A)	-1
coefficient ($\hat{\phi}$)	(0.100)	(0.117)		(N/A)
Log-likelihood	61.96	14.94	(N/A)	-104.48
(LL)				
$\sum_{i=1}^{8} T_i$	148	148	(N/A)	148
No. of est.	40	26	(N/A)	11
parameters				

9.5   Paper, Pulp and Printing

Data were available for this industry only for four countries: India, Korea, Taiwan and Thailand. In the other countries the energy consumption of this industry is probably included among industries not otherwise specified. India's share of total energy use for this industry in the region fell from 55 to 30 per cent, matched by Korea's rise from 2 to 35 per cent; though there are large fluctuations in between (see Figure 9.4). In all these countries energy consumption in the Paper industries is a relatively small proportion of total energy demand.

There are 19 observations used in the regressions for all countries except Taiwan, where there are only 15 observations available. The estimates for the

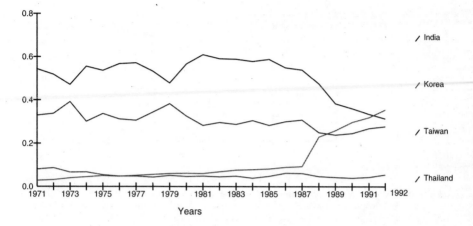

Figure 9.4: Share of energy consumption of paper industries of four Asian economies.

Table 9.16a: Country-specific estimates of the long-run production and price elasticities for the paper, pulp and printing industries based on ARDL(1, 0, 0) model and using weighted Stone prices.[1]

Country	Parameter estimates					
	$\hat{\varphi}$	$\hat{\theta}_y$	$\hat{\theta}_p$	$\hat{\sigma}$	$\bar{R}^2$	LL
India	−0.637	0.067	0.532	0.112	0.36	16.92
	(0.214)	(0.237)	(0.449)			
Korea	−0.444	1.887	−1.647	0.212	0.31	4.79
	(0.152)	(0.218)	(0.495)			
Taiwan	−0.463	0.478	−0.932	0.032	0.81	32.48
	(0.092)	(0.075)	(0.193)			
Thailand	−0.201	0.756	−0.050	0.165	−0.07	9.53
	(0.199)	(0.564)	(1.096)			

[1] See the notes to Table 9.1b.

ARDL(1, 0, 0) model using the Stone price index are given in Table 9.16. The average production elasticity is 0.8, but there is substantial heterogeneity, from 0.07 (0.2) in India to 1.9 (0.2) in Korea. The equation for Taiwan fits quite well, with over 80 per cent of the variation in annual changes in log energy consumption being explained and a standard error of 3 per cent. The $\bar{R}^2$ is negative in Thailand. The Korean equation fails the tests for functional form, normality and heteroskedasticity.

Equality of long-run coefficients cannot be rejected (just!) at the 1 per cent level using the Likelihood Ratio test, however the joint Hausman test would reject equality of the MG and PMG production and price elasticities, at this level. This is a reversal of the usual pattern. The individual Hausman tests do not reject equality of each coefficient, suggesting a high degree of covariation between the two estimates. The pattern of differences across the

Table 9.16b: Diagnostic statistics for the results in Table 9.16a.

Country	Diagnostic statistics			
	$\chi^2_{SC}(1)$	$\chi^2_{FF}(1)$	$\chi^2_N(2)$	$\chi^2_H(1)$
India	0.24	0.65	0.06	0.00
Korea	0.09	11.00	12.28	16.81
Taiwan	1.72	0.76	0.72	1.29
Thailand	1.94	0.08	0.72	0.03

Table 9.17: Alternative pooled estimators of the long-run production and price elasticities of energy demand for paper, pulp and printing industries in Asian developing economies (based on ARDL(1, 0, 0) specifications and weighted Stone energy price indices).

	Mean group estimators	Pooled mean group estimators	Dynamic fixed effects estimators	Static fixed effects estimators
Production	0.797	0.489	1.594	1.054
elasticity ($\hat{\theta}_y$)	(0.390)	(0.061)	(0.517)	(0.098)
Price	−0.524	−0.888	−2.253	−0.532
elasticity ($\hat{\theta}_p$)	(0.480)	(0.151)	(1.336)	(0.211)
Error correction	−0.436	−0.232	−0.114	−1
coefficient ($\hat{\phi}$)	(0.090)	(0.100)	(0.059)	(N/A)
Log-likelihood	63.72	56.07	31.03	−22.79
(LL)				
$\sum_{i=1}^{4} T_i$	72	72	72	72
No. of est.	20	14	8	7
parameters				

different estimators is similar to non-metallic products: The PMG procedure gives a lower production elasticity, 0.49 (0.06) compared to the MG estimates, 0.80 (0.39), and a larger price elasticity, −0.89 (0.15), compared to the MG estimates of −0.52 (0.48). As with non-metallic products, the DFE estimates are completely different again; with a production elasticity of 1.6 (0.5) and a price elasticity of −2.2 (1.3) (see Table 9.17).

When the lag order is chosen by the Schwarz criterion, a different order is chosen in each country: ARDL(0, 0, 1) for India, ARDL(1, 0, 0) for Korea, ARDL(1, 0, 1) for Taiwan and ARDL(1, 1, 0) for Thailand. The MG estimate of the production elasticity is almost identical at 0.8, but the price elasticity is somewhat lower, −0.36 (0.53). The PMG estimates show a somewhat higher production elasticity than the ARDL(1, 0, 0) 0.56 (0.03), and a significantly lower price elasticity −0.58 (0.16). The log-likelihood for the PMG using the Schwarz order is lower than for the PMG using ARDL(1, 0, 0) (see Table 9.18).

When the aggregate energy price is used, the MG production elasticity is 0.64 (0.22) and the price elasticity −0.86 (0.19), while the PMG estimates are

Table 9.18:   Alternative pooled estimators of the long-run production and price elasticities of energy demand for paper, pulp and printing industries in Asian developing economies (based on ARDL-SBC specifications and weighted Stone energy price indices).

	Mean group estimators	Pooled mean group estimators	Dynamic fixed effects estimators	Static fixed effects estimators
Production	0.795	0.563	(N/A)	1.054
elasticity ($\hat{\theta}_y$)	(0.404)	(0.033)		(0.098)
Price	−0.364	−0.585	(N/A)	−0.532
elasticity ($\hat{\theta}_p$)	(0.528)	(0.072)		(0.211)
Error correction	−0.641	−0.534	(N/A)	−1
coefficient ($\hat{\phi}$)	(0.134)	(0.226)		(N/A)
Log-likelihood	72.38	52.74	(N/A)	−22.79
(*LL*)				
$\sum_{i=1}^{4} T_i$	72	72	(N/A)	72
No. of est.	22	16	(N/A)	7
parameters				

Table 9.19:   Alternative pooled estimators of the long-run production and price elasticities of energy demand for paper, pulp and printing industries in Asian developing economies (based on ARDL(1, 0, 0) specifications and average real energy price indices).

	Mean group estimators	Pooled mean group estimators	Dynamic fixed effects estimators	Static fixed effects estimators
Production	0.640	1.210	1.072	0.952
elasticity ($\hat{\theta}_y$)	(0.217)	(0.067)	(0.189)	(0.078)
Price	−0.861	−1.179	−1.258	−0.676
elasticity ($\hat{\theta}_p$)	(0.191)	(0.100)	(0.310)	(0.099)
Error correction	−0.569	−0.326	−0.228	−1
coefficient ($\hat{\phi}$)	(0.097)	(0.159)	(0.061)	(N/A)
Log-likelihood	76.57	60.99	37.94	−6.96
(*LL*)				
$\sum_{i=1}^{4} T_i$	72	72	72	72
No. of est.	20	14	8	7
parameters				

1.21 (0.07) and −1.18 (0.1) (see Tables 9.19 and 9.20). The Hausman test rejects equality of the MG and PMG as with the Stone price index. Response to the aggregate price seems stronger than the industry specific price and the log-likelihood for the aggregate price is rather higher than for the industry price, 77 rather than 64 for the ARDL(1, 0, 0) specification. In this case it seems that the estimates using the aggregate price index are probably better. Looking at the individual country estimates, the fit of the equation using the aggregate price index is better in each case and the Indian price elasticity becomes negative. The price elasticities in India and Taiwan are significantly negative.

Table 9.20: Alternative pooled estimators of the long-run production and price elasticities of energy demand for paper, pulp and printing industries in Asian developing economies (based on ARDL-SBC specifications and average real energy price indices).

	Mean group estimators	Pooled mean group estimators	Dynamic fixed effects estimators	Static fixed effects estimators
Production	0.771	1.134	(N/A)	0.952
elasticity ($\hat{\theta}_y$)	(0.140)	(0.052)		(0.078)
Price	−0.574	−1.094	(N/A)	−0.676
elasticity ($\hat{\theta}_p$)	(0.210)	(0.070)		(0.099)
Error correction	−0.723	−0.599	(N/A)	−1
coefficient ($\hat{\phi}$)	(0.163)	(0.234)		(N/A)
Log-likelihood	86.93	47.69	(N/A)	−6.96
(LL)				
$\sum_{i=1}^{4} T_i$	72	72	(N/A)	72
No. of est.	22	16	(N/A)	7
parameters				

9.6   Conclusion

The broad conclusions drawn from our analysis at the level of individual industries reinforce those drawn in earlier chapters. There is more "noise" in the disaggregated data, and the reliability of the estimates differs considerably across countries and industries. Price elasticities seem to be greater on more disaggregated data, output elasticities are close to unity, but rather lower than the elasticities with respect to aggregate GDP found in earlier chapters. There is some evidence that the functional form is misspecified. For chemicals and iron and steel there is little difference between the MG and PMG. For the other two industries there is less agreement amongst the different estimates. There is still substantial heterogeneity across countries and the results are sensitive to dynamic specification. Using the Schwarz criterion to choose lag order tended to give lower estimates of the price elasticity. This seemed to happen partly because static models were chosen in a number of countries, making short-run and long-run price elasticities the same, and partly because lagged prices sometimes had a coefficient which was positive though smaller in absolute value than current prices.

CHAPTER 10

Forecasting Energy Demand

10.1 Introduction

One of the important uses of the estimated income and price elasticities of energy demand is in forecasting future energy demand. The motivation for the forecasts may be to assess the effect of Asian demand on the world energy market or on the world environment through Carbon Dioxide emissions, or to plan the required supply infrastructure needed in the individual countries. In this chapter we evaluate the forecasts for the period 1991–1994 and provide alternative energy forecasts for the period 1995–2015. In order to obtain the forecasts, we have to choose an appropriate level of aggregation from the variety that we have considered, choose a particular specification and project the exogenous variables. We consider each of these before presenting the forecasts.

In the preceding chapters we have analysed aggregate energy consumption; energy consumption by four industrial sectors; energy consumption by three types of fuel and energy consumption by four individual industries. In each case, we have provided estimates for the individual countries and for the average, using three estimators: Mean Group (MG) which is a simple average of the long-run coefficients across groups; Pooled Mean Group (PMG) which imposes equality of long-run slope coefficients across countries; and Dynamic Fixed Effects (DFE) which imposes equality of all slopes coefficients and error variances. In many cases, we have also experimented with alternative specifications of dynamics or variables included. This has generated a large number of estimates, which differ by country, estimation method, specification of functional forms and dynamics, and the level of disaggregation. While we have been able to draw some broad conclusions, these estimates have been very heterogeneous. We thus have to choose an appropriate level of aggregation for our forecasts and an appropriate degree of coefficient homogeneity. While it is quite possible in principle that large and significant differences in estimated elasticities between countries or between estimators do not matter in practice, because the differences cancel out in use, in practice this is unlikely.

In evaluating the heterogeneity it is important to be clear about the two tests that we have been using. The hypothesis that the parameters are the same in all countries, is almost invariably rejected by Likelihood Ratio Tests.

This suggests that if we wish to analyse a particular country, we should use the estimates for that particular country; though in some particular "outlier" cases these may have large variances. The hypothesis that the mean, over countries, of the long-run coefficients is the same as the pooled estimates obtained by assuming that the long-run coefficients are the same, is rarely rejected by the Hausman test. This suggests that if we are interested in forecasting the average or aggregate response over the region, the Pooled Mean Group estimates may be appropriate. The PMG estimates have the advantage that they take into account the differing precisions across countries, though the reported standard errors may underestimate the true degree of uncertainty, since the coefficients clearly do differ across countries. The pooled estimates also tend to suggest much slower adjustment than the country specific estimates.

We discussed the various ways of interpreting such significant heterogeneity in Section 5.4. Making a judgement in this case is difficult because of our sample size. Both N, the number of countries, 10, and T the number of years, 17, are small. If T were larger, we might have more faith in the individual country estimates, if N were larger then we might have more faith in the average estimates.[1] Disaggregation does not necessarily help in this respect, since in this particular case as we disaggregate, the signal-to-noise ratio falls, and the assumption of underlying homogeneity of coefficients becomes less plausible. In general, there are two ways we could forecast. We could forecast the disaggregate components using the aggregate estimates and aggregate the forecasts, or we could forecast the aggregate using the disaggregate estimates. Where reliable estimates of the disaggregate equations are available aggregating disaggregate forecasts is likely to be better. Here, where the disaggregate forecasts are sometimes based on rather unreliable estimates, using the aggregate equation seems more sensible.

Clearly, the choice of model will depend on the desired level of disaggregation of the forecasts. If we wish to obtain a forecast for the region as a whole, then using a common parameter model is more likely to be appropriate, if we wish to obtain a forecast for an individual country, industry or sector, the estimates particular to that industry or sector are appropriate. Below, after evaluating the models on the *ex ante* data for 1991–1994, we provide formal annual forecasts of aggregate energy demand on both bases, using country-specific estimates and the PMG long-run parameter estimates assumed to be common across countries.

10.2   Forecast Evaluation

Subsequent to estimation, data on real per-capita GDP and total energy consumption over the period 1991–1994 became available. This was used to

---

[1] Although with a large N we would have also needed a large T, for the asymptotics to work. See Hsiao, Pesaran and Tahmiscioglu (1997).

conduct forecasting tests. Data on GDP for Taiwan were not available and the average growth rate 1986–1990 was assumed to hold for 1990–1994, data for per-capita output growth in Sri Lanka were only available for 1990–1991 and this growth rate was assumed to hold for the whole period 1990–1994. No data on prices were available and it was assumed that energy prices remained at their 1990 level. The forecast errors will therefore be exaggerated, by lack of GDP data for Taiwan and Sri Lanka and by the effect of movements in energy prices. Four sets of forecasts for 1991–1994 were constructed for the logarithm of per-capita energy consumption:

(a) ARDL(1, 0, 0) country-specific estimates using forecast values of the lagged dependent variables for 1991–1993 (dynamic forecasts);
(b) ARDL(1, 0, 0) country-specific estimates using actual values of the lagged dependent variables for 1991–1993 (static forecasts);
(c) ARDL(1, 0, 0) Pooled Mean Group estimates using forecast values of the lagged dependent variable for 1991–1993 (dynamic forecasts);
(d) ARDL(1, 0, 0) Pooled Mean Group estimates using actual values of the lagged dependent variable for 1991–1993 (static forecasts).

With the dynamic forecasts, errors can accumulate; with the static forecasts, using the actual value of the lagged dependent variable should keep the forecast more on track. The ARDL(1, 0, 0) model explains the logarithm of per-capita energy consumption in terms of its lagged values and the current values of the logarithms of the ratio of the energy price to the CPI and of per-capita GDP. We base our forecasts on the ARDL(1, 0, 0) model in this and following sections because it was not rejected in most countries and tended to give sensible estimates. The Pooled Mean Group (PMG) estimator assumes that long-run income and price elasticities are identical across countries.

For the country-specific estimates predictive failure test statistics (the so-called Chow's second structural stability test) were also calculated.[2] Table 10.1 shows the p value for the predictive failure test and the Root Mean Square Errors of the four forecasts for the period 1991–1994; all are multiplied by 100 so they can be interpreted as percentages.[3] Only one of the ten countries, the Philippines, fails the predictive failure test at the 5 per cent level. In the Philippines real income fell substantially in the early 1990s but energy demand rose. A contributory factor was the fact that electricity consumption had been supply constrained in the late 1980s and this constraint was removed with the installation of new generating capacity after 1990. Consumption thus grew rapidly to return to equilibrium demand, despite falling income. Bangladesh and Malaya would fail at the 10 per cent level, though they pass at the 5 per cent level. In all but three cases (Malaysia for the country-specific estimates and

[2]For further details see, for example, Pesaran and Pesaran (1997, Section 18.5.2).
[3]The "p value" stands for the probability of falsely rejecting a correct null hypothesis.

Table 10.1:   Predictive failure tests and root mean squared forecast errors for the logarithm of per-capita energy consumption for the period 1991–1994.

Country	Predictive failure tests (p values)	Root mean squared forecast errors			
		Country specific		Pooled mean group	
		Dynamic	Static	Dynamic	Static
Bangladesh	5.4	12.02	8.80	7.49	6.09
India	55.0	3.27	2.95	2.35	2.01
Indonesia	15.4	7.91	5.43	14.11	7.61
Korea	95.0	3.77	2.28	1.05	0.99
Malaysia	8.2	4.54	7.02	13.94	8.85
Pakistan	60.9	4.69	3.72	2.27	3.96
Philippines	1.5	20.93	13.72	20.28	13.52
Sri Lanka	23.1	13.3	12.02	5.50	6.04
Taiwan	88.3	8.26	5.12	13.96	6.41
Thailand	20.6	4.23	3.64	3.78	3.28

Notes: Total energy consumption data in thousand TOE (Source: IEA). GDP per-capita were updated using GDP per-capita in real domestic units (Source: IFS). Data were available for all countries from 1990 to 1994 except for Sri Lanka and Taiwan. For Sri Lanka real GDP data were available only for 1990 and 1991, so the average rate of growth for this period was used to obtain the missing data for 1992–1994. For Taiwan no data were available at all, so the 1991–1994 data were obtained by simple extrapolations of the previous five years average growth rates. No data on energy prices were available and it was assumed that real energy prices remained at their 1990 level. Population data were available for all countries for 1990–1994 (Source: IFS), except Taiwan. For Taiwan population figures for the period 1990–1994 were extrapolated assuming the average population growth realized during 1986–1990 also holds over the 1990–1994 period.

Pakistan and Sri Lanka for the PMG) the static RMSE is smaller than the dynamic RMSE, as to be expected. The PMG estimates gave smaller RMSEs in six countries comparing static forecasts and seven countries comparing dynamic forecasts.

Figures 10.1–10.10, show the actual values of the logarithm of per-capita energy consumption and the values predicted by the country-specific and PMG equations for 1990–1994. The difference between actual and prediction in 1990 is the final estimated residual and is included to show how far the model was off track at the end of the estimation period. In most forecasting applications it is common to bring the model on track by making an intercept adjustment equal to the estimated residual in the final period from which forecasting starts. This makes actual and predicted the same in the final period. We have not done that. The predictions for 1991 use the actual value of the lagged dependent variable in 1990, the predictions for 1992–1994 are dynamic forecasts using the predicted values of the lagged dependent variable. In Bangladesh the PMG estimates have a larger initial error and the predictions miss the downturn in 1991–1992. India starts off right, misses the growth in 1991–1992, but the forecasts are on track at the end. In Indonesia, the growth in 1991 is missed, the country-specific estimates track quite well, the PMG estimates underpredict. In Korea all the estimates track very well. In Malaysia the country-specific estimates

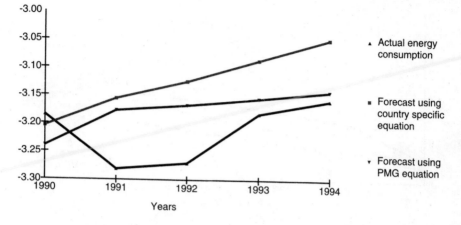

Figure 10.1: Actual per-capita energy consumption and the forecasts in Bangladesh.

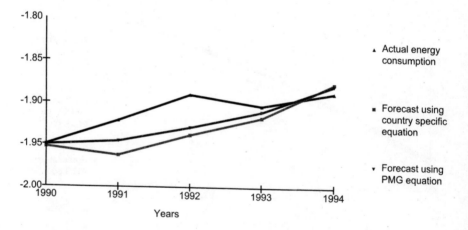

Figure 10.2: Actual per-capita energy consumption and the forecasts in India.

track quite well, but the PMG underestimates. In Pakistan, both sets of forecasts underestimate the end of the period actual values. In the Philippines the predictions go in the wrong direction, worsening the initial error. In Sri Lanka the PMG misses the downturn in 1991, otherwise it tracks the actual values reasonably well. In Thailand the country-specific and PMG predictions are very similar and slightly underestimate the level at the end. In Taiwan the PMG overestimates both growth and level of energy consumption, but this may have been due to the fact that GDP figures used in generating these forecasts for Taiwan were extrapolated.

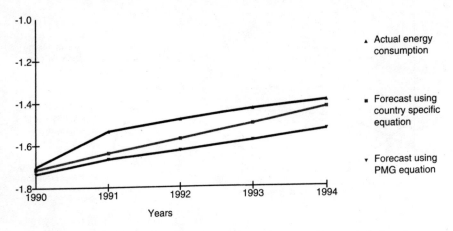

Figure 10.3:   Actual per-capita energy consumption and the forecasts in Indonesia.

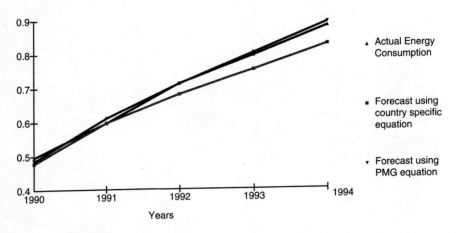

Figure 10.4:   Actual per-capita energy consumption and the forecasts in Korea.

For many purposes one would be interested in forecasting the level of total energy demand rather than the logarithm of per-capita energy demand so the forecasts for the levels were also evaluated. To provide forecasts of the levels, it is necessary to allow for the fact that the expected value of the level is not the exponential of the prediction of the logarithm. The equation that has been estimated has the form:

$$e_{it} = a_{0i} + \lambda_i e_{i,t-1} + \beta_i' x_{it} + \varepsilon_{it}, \quad t = 1, 2, \ldots, T,$$

where e_{it} is the logarithm of per-capita energy demand in country i, x_{it} is the vector containing price and income and $\lambda_i = (1 - \varphi_i)$.

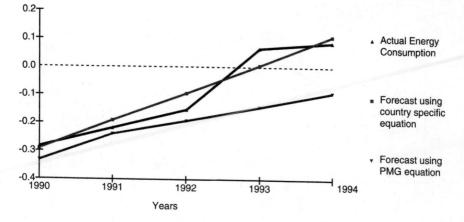

Figure 10.5: Actual per-capita energy consumption and the forecasts in Malaysia.

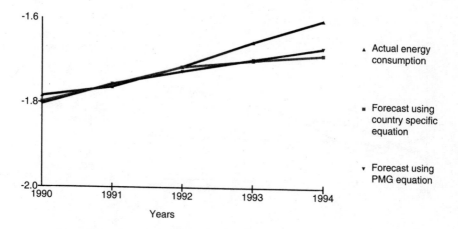

Figure 10.6: Actual per-capita energy consumption and the forecasts in Pakistan.

Starting from the end of the estimation period, the next period value of the logarithm of per-capita energy demand is:

$$e_{i,T+1} = (a_{0i} + \beta_i' \mathbf{x}_{i,T+1} + \varepsilon_{i,T+1}) + \lambda_i(a_{0i} + \lambda_i e_{i,T-1} + \beta_i' \mathbf{x}_{iT} + \varepsilon_T),$$

$$e_{i,T+1} = e^*_{i,T+1} + \varepsilon_{i,T+1} + \lambda_i \varepsilon_{iT},$$

where

$$e^*_{i,T+1} = a_{0i}(1 + \lambda_i) + \beta_i(\mathbf{x}_{i,T+1} + \lambda_i \mathbf{x}_{iT}) + \lambda_i^2 e_{i,T-1}.$$

Therefore the level of per-capita energy consumption is:

$$E_{i,T+1} = \exp(e^*_{i,T+1} + \varepsilon_{i,T+1} + \lambda_i \varepsilon_{i,T}),$$

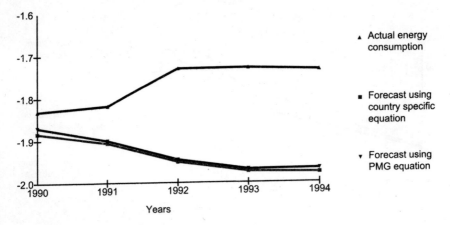

Figure 10.7: Actual per-capita energy consumption and the forecasts in Philippines.

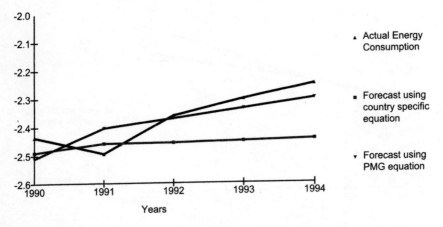

Figure 10.8: Actual per-capita energy consumption and the forecasts in Sri Lanka.

with expected value, given the information available at time T of

$$E(E_{i,T+1}|\Omega_T) = \exp(e^*_{i,T+1} + 0.5\sigma_i^2(1 + \lambda_i^2)),$$

where $\sigma_i^2 = \text{var}(\varepsilon_{it})$.[4] Correspondingly the expectations H steps ahead is

$$E(E_{i,T+H}|\Omega_T) = \exp\left(e^*_{i,T+H} + 0.5\sigma_i^2 \frac{(1 - \lambda_i^{2H})}{(1 - \lambda_i^2)}\right).$$

This formula was used to forecast the level of per-capita energy demand 1991–1994, for the same values of GDP as used in forecasting logarithms of per-capita energy consumption in Table 10.1 for each country and assuming no

---

[4]This result is obtained assuming ε_{it}'s are normally distributed.

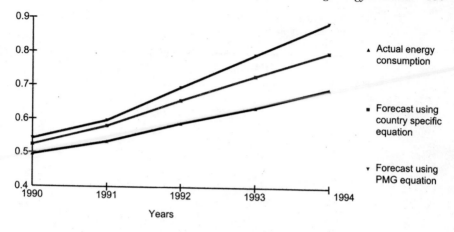

Figure 10.9:   Actual per-capita energy consumption and the forecasts in Taiwan.

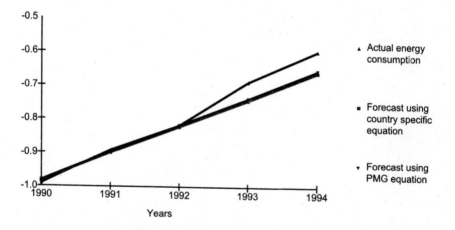

Figure 10.10:   Actual per-capita energy consumption and the forecasts in Thailand.

change in real energy prices after 1990. The parameters are chosen by either their country-specific or PMG estimates. This forecast is then multiplied by projected population to get a forecast of total energy consumption in thousand TOE. Notice that this formula does not allow for the uncertainty in the forecasts of the x_{it}. Table 10.2 gives the actual values and the two predictions for total energy consumption.

Table 10.3 gives the Root Mean Percentage Errors for the dynamic forecasts shown in Table 10.2. They are very similar, though a little smaller than the RMSEs for the corresponding dynamic forecasts of the logarithm of per-capita energy demand. The PMG estimates have smaller forecast errors in six countries. Total energy consumption over the ten countries in 1994 was 434,168

Table 10.2: Actual and *ex ante* forecasts of total energy consumption in thousand TOE over the period 1991–1994.

Country	Actual values[1]	Forecasts of total energy consumption	
		Country specific[2]	PMG[3]
Bangladesh			
1991	4129	4684	4591
1992	4282	4954	4732
1993	4780	5260	4872
1994	5008	5586	5026
India			
1991	124670	119702	121738
1992	131010	124958	126055
1993	131740	129940	130801
1994	139050	140633	140204
Indonesia			
1991	39109	35276	34281
1992	41974	38323	36272
1993	44779	41715	38531
1994	47249	45764	41199
Korea			
1991	78564	78660	79747
1992	88944	86159	88877
1993	97505	93422	98114
1994	107150	101484	108197
Malaysia			
1991	14619	15038	14321
1992	15977	16903	15323
1993	20361	19080	16447
1994	21452	21762	17816
Pakistan			
1991	19864	19972	20018
1992	21482	21473	21161
1993	23465	22460	22315
1994	25451	23429	23508
Philippines			
1991	10342	9479	9539
1992	11585	9292	9347
1993	11881	9305	9357
1994	12110	9504	9595
Sri Lanka			
1991	1423	1478	1562
1992	1641	1493	1626
1993	1762	1521	1701
1994	1882	1552	1783

Table 10.2 (*continued*)

Country	Actual values[1]	Forecasts of total energy consumption	
		Country specific[2]	PMG[3]
Taiwan			
1991	35075	36816	37420
1992	37496	40179	41643
1993	39740	43663	46261
1994	42526	47340	51317
Thailand			
1991	23169	22991	23060
1992	25271	25168	25285
1993	29117	27560	27717
1994	32290	30302	30499

[1] Actual values refer to total energy consumption in thousand TOE (Source: IEA).

[2] These are the forecasts based on the country-specific equations estimated over 1973–1990.

[3] These are the forecasts based on the Pooled Mean Group (PMG) equations. Both the country-specific and PMG forecasts are based on updated observations on the GDP per capita and price data to 1994. The data used are
(1) population (Source: IFS (1990–1995), UN (2000–2010)). Data were available for all countries for 1990–1994, except Taiwan. For Taiwan post 1990 the average rate of growth of the previous five years was assumed to continue;
(2) GDP per capita was updated using GDP per capita in real domestic units (Source: IFS). Data were available for all countries over the period 1990–1994 except for Sri Lanka and Taiwan. For Sri Lanka data were available for 1990 and 1991, so this rate of growth was used to get the 1992–1994 data. For Taiwan no data were available at all, so the 1991–1994 data were obtained by assuming that the previous five years average growth rate continued and
(3) real energy prices were assumed to stay at their 1990 value.

thousand TOE, the country-specific estimates predicted 427,356 and the PMG 429,144; thus although there are some large errors for individual countries in aggregate they cancel out to a large extent and the error in the PMG, an underestimate of only 1 per cent, suggests that the forecast for the aggregate is unbiased.

What can one conclude from the forecast evaluation over the period 1991–1994? Firstly, the prediction errors are significant in only one country, the Philippines. This indicates that in the other countries the forecast errors are

Table 10.3:   Forecast evaluation of total energy consumption over 1991–1994.

Country	Root mean square country specific	Average percentage errors PMG
Bangladesh	12.86	7.74
India	3.18	2.29
Indonesia	7.56	13.19
Korea	3.72	0.95
Malaysia	4.57	13.02
Pakistan	4.52	4.61
Philippines	18.67	18.14
Sri Lanka	12.16	5.81
Taiwan	8.68	14.69
Thailand	4.10	3.68

Notes: Based on actual and *ex ante* forecasts of energy consumption (1000 TOE) – 1991–1994 (Table 10.2).

no larger than we would expect from the in sample fit. This is not necessarily reassuring because the in sample fit was not very high in some countries. Secondly, the PMG estimator does rather well. Its dynamic RMSE of forecasts for the logarithm of per-capita energy demand is smaller than the country-specific estimates in seven out of ten countries. Imposing homogeneous long-run coefficients improves forecast performance in most cases. Thirdly, in absolute terms the PMG dynamic forecast errors for some countries are rather large, over 10 per cent for Indonesia, Malaysia, Philippines and Taiwan (where the problem may be lack of income data). Fourthly, there is no obvious pattern of bias, so the forecasts for the region as a whole are not only more accurate than those for the individual countries, but very close to the actual in 1994. Fifthly, there is not much difference between the forecast performance of the logarithm of per-capita demand and the level of total demand. Bearing these conclusions in mind, we shall go on to use the models for forecasting.

10.3   Energy Forecasts to 2015

For the long-term forecasts, it was assumed that real energy prices were constant and the rates of growth of per-capita GDP and population were as given in Table 10.4.[5]

---

[5]There are various views on the energy price prospects, many of them conflicting. The World Bank's view is that of international oil prices declining slowly in real terms. (See recent issues of "Commodity Markets and the Developing Countries", Commodity Policy and Analysis Unit, World Bank.) This view is based on the expectation that improvements, and hence cost reductions, will be made with respect to oil production technologies. An opposite view is for the real price of oil to increase. This view is advanced in Campbell (1998) based on the argument that the bunched discoveries of 'giant' oil fields of the 1960s pass their peak output and are substituted by much higher cost supplies. We have taken a middle-ground position by assuming that on average real energy prices over the next two decades will remain at their current levels. The GDP growth forecasts are also based on World Bank projections and the *Asia Pacific Consensus Forecasts*.

Table 10.4: Rates of growth of per-capita GDP and population assumed over the period 1990–2015.

Country	Per-capita GDP growth[1]			Population growth[2]		
	1990–94	*1994–2005*	*2005–2015*	*1990–94*	*1994–2005*	*2005–2015*
Bangladesh	1.86	3.64	4.05	2.14	1.62	1.65
India	2.04	4.93	5.08	2.39	1.69	1.27
Indonesia	5.16	6.28	6.91	1.51	1.59	1.09
Korea	5.97	5.78	5.30	0.90	0.82	0.60
Malaysia	5.58	5.64	5.72	2.53	2.03	1.53
Pakistan	1.67	2.37	3.30	2.95	3.08	2.45
Philippines	−1.19	4.00	4.41	2.75	1.70	1.59
Sri Lanka	3.13	3.86	4.52	1.25	1.00	0.28
Taiwan	7.55	5.36	4.89	1.10	1.10	1.10
Thailand	6.73	6.14	6.03	1.25	0.64	0.62

[1] GDP per capita was updated using GDP per capita in real domestic units (Source: IFS). Data were available for all countries from 1990 to 1995 except for Sri Lanka and Taiwan. For Sri Lanka data were available only for 1990 and 1991. The figures for 1992–1995 were obtained by assuming that the previous five years average growth rate is also valid for the 1992–1995 period.

From 1995 onwards forecasts of GDP growth were used (Source: Consensus Economics, Consensus Forecasts, April 14, 1997). For all countries except Korea, Sri Lanka and Taiwan forecasts were available for 1996–2000 and 2005. The 2000–2015 growth rate was assumed to be the average of the 2000 and 2005 values. For Korea, Sri Lanka and Taiwan forecasts were available for the two periods 1996–2002 and 2003–2007.

The growth post 2007 was assumed to be the same as the ones projected for the 2003–2007 period. These were converted to a per-capita basis using UN forecasts of population.

[2] Population data (Source: IFS (1990–1995), UN (2000–2010)) were available for all countries for 1990–1995, and for the years 2000, 2005 and 2010, except for Taiwan. The missing values were estimated by assuming an exponential trend throughout the period. The average growth rate over the period 2010–2015 was assumed to be the same as those projected for the period 2005–2010. In the absence of output projections for Taiwan, the average growth realized over the period 1985–1990 was assumed to hold for the whole period 1991–2015.

Again, we base our forecasts on the ARDL(1, 0, 0) model where the logarithm of per-capita energy consumption is explained in terms of its lagged values and the current values of the logarithm of the ratio of the energy price, P_{it} to the Consumer Price Index, CPI_{it}, and the logarithm of per-capita GDP, y_{it}. The ARDL(1, 0, 0) seems appropriate since it was not rejected in most countries and tended to give sensible estimates.

The forecasts are graphed in Figures 10.11–10.20 for each of the ten countries in our sample. There are a number of features of these forecasts. Firstly, the short-run dynamics die out quite fast and there is a clear tendency for the forecasts to return to the underlying trends in per-capita output quite quickly. The forecasts based on the individual country estimates, broadly follow historical trends in energy growth. However, in some countries the forecasts based on the Pooled Mean Group estimates show a marked break in trend growth, because the country-specific income elasticity is very different from the average; Bangladesh and Malaysia are obvious cases. India and Thailand are representative countries in that their estimated elasticities are very close to the average so

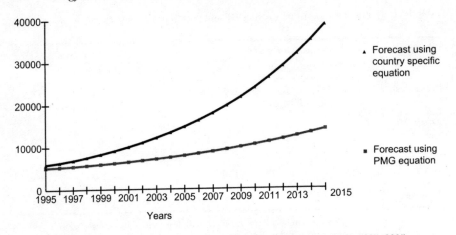

Figure 10.11:   Forecasts of total energy consumption in Bangladesh, 1995–2015.

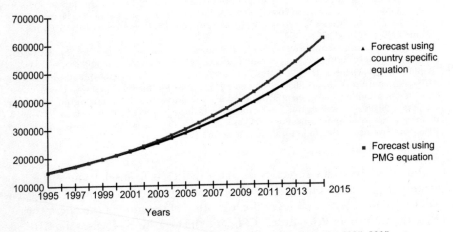

Figure 10.12:   Forecasts of total energy consumption in India, 1995–2015.

there is little difference between the country specific and pooled mean group forecast.

Table 10.5 gives the total energy demand in 1994 and the forecasts from the country-specific equations and the pooled mean group equations for the years 2005 and 2015, for each country and the average per-capita energy consumption in the region as a whole. Energy demand by these ten countries grew by 30 per cent between 1990 and 1994. Considering the average first, there is little difference between the forecasts based on the pooled or unpooled individual country regressions. Both suggest that average per-capita energy consumption

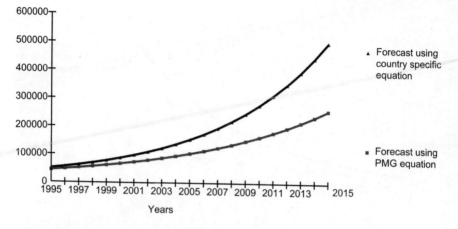

Figure 10.13: Forecasts of total energy consumption in Indonesia, 1995–2015.

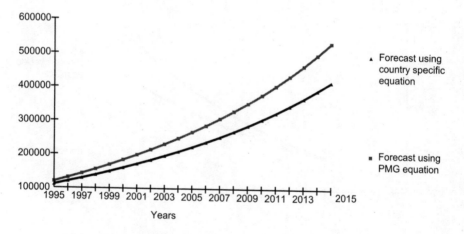

Figure 10.14: Forecasts of total energy consumption in Korea, 1995–2015.

in this region will more than double between 1994 and 2005 and then double again to 2015. The differences between the two forecasts for individual countries are much more marked, confirming the impression obtained from the figures.

It is clear that the heterogeneity issue reappears in the individual forecasts. For some countries, the individual forecasts and the PMG forecasts are similar: India, Pakistan, Philippines and Thailand. For other countries we may not have very much faith either in the estimates based on the average or on those based on the individual country estimates, Sri Lanka would be a case in point. In these

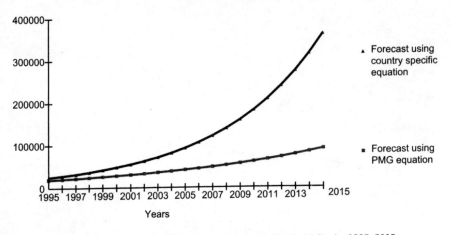

Figure 10.15:   Forecasts of total energy consumption in Malaysia, 1995–2015.

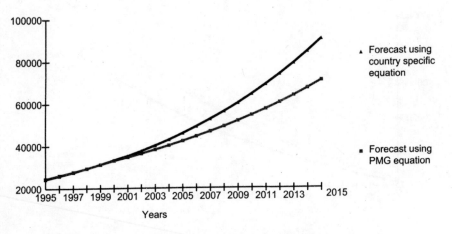

Figure 10.16:   Forecasts of total energy consumption in Pakistan, 1995–2015.

circumstances, a weighted average of the two might be sensible, the weights based on the significance of the difference from the mean. In Bangladesh, where all the estimates have suggested very high GDP elasticities and one would expect energy intensity to grow from its very low levels, more weight would be given to the country-specific estimates. Similarly for Taiwan and Korea, which have relatively high energy intensities, lower than average GDP elasticities and are likely to be able to adopt energy saving technologies, more weight would be put on the individual country estimates. For Malaysia where the country-specific forecast seems out of line, the PMG forecast would get most weight.

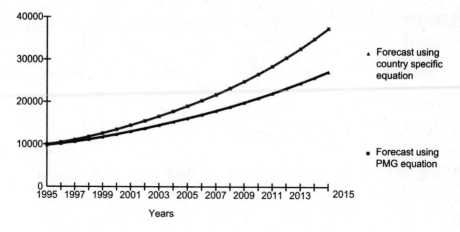

Figure 10.17:   Forecasts of total energy consumption in Philippines, 1995–2015.

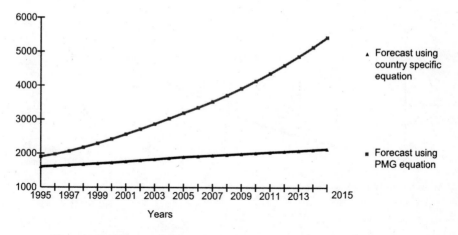

Figure 10.18:   Forecasts of total energy consumption in Sri Lanka, 1995–2015.

For the others, putting equal weights on PMG and individual forecasts would be sensible.

Table 10.6 gives the actual average annual growth rates in total energy demand over the 1990–1994 period, and the forecast of average annual growth rates over the decades 1994–2005 and 2005–2015, using country-specific and pooled mean group estimates. Unlike the forecast of the level of per-capita energy consumption, the choice of estimator does make a difference to the forecast of the growth rates. The country-specific estimates give higher growth rates. This is largely because of the high growth rates forecast for Bangladesh

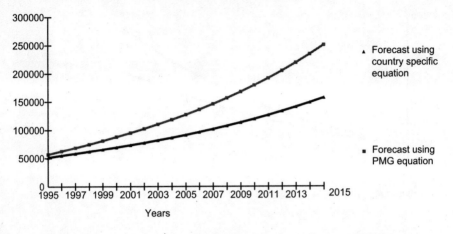

Figure 10.19:   Forecasts of total energy consumption in Taiwan, 1995–2015.

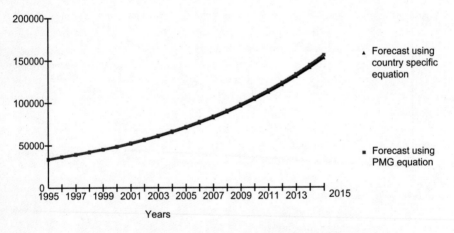

Figure 10.20:   Forecasts of total energy consumption in Thailand, 1995–2015.

and Malaysia. However, the fast rates of growth of energy consumption forecast for these countries do not have much affect on the forecast of total energy consumption in the region because of the relatively small weights that these countries have in the total per-capita energy consumption in the region. Broadly the forecasts suggest that energy demand will grow at about 7 per cent per annum, similar to the average growth rate in the early 1990s, but that there is considerable heterogeneity at a country level.

Table 10.5: Total energy consumption in thousand TOE, actual and forecast (based on ARDL(1, 0, 0) specifications in logarithms of per-capita output and relative energy prices).

Country	Actual	Country specific		Pooled mean group	
	1994	*2005*	*2015*	*2005*	*2015*
Bangladesh	5008	14724	38640	7951	13981
India	139050	286417	541808	299678	616175
Indonesia	42749	153950	500542	104071	258527
Korea	107150	223166	417169	267217	532404
Malaysia	21452	93328	361807	41603	90714
Pakistan	25451	45909	90296	42292	70708
Philippines	12110	16102	27156	18962	37303
Sri Lanka	1882	1894	2133	3191	5422
Taiwan	42526	91176	156951	126995	250347
Thailand	32290	70824	152747	71867	156080
Average	42967	99749	228925	98383	203166

See the notes to Tables 10.1 and 10.4.

Table 10.6: Average growth rates of total energy consumption, actual and forecast (based on ARDL(1, 0, 0) specifications in logarithms of per-capita output and relative prices).

Country	Actual[1] values	Country specific[2]		Pooled mean group[3]	
	1990–94	*1994–2005*	*2005–2015*	*1994–2005*	*2005–2015*
Bangladesh	3.08	8.58	9.64	4.08	5.62
India	3.00	6.59	6.37	6.91	7.21
Indonesia	7.10	10.88	11.78	8.28	9.09
Korea	10.59	7.26	6.27	8.35	6.92
Malaysia	11.30	13.23	13.53	7.73	7.79
Pakistan	6.25	5.96	6.76	5.33	5.13
Philippines	5.39	4.57	5.23	5.89	6.77
Sri Lanka	7.24	1.83	1.25	5.24	5.31
Taiwan	6.03	6.14	5.43	8.42	6.81
Thailand	10.16	7.87	7.69	7.94	7.75
Average	7.01	7.29	7.40	6.82	6.84

[1] Actual values here refer to average growth of total energy consumption, Source IEA.

[2] These are the forecasts based on the country specific equations estimated over the period 1973–1990.

[3] These are the forecasts based on the PMG equations estimated over the period 1973–1990.
See Table 10.4 for a description of the data used to project the exogenous variables to the year 2015.

10.4 Conclusion

After evaluating the forecasts on 1991–1994 data, this chapter has presented forecasts for per-capita energy consumption for the ten countries over the period 1995–2015. The forecasts are based on the ARDL(1, 0, 0) model which relates the logarithm of aggregate energy demand in each country to the logarithm of the energy price relative to the CPI and the logarithm of per-capita income. The forecasts were constructed using both individual country estimates and the pooled mean group estimates. There was very little difference between their forecasts for the average per-capita energy demand for the region. Both models suggested that it would double between 1994 and 2005 and double again between 2005 and 2015. There were large differences between the two models for individual country estimates, though in many cases there would be sensible ways of averaging them. The forecasts can of course only be illustrative, there are too many uncertainties to make long-term forecasts with confidence and the projections will be sensitive to a variety of factors which were discussed.

Part IV

Summary and Conclusions

TWELVE

Summary and Conclusions

CHAPTER 11

Summary and Conclusions

This study has used a new data set and new econometric techniques to estimate total energy demand functions at aggregate, sectoral and industrial levels together with demand functions for individual fuels for ten developing Asian countries. The topic is of obvious importance. Prior to the 1997 financial crisis, Asia was the fastest growing region of the world and taking an increasing share of global energy supplies. This increase in demand for energy, which is likely to continue despite the financial crisis, will have implications for global energy markets and the world price of energy and for the global environment as emissions of greenhouse gases from these economies grow rapidly. This growth in demand will also pose difficult policy problems for national governments in the region as they try to ensure that the energy supply infrastructure necessary to allow growth to continue is installed. In this concluding chapter we evaluate the estimates and discuss the implications of the forecasts for policy.

11.1 Estimates

The average estimates, for the region as a whole, obtained from the preferred specifications tended to be sensible and often quite robust to alternative specifications. At the aggregate level they suggest an elasticity of about 1.2 with respect to per-capita GDP and an elasticity of about -0.3 with respect to energy prices. Both these estimates are higher (in absolute values) than those obtained for Asian countries by Siddayao (1985, Chapter 4) using data over the 1960–1980 period.[1] However, our estimates are quite close to the long-run price and income elasticities reported in Table 2 of Ibrahim and Hurst (1990) for six of the Asian economies in our sample. Averaging the estimates obtained

---

[1] It is worth noting that Siddayao uses price of Saudi Arabian light crude as a proxy for energy prices, which does not take account of differences in energy taxes and supply availabilities across the countries in the region. With the Summers and Heston GDP series not available to her, she uses national GDP estimates in her pooled regressions which, due to incomparability of output series across countries, may also bias the output elasticities. Finally, many of the regressions that she reports are based on static OLS regressions that could further bias the elasticity estimates in the downward direction.

171

by Ibrahim and Hurst across these Asian economies yields income and price elasticities of 1.26 and −0.27, respectively. In her survey of oil demand elasticities in developing countries, Dahl (1993: 401) also finds that the "bulk of [long-run] price elasticities lies between −0.13 and −0.26", and "Income elasticities fall between 0.79 and 1.40".

As compared to the estimates obtained for the OECD countries, our price elasticity is similar or slightly lower than comparable OECD elasticities and the output elasticity seems to be rather higher than OECD countries. Atkinson and Manning, in Chapter 3 of Barker *et al.* (1995) provide a survey of international energy elasticities. What is clear from their Table 2.1 is how sensitive the elasticity estimates are to model specification, the level of disaggregation and the sample used.

This sensitivity to sample is a feature of our analysis and there is very substantial heterogeneity across countries in estimated elasticities. Given this heterogeneity it is difficult to determine the extent to which countries are really different and the extent to which the small sample available and poor quality data are making the estimates for particular countries unreliable. This heterogeneity in national estimates is a common feature of every level of disaggregation. As one moves to more disaggregated data, there seems to be more noise in the data and the precision of the estimates reduces. There is some indication that price elasticities are larger at disaggregated levels but they are not very precisely determined. At the sectoral levels GDP elasticities differ substantially across sectors and countries with no obvious pattern. However, the average is somewhat above unity, and thus consistent with the aggregate results. At the more detailed industrial level, energy demand elasticities with respect to industrial production seem to be below unity. The above unity estimates of aggregate energy demand obtained with respect to GDP is thus probably reflecting the growing share of industrial sectors in GDP.

The models seemed well specified and structurally stable, in that they passed a battery of diagnostic tests and produced reasonable out of sample forecasts, passing predictive failure tests. This suggests that there are no major factors omitted. However, since these tests may have low power it is important to consider possible sources of misspecification; in particular inappropriate functional form, omitted variables and inadequate dynamics. In addition, it is important to consider to what extent the unexplained heterogeneity between countries could be a product of other structural factors not included in the models.

One possibility is that the constant elasticity formulation misses important non-linearities, which could arise from possible asymmetries in the response of energy demand to price and output changes. Asymmetry of energy demand to oil price changes in the case of the OECD countries has been researched extensively. See, for example, Dargay (1992), Gately (1992, 1993), Hogan (1993) and Dargay and Gately (1994, 1995). Dargay and Gately find evidence in support of asymmetric price effects, while Hogan remains sceptical about the importance of such irreversible price effects in the long run. Moreover, the evidence of price irreversibility tends to be less pronounced when total energy demand (as compared to oil demand) is considered. For the non-OECD countries, the case for price irreversibility hypothesis is even weaker, and more difficult to evaluate due to data limitations. For example, Dargay and Gately (1995: 174–175), who do find evidence of price irreversibility in the case of the OECD countries, are unable to find any significant statistical evidence of asymmetric price effects on oil or total energy demand in Less Developed Countries (LDC).

A second type of non-linearity (asymmetry) in energy demand often considered in the literature concerns the relationship between energy intensities and per-capita output levels. At low levels of income, the income elasticity is likely to rise with income as commercial energy sources are substituted for biomass fuels (wood, etc.) and industry replaces agriculture. At high levels of income, the income elasticity is likely to fall with income as information-intensive production replaces material-intensive production. This would be consistent with an "environmental Kuznets curve" in which the energy intensity rises and then falls with per-capita GDP. There is some suggestion of such an effect in indications of misspecification of functional form in some of our equations and in the global cross-section pattern, though it would not explain the differences in energy intensity between the countries in our sample.[2] It is not obvious what such non-linearity would imply for the forecasts, since it would depend on the number and size of the countries that were below the peak, where assuming a constant elasticity will underestimate future demand, relative to those that are above the peak, where a constant elasticity assumption will tend to overestimate demand. It is certainly possible that as these countries develop and information-intensive rather than material-intensive products become more important the GDP elasticity will fall towards OECD values where it tends to be below unity. However, such effects may be very long-term. In our sample, experiments with a variety of functional forms do not show one that is clearly preferred; though there was considerable evidence that using the logarithm of energy demand as the dependent variable was better than using the value share.

There are a range of possible variables that may be relevant to energy demand that we have not included in the models. These include urbanization, the distribution of income, the age structure of the population, and energy supply factors. While we admit that these and other omitted variables may be important we are inclined to think they are of second order importance for long-term analysis and forecasting. Most such variables we have considered are

---

[2]Using our data set, this issue is further examined by Galli (1997), who finds some evidence of a non-linear relationship between energy intensities and per-capita output across the Asian economies.

very difficult to measure precisely, change rather slowly over time, and do not seem to account for the heterogeneity in energy intensity or elasticities across countries. The heterogeneity seems to be idiosyncratic, reflecting structural features of each country, rather than systematic.

Given the short time series in our samples, 18 years, it was only possible to investigate simple dynamics. Although the estimated equations do not show evidence of dynamic misspecification one would expect dynamic adjustments between price and output changes and energy demand to be more complicated and perhaps slower than those suggested by the estimates we have obtained. As discussed in Section 3.1 the demand for energy is a derived demand depending on the structure of capital stock, and it often takes many years to adjust the capital stock – industrial equipment, vehicles, residential heating, and so on – in response to relative price changes. The speed of adjustment will also depend on whether the price changes are perceived to be permanent or transitory and the extent to which the degree of utilization (e.g. number of miles driven per vehicle) can be varied. The slow adjustment imposed by embodied capital stock may also give the impression of asymmetric adjustment to price changes which we have already discussed above.

Although there are inevitable uncertainties surrounding the estimates, the models developed in this study seem to provide a reliable historical basis for forecasting and policy analysis. It is the strength of the econometric approach in contrast to calibrated models, where the parameters are imposed *a priori*, that their fit to the data and sensitivity to specification can be evaluated empirically. As it is forcefully argued by Granger (1998), model evaluation *must* form an integral part of any empirical analysis aimed at forecasting or policy analysis.

11.2   Forecasts and Policy Implications

The purpose of assembling the very detailed energy data and conducting an intensive econometric analysis to obtain better estimates of the price and income elasticities of the demand for energy is to address the policy issues raised in the introduction. The Asian developing countries were and probably will be a region of very rapid growth of GDP, which is why we have focused on them, and of very rapid growth in energy demand: per-capita energy consumption has increased sharply in all of them. The OECD countries which have been the focus of most analysis are a less important source of growth and OECD estimates are less likely to be informative either about these countries, or about China whose future energy demands are likely to have a major impact. If this Asian growth continues, as seems likely, this will have implications for world energy markets, for the environment and for energy supply policy within these countries.

It is likely that the world energy market will be able to adjust to this growing demand. Contrary to what was feared in the 1970s, depletion of non-renewable resources such as oil has not proved to be a major problem. Markets and the price mechanism have worked reasonably well inducing substitution both across fuels and between energy and non-energy products, and have provided incentives for exploration of new energy resources and the development of the existing oil and gas fields, and various other adjustments. Ironically, the major problem has been with renewable resources, such as air, water, soil, forests and fish, where property rights are often less well defined and markets operate less effectively. In the case of energy demand by the developing Asian economies, the major environmental impact is through the emission of greenhouse gases, as fossil fuels such as coal, oil and natural gas are burned. These fuels have different rates of emission and substitution of natural gas for coal or oil would reduce greenhouse gas emissions. Processing and transporting natural gas to Asian economies which do not have their own supplies, or exploration and development of the gas reserves in those Asian economies that have their own sources notably Bangladesh, would require substantial infrastructure invest-ment, but might well be a medium-term response to Kyoto objectives and mar-ket signals. Given increasing demand for electricity, countries have to choose how to generate it and they face severe constraints on generating electricity by the two main non-fossil methods: nuclear and hydroelectric. Korea and Taiwan generate significant amounts of their total energy supply from nuclear, 12 per cent and 16 per cent in 1992, India a small amount. The obstacles to further expansion of nuclear are economic, the large capital costs; public safety concerns in some countries; and concerns over proliferation of nuclear weapons in some countries reinforced by the 1998 nuclear tests of India and Pakistan. All the countries except Taiwan use some Hydropower, but with the exception of Sri Lanka where it accounts for 12 per cent of total supply, it is not a significant source as yet. One obstacle to hydroelectric power is that even if there are suitable sites, which in many countries there are not, there is growing environmental and local opposition to the large dams and reservoirs often required.

To provide forecasts of energy demand, we required forecasts of GDP and real energy prices. For energy prices, one might start from an estimate of the growth in world prices assuming that the feedback from Asian energy demand to prices was small. While this assumption might have been valid in the past it is less likely to be so in the future. As the Asian share of world energy demand increases, as is likely, Asian demand will have implications for world prices.[3] Even given a baseline assumption for world energy prices, we also need to make an assumption about national energy taxes. Government policy on energy

---

[3]The sharp petroleum price decline during late 1997 and early 1998 is considered to be partly due to the economic slowdown in Asia.

taxes is likely to be influenced by development targets, pollution and road transport congestion concerns. GDP projections are more straightforward since a sensible baseline is to assume that recent growth rates will continue. While this is a sensible baseline, it is dependent on the policies adopted by the governments of these countries and of their political stability. This is a region of geo-political instability with many disputed borders and various internal tensions, thus major internal or external conflicts which disrupt the growth process in one or more of the countries are not unlikely, even if those affected recover from the 1997 financial crisis. More directly relevant to energy forecasting are possible feedbacks from energy to growth: growth may be constrained if energy supply cannot meet demand, because of lack of infrastructure, or if energy prices increase very sharply to balance demand and supply. While we have not formally modelled GDP or energy prices, we need to be aware of such feedbacks in interpreting forecasts which do not allow for them, as ours do not. In interpreting the forecasts we must also be aware of the factors discussed in the previous section which may have been left out of the models.

The forecasts in the previous chapter provide a quantitative picture of the implication of one particular scenario, which might be called the "business as usual" scenario. It assumes that the Asian economies, some of whose growth has been interrupted by the financial crisis, will return to their historical trend. It also assumes that (outside China, which is a special case because of its high initial energy intensity) there will be no major structural change which will cause energy demand to respond very differently to income and price. One possible source of such a structural change is effective energy conservation policies in these countries. If one adopts the end-use or techno-economic approach discussed in Section 3.2, it is possible to identify a large range of engineering measures that would increase energy efficiency per unit of output and thus change the income and price elasticities in these countries. Such measures could include construction of efficient mass-transit systems, limitations on the use of motorized vehicles in certain parts of cities, and enforcement of pollution reducing devices. Some of the technologies that can be adopted in these countries to make energy use cleaner and more efficient are discussed in Ishiguro and Akiyama (1995a, 1995b). Given the environmental problems of these countries and the high income elasticities of demand, measures, especially in electricity generation and transport, are urgently needed.

Ishiguro and Akiyama have demonstrated that compared with industrialized countries, technologies used in the household, industry, transport, and electricity generation of developing Asian countries are considerably less energy efficient and more polluting. They have looked into ways for many of these countries to increase energy efficiency and reduce pollution from energy use. The governments of these countries have been reluctant to enforce adoption of these methods because of their concern about the large investment required. However, the social costs of energy use and the consequent pollution should not be ignored, especially in terms of the environmental problems suffered by people in large cities. Given the recent relatively low world price of energy, the low price elasticity of demand this study has identified, and the expected rapid increase in energy demand in these countries, mandatory adoption of energy efficient and low polluting facilities and machines for electricity generation, industry and transport should be considered. Other measures include introduction of tax and subsidies that discourage the use of inefficient and high polluting equipments and machinery, in favour of the more efficient and low polluting ones. Such measures may be justified in view of the high costs of pollution and inefficient use of energy. Since the late 1970s, many of these measures have worked well in the industrialized countries; as a result energy intensities has been declining and the absolute level of energy consumption has been increasing at much lower rates.

The estimates using demeaned data, which allow for a flexible trend in energy efficiency across countries, did not indicate any large and systematic effects in the ten countries we analysed. Big improvements certainly seem possible in China. With the opening up of China's economy and her increased reliance on market forces as the primary resource allocation mechanism there will be pressures for increased efficiency in energy use, particularly as GDP grows, and energy prices start to move towards free market levels. In the case of the other countries, which have much lower energy intensities and have more pressing demands for scarce investment funds, this seems less probable. It is possible that foreign direct investment by multinationals in the energy supply industries of some of these countries could improve efficiency, but such investment would equally remove supply constraints, in particular in electricity production, which are currently constraining demand. Again one cannot be certain, but there are few indications of the possibility of sharp falls in energy intensity in the region outside China.

While we would be delighted if our forecasts were proved wrong by energy conservation measures, we are sceptical. Firstly, there has to be the political will to implement such measures.[4] This is often lacking because of the distributional consequences; the unwillingness of the US government to increase tax on gasoline is an obvious example. This is not just a problem for democracies, autocracies are often highly constrained by their dependence on particular interest groups. Secondly, if the political will is there, it has to be implemented in regulations that meet the objectives. Writing the regulations is often technically very demanding and the necessary technical expertise is often limited to those who have a vested interest: the energy users. Often well intended regulations have unintended, perverse, consequences. Thirdly, the

---

[4]For example, it is noteworthy that none of the fast growing Asian developing countries have committed to the reduction of the greenhouse gases at the Kyoto Conference held in December 1997 (see UN-FCCC, 1998).

regulations have to be enforced. Avoidance and evasion of the regulations is often quite easy given the limited enforcement power of the state in most of the countries in our sample. Almost all the sample have institutional limitations (and indigenous guerrilla movements) which restrict their ability to enforce law and order, let alone energy conservation measures, in parts of their country. The political economy of energy conservation measures, largely ignored by the techno-economic approach, is clearly a subject for further research. While effective national political action may be unlikely, an international programme may be possible: giving incentives to national governments to act; providing the expertise and technology and using market incentives to diffuse more efficient less polluting energy using technologies.

Supposing we assume no major structural break, like effective energy conservation policies in these countries, the broad features of our results have clear qualitative implications both for the forecast and for policy. The broad features are an average aggregate elasticity with respect to per-capita GDP rather greater than unity, about 1.2, and an aggregate price elasticity about -0.3. This implies that with constant real energy prices energy demand per capita would grow about 20 per cent faster than GDP in the region. If the target was to have energy intensity constant, real energy prices would have to grow at two-thirds the rate of per-capita GDP growth. In an economy growing by 6 per cent a year, as many of the Asian countries were, this would mean annual increases in real energy prices of 4 per cent a year, substantially higher than we assumed above and higher than the likely growth of world energy prices. Energy price growth (in real terms) of this order would require steady escalation in energy taxes. This might be feasible in some circumstances. What would certainly not be feasible are price increases to keep per-capita energy demand constant. This would require the rate of increase of real energy demand to be four times the rate of growth of per-capita income: 24 per cent per annum for an economy growing at 6 per cent a year. The effect of price increases might be somewhat greater if they also reduced the rate of growth, something that we have not modelled.

To get lower forecasts of energy demand requires either lower growth, higher energy prices or a change in the parameters. We do not think lower growth should be an objective for these countries, most of whom are still very poor. We do not think the magnitude of the energy price rises required to have a substantial effect on demand are feasible. Therefore to deal with the problem the growth in energy demand in this region poses for the environment requires changes in the parameters. This is primarily a matter of changing the energy using technology to increase efficiency and reduce emissions. As we noted above such technologies are available, but we were sceptical about the willingness or ability of these governments on their own to take energy conservation measures. However, it is possible that with international support and action, multilateral programmes to transform the technology may be feasible.

While there are very large technological, geopolitical and economic uncertainties, the high rates of growth of these economies, the fairly high income elasticities, the relatively low price elasticities and the political and economic constraints on energy conservation, mean that it is difficult to construct plausible scenarios which do not involve rapid growth in energy demand and emissions. This has to be seen as an urgent policy challenge: how can international action change these projections?

Part V

Appendices

Appendix A

An Energy Databank for Asian Developing Economies

A.1   Introduction

Long time series of consistent, comparative data on energy demands and supplies together with the factors that influence them are essential both to estimate reliable econometric energy models and to develop appropriate energy policies. This appendix describes the energy databank which we have constructed and used to implement the empirical analysis reported in this volume.

The databank and the Gauss program for the computation of pooled mean group estimators are available on request from the Oxford Institute for Energy Studies in easy readable formats, to enable other researchers to double check our estimates/forecasts, and in the hope that the ready availability of the data promotes further econometric research in the area of energy demand in Asian developing economies.

The databank is part of a special demonstration version of the new databank access package called *DETS* (*Data Extractor for Time Series*), recently developed as a companion to the econometric package *Microfit 4.0*, published by *Oxford University Press*, 1997 (see Holley (1997)).

A.2   Content of the Databank

The databank consists of three main modules:

Energy Balances (file name **ASIA-IEA.DTS**),
Energy Prices and Consumer Price Indices (file name **ASIA-PR.DTS**), and
Activity Measures (file name **ASIA-ACT.DTS**).

Each module contains annual observations over the period 1970–1993 for the following eleven countries:

Bangladesh (BGD)	Pakistan (PAK)
China (CHA)	Philippines (PHI)
India (IND)	Sri Lanka (LKA)
Indonesia (IDN)	Taiwan (TWN)
South Korea (KOR)	Thailand (THA).
Malaysia (MYS)	

A.2.1   Energy Balances

This module (supplied in the file **ASIA-IEA.DTS**) provides consistent energy balances, disaggregated by fuel types, sources of supply and end use, measured in Tons of Oil Equivalent (TOE). The method of conversion from original units to TOE is described in *International Energy Agency* (IEA, 1994).

The *Energy Balances Databank* is constructed from individual country Excel files. Each Excel file (e.g. **BGD-IEA.XLS**, or **TWN-IEA.XLS**) contains data on 175 variables. The number of variables (for each country) with a complete set of observations in these files are:

BGD 121; *CHA* 152; *IDN* 135; *IND* 153; *KOR* 144; *LKA* 104;

MYS 122; *PAK* 120; *PHI* 141; *THA* 145; *TWN* 154;

making a total of 1491 series with data.

The Fuels included are the relevant country specific subset of: Coal, Crude oil, Petroleum products, Gas, Nuclear, Hydro/other, electricity, and total energy.

The sources of supply which make up *Total Primary Energy Supply* include: Indigenous production, Imports, Exports, International Marine Bunkers, and Stock changes.

Total Primary Energy Supply is then related to *Total Final Consumption* by taking account of the use of energy in the energy producing industries.

Total Final Energy Consumption is then broken down into use by fuel by the Agriculture, Industry, Transport, Public and Commercial Sector, and Residential Sector, with Transport and Industrial sectors further disaggregated in the case of some countries.

The industrial sub-sectors in the *Energy Balances Databank* and their ISIC numbers are:

Iron and Steel [371]
Chemical [352, 355, 356 and part of 351 and 354]
Non ferrous metals [372]
Non metallic mineral products [6]
Transport equipment [384]
Machinery [38 except 384]
Mining (excluding fuel and quarrying) [23 and 29]
Food processing, beverages and tobacco [31]
Pulp, paper and printing [34]
Wood and wood products (other than pulp and paper) [33]
Construction [50]
Textiles and Leather [32]
Non specified, any use not classified above.

Warning

It should be noted that the data need to be inspected carefully and checked, since there are a number of anomalies. Consider some examples from Bangladesh, though they are common throughout the database. Total energy consumption for 1990 at 2402.5 is out of line with the previous year 4088.9 and the following year at 4293.9. This seems to result from zero consumption of *Natural Gas* being recorded in 1990 for some industrial sectors. There is very little variation in *Natural Gas Supply* and the adjustment is taken by the statistical discrepancy. Crude oil own use is very erratic and disappears in the last few years. Before that it was equal and opposite to the statistical discrepancy. For a range of industries observations on electricity consumption are available only for 1974 and no other years. Depending on the purpose of the particular exercise, the data could be adjusted to deal with such outliers.

A.2.2   Energy Prices and Consumer Price Indices

The energy price component of the databank (supplied in the file **ASIA-PRI.DTS**) contains time series data for the individual countries (excluding China) on the prices of various fuels in both local currency per TOE and real local currency per TOE. The list of price variables differs depending on the range of products available in each country. It includes average energy prices, electricity, coal/anthracite, natural/town gas, oil products and disaggregated oil products such as gasoline, diesel, kerosene, fuel oil.

A.2.3   Activity or Output Measures

The activity data (supplied in the file **ASIA-ACT.DTS**) consists of sectorally disaggregated data on

The Index of Industrial Production,
Value Added in Current Prices,
Value Added in Constant Prices,
The Wage Bill.

The sectoral disaggregation is based on the ISIC and the match to the energy balance data is described above.

For the transport sector, there is also more detailed information, which will be made available in a future release of the databank.

A full list of the variables in this databank, by country and the range of available data, are given in *Microsoft Word 6.0* file, **LIST-ACT.DOC** which can be obtained from the Oxford Institute for Energy Studies.

A.2.4   National Product

The full Penn World Tables, Summers and Heston (1991) is also provided as a part of the *DETS* program in the file **PWT56.DTS**. This file provides Data on GDP and its components at international prices, population and exchange rates.

A.3   The Data Files

A.3.1   Energy Balances

The energy balance statistics are supplied in 11 separate *Excel Worksheet 4.0* files (namely <country>-IEA.XLS), and combined in the *DETS* file **ASIA-IEA.DTS**.

A.3.2   Prices

Energy prices are supplied in 10 country-specific *Excel Worksheet 4.0* files (namely <country>-PR.XLS), and combined in the *DETS* file **ASIA-PR.DTS**. There are no energy prices available for China.

A.3.3   Activity Data

For each country there are three sets of *Excel Worksheet 4.0* files, covering industrial output, value added in current and constant prices, and wages. The industrial data for all the countries are combined in the *DETS* file **ASIA-ACT.DTS**.

A full list of the variables in all the three databanks together with a description and the range of available data, are available from the authors on request.

A.4   Penn World Tables

These are in the database file **PWT56.DTS**.

A.4.1   Accessing the Databank Using the DETS Package

The most effective and efficient method of accessing the databank is via the *DETS* package. This software program has been developed by Holley (1997) and is ideally suited for searching, plotting, viewing, and saving a selection of the series from the databank. Selected data series can be saved in a file in a variety of formats, including the WKS format and the file format used by the *Microfit* econometric package.

To access the databank via the *DETS* package you need first to install the demonstration version of the package on your PC. This demonstration version is on two 3.5″ floppy disks. The two program disks are labelled: *DETS*: Energy Demand for Asian Developing Economies, Disk 1/2 and Disk 2/2. Assuming you are running Windows 95, place disk 1 in the floppy disk drive **a:** click on **Start**, then **Run** A:SETUP. The databanks **ASIA-IEA.DTS**, **ASIA-PR.DTS**, **ASIA-ACT.DTS** and **PWT56.DTS** will also be automatically copied into your PC, in the default directory **C:\DETSASIA**.

A.5   Extension and Updating of the Databank

The databank is constructed so that it can be easily updated and extended by changing the basic country-specific Excel files and then converting the updated Excel files into *DETS* databank files using the converter program (**DETSCONV.EXE**) supplied with the full *DETS* package, but not included in the demonstration version.[1] Since Lotus and Excel spreadsheet packages are standard primary data processing tools, the use of spreadsheets as the basic building block in construction of the databank also simplifies the important task of updating it.

A.6   Sources of Data

Energy Balance Statistics are taken from the *International Energy Agency Yearbook. Energy Statistics and Balances of Non-OECD countries, OECD Paris,* various issues. They were retrieved and processed in individual country Excel files on a consistent basis by Jonathan Coleman and Jamshid Heidarian, at the *World Bank.*

The energy price statistics were taken from the *Asian Development Bank Yearbook: Energy Indicators of Developing Member Countries, Manila,* various issues.

The industrial data were taken from *Industrial Commodity Statistics Yearbooks and Key Indicators of Developing Asia and Pacific Countries,* UNIDO (1994).

A.7   An Example of the Use of the Databank

To illustrate the use of the databank, suppose that you wish to estimate an aggregate energy demand function for Bangladesh. In the following example, it will be assumed that you have installed the demonstration version of the *DETS* program on your PC and the databanks **ASIA-IEA.DTS**, **ASIA-PR.DTS** and **PWT56.DTS** are in the directory **C:\DETSASIA**; that you are running the system under Windows; and that you will be running the energy regressions using *Microfit for Windows* which is installed in the directory **C:\MFIT4WIN.**

Run the *DETS* program by double-clicking the *DETS* (Demonstration) icon and when prompted click **OK.** You will be presented with a data file menu, which will include **ASIA-IEA, ASIA-PR** and **PWT56** databanks. Otherwise, you can change directories to find these files. Move the highlight to **ASIA-IEA** and click **OK** or press **ENTER.** You will be presented with a set up search criteria menu: type in the "search for" box "Bangladesh total" and click **OK.** You will be presented with a list of 43 variables which match your criteria, i.e. include "Bangladesh" and "total" in their description. The list will give you the name

---

[1]For details of the commercial version of the DETS program see http:\\www.intecc.co.uk\camfit\.

of the variable, the description and the range of data available. Use the arrow-down key to move the highlight down till you come to BGDTOTC, Bangladesh Total Final Energy Consumption, variable number 17. You will see that there are data on this variable for 1971–1992. You can use the options on the menu bar to view or graph the series.

Return to the main menu and with BGDTOTC highlighted press **ENTER**. This variable will then appear in the output screen. Click the Search option on the menu bar and choose New Search. Alternatively, type **ALT + S + N**. Click on the database files box and then press the down-arrow key. You will then be presented with a list of files.

Choose the databank **ASIA-PR**. Edit the search for box from "Bangladesh total" to "Bangladesh" and press **ENTER**. A list of variables will appear. Use the down-arrow key to move the highlight down to BGDAERP, average energy price in constant 1992 prices (Taka/TOE). It is variable 21 out of 21. Notice that there are data for 1973–1992. Press **ENTER** to put it in the output box. Use **ALT + S + N**, highlight the data file box, use the down-arrow key to get the menu and choose **PWT56**, leave the search criteria as Bangladesh and click **OK** to get the list of variables. Highlight BGDPOP and press **ENTER**, then move down the list and highlight BGDRGDPL and press **ENTER**. Notice that there are data on these variables for 1959–1992. You now have four variables in your output list. Click File on the menu bar and choose the Save Output File option. You will get a menu asking for name, format, range etc. Give the file name as **bgden.fit**. The PWT has a longer data range than the energy data and we do not want all the observations. Click the Starting Period box. You will get a list of years. Move down to 1970 and click on that. *Microfit* files are the default option for saving, but you could choose a different format. Then click **OK**. Press **Yes** to clear the output list. Close the *DETS* program.

Run the *Microfit* program by double-clicking on the *Microfit for Windows* icon. Click on **File** and then click on **Open** to Input Data from a special Microfit file. Move to the sub-directory **C:\DETSASIA** and double-click on **bgden.fit** to open this special Microfit data file (already created using the *DETS* program). To see the 4 variables saved using the *DETS* program click on the **Data** button.

To create the logarithms of per-capita energy consumption, per-capita income and relative prices click on the **Process** button to return to the Data Processing Stage and in the screen editor type

$$le = log(bgdtotc/bgdpop); \quad ly = log(bgdrgdpl);$$
$$lpc = log(bgdaerp); \quad inpt = 1$$

and click the **Go** button to create these variables.

You can now estimate energy demand equations for Bangladesh using appropriate options from *Microfit for Windows*.

Appendix B

Fuel Share Equations in Terms of Elasticities

Suppose we have time series data on prices, p_i, and quantities, q_i, for goods $i = 1, 2, \ldots, m$, with total expenditure $Z = \sum_{i=1}^{m} p_i q_i$, and define an aggregate price index such that: $\ln(P) = \sum_{i=1}^{m} w_i \ln(p_i)$, where $w_i = p_i q_i / \sum_{i=1}^{m} p_i q_i$, $i = 1, 2, \ldots, m$ are value shares. The Almost Ideal Demand System is

$$w_i = \alpha_i + \sum_{j=1}^{m} \beta_{ij} \ln(p_j) + \gamma_i \ln(Z/P), \quad i = 1, 2, \ldots, m. \tag{B.1}$$

This model can be written equivalently as:

$$\ln(p_i) + \ln(q_i) - \ln(Z) = \ln\left[\alpha_i + \sum_{j=1}^{m} \beta_{ij} \ln(p_j) + \gamma_i \ln(Z/P)\right].$$

Taking all prices as given, the expenditure elasticity is:

$$\varepsilon_i = \frac{\partial \ln(q_i)}{\partial \ln(Z)} = 1 + \frac{\gamma_i}{w_i}. \tag{B.2}$$

Taking Z and all prices except one, say the i-th price, as given by:[1]

$$\frac{\partial \ln(q_i)}{\partial \ln(p_i)} + 1 = \frac{\beta_{ii} - \gamma_i w_i}{w_i},$$

so the own price elasticity is

$$\varepsilon_{ii} = \frac{\partial \ln(q_i)}{\partial \ln(p_i)} = \frac{\beta_{ii} - \gamma_i w_i}{w_i} - 1, \tag{B.3}$$

and the cross-price elasticity is

$$\varepsilon_{ij} = \frac{\partial \ln(q_i)}{\partial \ln(p_j)} = \frac{\beta_{ij} - \gamma_i w_j}{w_i}, \quad i \neq j. \tag{B.4}$$

---

[1] Note that $\partial \ln P / \partial \ln P_i = w_i$, or $\partial P / \partial P_i = w_i P / P_i$.

Evaluating (B.2), (B.3) and (B.4) at some base values of w_i, w_j, say $\bar{w}_i$, and $\bar{w}_j$, respectively we have:

$$\gamma_i = (\varepsilon_i - 1)\bar{w}_i,$$
$$\beta_{ii} = \bar{w}_i(\varepsilon_{ii} + 1 + \gamma_i),$$
$$\beta_{ij} = \bar{w}_i\varepsilon_{ij} + \gamma_i\bar{w}_j, \quad \text{for } i \neq j.$$

In practice, it is often more convenient to work with a version of (B.1) which is formulated directly in terms of the (average) elasticities ε_i and ε_{ij} rather than the coefficients, β_{ij} and γ_i. Using the above relations between the two sets of parameters, (B.1) can also be written, after some algebra, as:

$$\frac{w_i}{\bar{w}_i} - \ln(p_i) = \frac{\alpha_i}{\bar{w}_i} + \sum_{j=1}^{m} \varepsilon_{ij}\ln(p_j) + (\varepsilon_i - 1)\left[\ln(Z/P) + \sum_{i=1}^{m} \bar{w}_i\ln(p_i)\right]. \quad \text{(B.5)}$$

Notice that in the base year, used to define $\bar{w}_i$, the term in square brackets is just Z. In addition if prices indices and Z are scaled to be unity in the base year, then $\alpha_i = \bar{w}_i$, and $\alpha_i/\bar{w}_i = 1$. Statistically, the two formulations, (B.1) and (B.5) are identical, though the log-likelihoods will differ because of the different scaling of the dependent variable.

The homogeneity hypothesis $\sum_{j=1}^{m} \beta_{ij} = 0$, implies $\sum_{j=1}^{m} \eta_{ij} + \eta_i = 0$. Symmetry implies $\bar{w}_i\eta_{ij} + \gamma_i\bar{w}_j = \bar{w}_j\eta_{ji} + \gamma_j\bar{w}_i$. Thus it will be more convenient to test symmetry and homogeneity in (B.1) rather than (B.5). With homogeneity imposed (B.5) becomes:

$$\frac{w_i}{\bar{w}_i} - \ln(p_i/p_m) = \frac{\alpha_i}{\bar{w}_i} + \sum_{j=1}^{m-1} \eta_{ij}\ln(p_j/p_m)$$

$$+ (\eta_i - 1)\left[\ln(Z/P) + \sum_{i=1}^{m-1} \bar{w}_i\ln(p_i/p_m)\right]. \quad \text{(B.6)}$$

Consider now the model using the reciprocal rather than the logarithm of real expenditure, and denote real expenditure Z/P by e. We then obtain

$$w_i = \alpha_i + \sum_{j=1}^{m} \beta_{ij}\ln(p_j) + \delta_i/e, \quad i = 1, 2, \ldots, m, \quad \text{(B.7)}$$

using the same procedure as above

$$\varepsilon_i = \frac{\partial \ln(q_i)}{\partial \ln(Z)} = 1 - \frac{\delta_i/e}{w_i}, \tag{B.8}$$

$$\varepsilon_{ii} = \frac{\partial \ln(q_i)}{\partial \ln(p_i)} = \frac{\beta_{ii} + \delta_i w_i/e}{w_i} - 1, \tag{B.9}$$

$$\varepsilon_{ij} = \frac{\partial \ln(q_i)}{\partial \ln(p_j)} = \frac{\beta_{ij} + \delta_i w_j/e}{w_i}, \quad \text{for } i \neq j. \tag{B.10}$$

Evaluating these elasticities at base values, $\bar{e}$ and $\bar{w}_i$ we have:

$$\delta_i = -(\varepsilon_i - 1)\bar{w}_i\bar{e}, \tag{B.11}$$

$$\beta_{ii} = (\varepsilon_{ii} + 1 - \delta_i/\bar{e})\bar{w}_i, \tag{B.12}$$

$$\beta_{ij} = \varepsilon_{ij}\bar{w}_i - \delta_i\bar{w}_j/\bar{e}. \tag{B.13}$$

The relations corresponding to (B.7), but in terms of elasticities are

$$\frac{w_i}{\bar{w}_i} - \ln(p_i) = \frac{\alpha_i}{\bar{w}_i} + \sum_{j=1}^{m} \varepsilon_{ij}\ln(p_j) + (\varepsilon_i - 1)\left(\sum_{j=1}^{m} \bar{w}_j\ln(p_j) - \frac{\bar{e}}{e}\right),$$

$$i = 1, 2, \ldots, m.$$

If the data are scaled so that $Z = p_i = 1$ in the base year, then $\alpha_i = \varepsilon_i\bar{w}_i$.

Appendix C

Result Tables for Chapter 7

Table C.1a: Country-specific estimates of the long-run output and price elasticities of industrial energy demand based on ARDL(1, 0, 0) specifications.[1]

Country	Parameter estimates					
	$\hat{\varphi}$	$\hat{\theta}_y$	$\hat{\theta}_p$	$\hat{\sigma}$	$\bar{R}^2$	LL
Bangladesh	−0.761	1.960	0.012	0.078	0.52	21.60
	(0.186)	(0.235)	(0.108)			
India	−1.038	1.156	−0.269	0.040	0.53	32.71
	(0.234)	(0.124)	(0.185)			
Indonesia	−0.216	1.508	−0.697	0.079	0.24	21.40
	(0.212)	(1.154)	(0.939)			
Korea	−0.218	1.094	−0.520	0.036	0.57	34.84
	(0.126)	(0.173)	(0.480)			
Malaysia	−0.130	1.597	−0.376	0.072	−0.16	22.97
	(0.202)	(1.612)	(1.105)			
Pakistan	−0.399	1.675	−0.181	0.046	0.02	30.33
	(0.242)	(0.898)	(0.560)			
Philippines	−0.313	0.194	−1.009	0.086	0.25	19.90
	(0.155)	(1.020)	(0.529)			
Sri Lanka	−0.300	−0.008	−0.302	0.153	0.02	10.12
	(0.211)	(2.435)	(0.993)			
Taiwan	−0.263	0.810	−0.413	0.067	0.07	24.09
	(0.243)	(0.230)	(0.729)			
Thailand	−0.547	1.244	−0.558	0.038	0.76	33.76
	(0.151)	(0.188)	(0.159)			

[1] All the regressions are estimated over the period 1974–1990 inclusive ($T = 17$). The figures in brackets are standard errors, $\hat{\sigma}$ is the estimated standard error of the regression, $\bar{R}^2$ is the adjusted squared multiple correlation coefficient of the error correction model, $\hat{\varphi}$ is the coefficient of the error correction term which is imposed to be equal to −1 in case of models without lagged dependent variables. LL is the maximized value of the log-likelihood of the estimated equation.

Table C.1b: Diagnostic statistics for the results in Table C.1a.[1]

Country	Diagnostic statistics			
	$\chi^2_{SC}(1)$	$\chi^2_{FF}(1)$	$\chi^2_N(2)$	$\chi^2_H(1)$
Bangladesh	3.76	0.73	1.90	0.01
India	2.10	1.00	0.38	0.14
Indonesia	0.64	2.64	0.61	1.73
Korea	0.22	1.13	0.57	0.00
Malaysia	0.02	0.65	0.32	0.00
Pakistan	0.59	1.95	1.62	0.27
Philippines	1.47	0.09	2.06	0.11
Sri Lanka	0.07	0.32	0.56	1.69
Taiwan	1.30	2.85	1.49	2.74
Thailand	1.47	0.61	1.10	1.75

[1] $\chi^2_{SC}(1)$, $\chi^2_{FF}(1)$, $\chi^2_N(2)$, $\chi^2_H(1)$, are Lagrange multiplier statistics for tests of residual serial correlation, functional form mis-specification, non-normal errors, and heteroskedasticity.

Table C.2a: Country-specific estimates of the long-run output and price elasticities of industrial energy demand based on ARDL(1, 1, 1) specifications.[1]

Country	Parameter estimates					
	$\hat{\varphi}$	$\hat{\theta}_y$	$\hat{\theta}_p$	$\hat{\sigma}$	$\bar{R}^2$	LL
Bangladesh	−0.744	1.927	0.048	0.084	0.45	21.77
	(0.230)	(0.267)	(0.172)			
India	−1.120	1.172	−0.260	0.042	0.50	33.54
	(0.265)	(0.129)	(0.188)			
Indonesia	−0.118	−0.056	0.061	0.083	0.15	21.94
	(0.252)	(5.679)	(2.659)			
Korea	−0.215	1.100	−0.528	0.039	0.49	34.84
	(0.199)	(0.228)	(0.665)			
Malaysia	−0.265	0.118	0.716	0.068	−0.04	25.34
	(0.230)	(0.983)	(0.839)			
Pakistan	−0.284	−0.588	1.321	0.038	0.33	35.02
	(0.228)	(2.858)	(1.881)			
Philippines	−0.431	0.363	−1.390	0.070	0.50	24.83
	(0.141)	(0.603)	(0.419)			
Sri Lanka	−0.402	−0.460	−0.056	0.165	−0.15	10.25
	(0.335)	(2.464)	(0.998)			
Taiwan	0.098	2.418	0.710	0.041	0.66	33.94
	(0.194)	(2.860)	(1.201)			
Thailand	−0.798	1.206	−0.564	0.036	0.78	36.23
	(0.198)	(0.121)	(0.106)			

[1] All the regressions are estimated over the period 1974–1990 inclusive ($T = 17$). The figures in brackets are standard errors, $\hat{\sigma}$ is the estimated standard error of the regression, $\bar{R}^2$ is the adjusted squared multiple correlation coefficient of the error correction model, $\hat{\varphi}$ is the coefficient of the error correction term which is imposed to be equal to −1 in case of models without lagged dependent variables. LL is the maximized value of the log-likelihood of the estimated equation.

Table C.2b: Diagnostic statistics for the results in Table C.2a.[1]

Country	Diagnostic statistics			
	$\chi^2_{SC}(1)$	$\chi^2_{FF}(1)$	$\chi^2_N(2)$	$\chi^2_H(1)$
Bangladesh	3.83	0.21	1.81	0.62
India	0.55	0.46	0.46	0.81
Indonesia	2.86	1.54	0.51	2.17
Korea	0.23	1.26	0.58	0.00
Malaysia	0.05	1.70	1.80	0.38
Pakistan	0.62	0.01	1.17	0.15
Philippines	4.99	3.46	0.72	5.59
Sri Lanka	0.08	1.07	0.57	1.21
Taiwan	2.20	0.34	1.48	0.43
Thailand	0.03	2.38	1.04	1.28

[1] $\chi^2_{SC}(1)$, $\chi^2_{FF}(1)$, $\chi^2_N(2)$, $\chi^2_H(1)$, are Lagrange multiplier statistics for tests of residual serial correlation, functional form mis-specification, non-normal errors, and heteroskedasticity.

Table C.3a: Country-specific estimates of the long-run output and price elasticities of industrial energy demand based on ARDL specifications selected using the Schwarz criterion.[1]

Country	Parameter estimates					
	$\hat{\varphi}$	$\hat{\theta}_y$	$\hat{\theta}_p$	$\hat{\sigma}$	$\bar{R}^2$	LL
Bangladesh	−1.000	1.861	0.029	0.079	0.50	20.58
(0, 0, 0)	(N/A)	(0.165)	(0.083)			
India	−1.000	1.161	−0.277	0.039	0.56	32.69
(0, 0, 0)	(N/A)	(0.120)	(0.179)			
Indonesia	−0.216	1.508	−0.697	0.079	0.24	21.40
(1, 0, 0)	(0.212)	(1.154)	(0.939)			
Korea	−0.218	1.094	−0.520	0.036	0.57	34.84
(1, 0, 0)	(0.126)	(0.173)	(0.480)			
Malaysia	−0.130	1.597	−0.376	0.072	−0.17	22.97
(1, 0, 0)	(0.202)	(1.612)	(1.105)			
Pakistan	−0.310	−0.238	1.090	0.037	0.38	34.97
(1, 0, 1)	(0.194)	(1.941)	(1.274)			
Philippines	−0.463	0.464	−1.234	0.073	0.46	23.44
(1, 1, 0)	(0.144)	(0.572)	(0.356)			
SriLanka	−0.300	−0.008	−0.302	0.153	0.02	10.12
(1, 0, 0)	(0.211)	(2.435)	(0.993)			
Taiwan	0.194	1.686	0.625	0.042	0.64	32.89
(1, 0, 1)	(0.180)	(0.673)	(0.551)			
Thailand	−1.000	1.147	−0.524	0.036	0.78	35.46
(0, 1, 1)	(N/A)	(0.078)	(0.076)			

[1] All the regressions are estimated over the period 1974–1990 inclusive ($T = 17$). The figures in brackets are standard errors, $\hat{\sigma}$ is the estimated standard error of the regression, $\bar{R}^2$ is the adjusted squared multiple correlation coefficient of the error correction model, $\hat{\varphi}$ is the coefficient of the error correction term which is imposed to be equal to −1 in case of models without lagged dependent variables. LL is the maximized value of the log-likelihood of the estimated equation.

Table C.3b: Diagnostic statistics for the results in Table C.3a.[1]

Country	Diagnostic statistics			
	$\chi^2_{SC}(1)$	$\chi^2_{FF}(1)$	$\chi^2_N(2)$	$\chi^2_H(1)$
Bangladesh (0, 0, 0)	0.09	0.02	1.41	0.03
India (0, 0, 0)	2.26	1.72	0.39	0.18
Indonesia (1, 0, 0)	0.64	2.64	0.61	1.73
Korea (1, 0, 0)	0.22	1.13	0.57	0.00
Malaysia (1, 0, 0)	0.02	0.65	0.32	0.00
Pakistan (1, 0, 1)	0.31	0.02	1.17	0.14
Philippines (1, 1, 0)	5.21	3.93	0.23	3.20
Sri Lanka (1, 0, 0)	0.07	0.32	0.56	1.69
Taiwan (1, 0, 1)	0.82	2.00	1.20	0.35
Thailand (1, 0, 1)	1.09	1.92	1.52	0.51

[1] $\chi^2_{SC}(1)$, $\chi^2_{FF}(1)$, $\chi^2_N(2)$, $\chi^2_H(1)$, are Lagrange multiplier statistics for tests of residual serial correlation, functional form mis-specification, non-normal errors, and heteroskedasticity.

Table C.4a: Country-specific estimates of the long-run output and price elasticities of industrial energy demand based on ARDL(1, 0, 0, 0) specifications.[1]

Country	Parameter estimates						
	$\hat{\varphi}$	$\hat{\theta}_y$	$\hat{\theta}_p$	$\hat{\theta}_x$	$\hat{\sigma}$	$\bar{R}^2$	LL
Bangladesh	−0.728	1.691	−0.159	0.262	0.077	0.54	22.52
	(0.185)	(0.327)	(0.198)	(0.243)			
India	−1.024	0.856	−0.384	0.376	0.036	0.64	35.51
	(0.207)	(0.179)	(0.181)	(0.192)			
Indonesia	−0.318	1.899	−0.303	−0.431	0.079	0.24	22.06
	(0.236)	(0.779)	(0.640)	(0.415)			
Korea	−0.576	1.000	0.123	−0.625	0.027	0.75	40.29
	(0.145)	(0.042)	(0.093)	(0.126)			
Malaysia	−0.963	0.411	−0.171	1.035	0.058	0.24	27.25
	(0.339)	(0.169)	(0.108)	(0.182)			
Pakistan	−0.276	2.867	−0.297	−0.734	0.045	0.08	31.50
	(0.253)	(1.815)	(0.760)	(1.010)			
Philippines	−0.322	0.172	−0.962	−0.050	0.089	0.19	19.90
	(0.235)	(1.108)	(0.999)	(0.899)			
Sri Lanka	−0.390	−2.309	−0.057	0.967	0.141	0.16	12.18
	(0.200)	(1.793)	(0.647)	(0.630)			
Taiwan	−0.193	1.564	−2.279	3.875	0.055	0.37	28.03
	(0.202)	(0.810)	(2.818)	(4.483)			
Thailand	−0.595	1.254	−0.514	−0.168	0.039	0.74	34.01
	(0.174)	(0.180)	(0.156)	(0.261)			

[1] All the regressions are estimated over the period 1974–1990 inclusive ($T = 17$). The figures in brackets are standard errors, $\hat{\sigma}$ is the estimated standard error of the regression, $\bar{R}^2$ is the adjusted squared multiple correlation coefficient of the error correction model, $\hat{\varphi}$ is the coefficient of the error correction term which is imposed to be equal to −1 in case of models without lagged dependent variables. *LL* is the maximized value of the log-likelihood of the estimated equation.

Table C.4b: Diagnostic statistics for the results in Table C.4a.[1]

Country	Diagnostic statistics			
	$\chi^2_{SC}(1)$	$\chi^2_{FF}(1)$	$\chi^2_N(2)$	$\chi^2_H(1)$
Bangladesh	3.36	0.00	1.70	0.60
India	3.64	0.02	0.22	6.28
Indonesia	0.31	0.00	0.52	1.85
Korea	0.46	0.44	0.57	0.08
Malaysia	4.22	0.51	0.63	0.28
Pakistan	0.14	0.07	0.56	0.43
Philippines	2.11	0.13	1.97	0.18
Sri Lanka	1.19	0.10	1.05	1.44
Taiwan	0.00	1.55	1.20	0.58
Thailand	1.77	0.13	0.74	0.98

[1] $\chi^2_{SC}(1)$, $\chi^2_{FF}(1)$, $\chi^2_N(2)$, $\chi^2_H(1)$, are Lagrange multiplier statistics for tests of residual serial correlation, functional form mis-specification, non-normal errors, and heteroskedasticity.

Table C.5a: Country-specific estimates of the long-run output and price elasticities of transportation energy demand based on ARDL(1, 0, 0) specifications.[1]

Country	Parameter estimates					
	$\hat{\varphi}$	$\hat{\theta}_y$	$\hat{\theta}_p$	$\hat{\sigma}$	$\bar{R}^2$	LL
Bangladesh	−0.721	1.625	0.000	0.068	0.81	23.88
	(0.126)	(0.256)	(0.123)			
India	−0.767	0.436	−0.033	0.022	0.28	43.02
	(0.266)	(0.066)	(0.070)			
Indonesia	−0.532	1.286	−0.324	0.033	0.35	36.11
	(0.243)	(0.158)	(0.120)			
Korea	−0.718	1.387	−0.203	0.091	0.59	18.87
	(0.167)	(0.101)	(0.120)			
Malaysia	−0.095	3.318	−1.753	0.041	0.23	32.55
	(0.089)	(2.459)	(2.067)			
Pakistan	−0.415	1.425	0.165	0.043	−0.01	31.80
	(0.299)	(0.235)	(0.160)			
Philippines	−0.345	1.187	−1.324	0.152	0.32	10.13
	(0.158)	(1.579)	(0.651)			
Sri Lanka	−0.897	0.578	0.101	0.067	0.39	24.06
	(0.254)	(0.184)	(0.086)			
Taiwan	−1.070	1.038	−0.005	0.064	0.50	24.94
	(0.269)	(0.052)	(0.081)			
Thailand	−0.719	1.474	−0.375	0.038	0.76	33.58
	(0.141)	(0.088)	(0.075)			

[1] All the regressions are estimated over the period 1974–1990 inclusive ($T = 17$). The figures in brackets are standard errors, $\hat{\sigma}$ is the estimated standard error of the regression, $\bar{R}^2$ is the adjusted squared multiple correlation coefficient of the error correction model, $\hat{\varphi}$ is the coefficient of the error correction term which is imposed to be equal to −1 in case of models without lagged dependent variables. LL is the maximized value of the log-likelihood of the estimated equation.

Table C.5b: Diagnostic statistics for the results in Table C.5a.[1]

Country	Diagnostic Statistics			
	$\chi^2_{SC}(1)$	$\chi^2_{FF}(1)$	$\chi^2_N(2)$	$\chi^2_H(1)$
Bangladesh	1.73	0.96	1.04	0.49
India	1.32	1.57	1.11	2.93
Indonesia	0.20	7.25	0.14	0.18
Korea	2.45	0.26	0.62	1.01
Malaysia	0.22	2.65	2.77	0.60
Pakistan	0.24	0.32	0.92	2.00
Philippines	2.72	12.99	15.68	9.33
Sri Lanka	2.15	0.00	0.03	1.75
Taiwan	5.02	11.01	5.78	0.08
Thailand	2.99	2.01	0.13	0.00

[1] $\chi^2_{SC}(1)$, $\chi^2_{FF}(1)$, $\chi^2_N(2)$, $\chi^2_H(1)$, are Lagrange multiplier statistics for tests of residual serial correlation, functional form mis-specification, non-normal errors, and heteroskedasticity.

Table C.6a: Country-specific estimates of the long-run output and price elasticities of transportation energy demand based on ARDL(1, 1, 1) specifications.[1]

Country	Parameter estimates					
	$\hat{\varphi}$	$\hat{\theta}_y$	$\hat{\theta}_p$	$\hat{\sigma}$	$\bar{R}^2$	*LL*
Bangladesh	−1.082	1.707	0.018	0.060	0.85	27.53
	(0.186)	(0.161)	(0.072)			
India	−1.159	0.461	−0.037	0.016	0.60	49.43
	(0.228)	(0.034)	(0.035)			
Indonesia	−0.460	1.330	−0.367	0.035	0.26	36.45
	(0.460)	(0.228)	(0.195)			
Korea	−0.754	1.384	−0.205	0.099	0.51	18.93
	(0.326)	(0.114)	(0.123)			
Malaysia	−0.141	3.692	−2.858	0.040	0.27	34.45
	(0.098)	(2.048)	(2.257)			
Pakistan	−0.397	1.405	0.168	0.046	−0.18	31.92
	(0.403)	(0.278)	(0.212)			
Philippines	−0.297	1.650	−1.720	0.165	0.21	10.24
	(0.318)	(2.456)	(1.672)			
Sri Lanka	−0.912	0.683	0.069	0.068	0.37	25.19
	(0.303)	(0.212)	(0.092)			
Taiwan	−1.035	1.030	0.005	0.069	0.42	25.05
	(0.304)	(0.062)	(0.102)			
Thailand	−0.613	1.487	−0.355	0.039	0.75	34.56
	(0.258)	(0.112)	(0.124)			

[1] All the regressions are estimated over the period 1974–1990 inclusive ($T = 17$). The figures in brackets are standard errors, $\hat{\sigma}$ is the estimated standard error of the regression, $\bar{R}^2$ is the adjusted squared multiple correlation coefficient of the error correction model, $\hat{\varphi}$ is the coefficient of the error correction term which is imposed to be equal to -1 in case of models without lagged dependent variables. *LL* is the maximized value of the log-likelihood of the estimated equation.

Table C.6b: Diagnostic statistics for the results in Table C.6a.[1]

Country	Diagnostic statistics			
	$\chi^2_{SC}(1)$	$\chi^2_{FF}(1)$	$\chi^2_N(2)$	$\chi^2_H(1)$
Bangladesh	0.00	0.67	2.81	0.51
India	3.49	0.55	0.56	0.08
Indonesia	0.20	6.86	0.84	0.78
Korea	7.62	0.10	0.66	0.93
Malaysia	0.50	0.64	3.22	0.55
Pakistan	0.37	0.01	0.75	1.82
Philippines	4.07	14.30	14.19	10.76
Sri Lanka	0.79	0.02	0.43	1.59
Taiwan	13.80	14.35	5.27	0.03
Thailand	0.65	1.30	0.55	0.28

[1] $\chi^2_{SC}(1)$, $\chi^2_{FF}(1)$, $\chi^2_N(2)$, $\chi^2_H(1)$, are Lagrange multiplier statistics for tests of residual serial correlation, functional form mis-specification, non-normal errors, and heteroskedasticity.

Table C.7a: Country-specific estimates of the long-run output and price elasticities of transportation energy demand based on ARDL specifications selected using the Schwarz criterion.[1]

Country	Parameter estimates					
	$\hat{\varphi}$	$\hat{\theta}_y$	$\hat{\theta}_p$	$\hat{\sigma}$	$\bar{R}^2$	LL
Bangladesh	−1.000	1.742	−0.000	0.058	0.86	26.70
(0, 1, 0)	(N/A)	(0.165)	(0.067)			
India	−1.000	0.466	−0.046	0.016	0.63	48.79
(0, 0, 1)	(N/A)	(0.036)	(0.037)			
Indonesia	−0.532	1.286	−0.324	0.033	0.35	36.11
(1, 0, 0)	(0.243)	(0.158)	(0.120)			
Korea	−0.718	1.387	−0.204	0.091	0.59	18.87
(1, 0, 0)	(0.167)	(0.101)	(0.120)			
Malaysia	−0.095	3.318	−1.753	0.041	0.23	32.55
(1, 0, 0)	(0.089)	(2.459)	(2.067)			
Pakistan	−0.415	1.425	0.165	0.043	−0.01	31.80
(1, 0, 0)	(0.299)	(0.235)	(0.160)			
Philippines	−0.345	1.187	−1.324	0.152	0.32	10.13
(1, 0, 0)	(0.158)	(1.579)	(0.651)			
Sri Lanka	−1.000	0.560	0.107	0.065	0.43	23.95
(0, 0, 0)	(N/A)	(0.155)	(0.073)			
Taiwan	−1.000	1.043	−0.012	0.062	0.53	24.89
(0, 0, 0)	(N/A)	(0.050)	(0.080)			
Thailand	−0.719	1.474	−0.375	0.038	0.76	33.58
(1, 0, 0)	(0.141)	(0.088)	(0.075)			

[1]All the regressions are estimated over the period 1974–1990 inclusive ($T = 17$). The figures in brackets are standard errors, $\hat{\sigma}$ is the estimated standard error of the regression, $\bar{R}^2$ is the adjusted squared multiple correlation coefficient of the error correction model, $\hat{\varphi}$ is the coefficient of the error correction term which is imposed to be equal to −1 in case of models without lagged dependent variables. LL is the maximized value of the log-likelihood of the estimated equation.

Table C.7b: Diagnostic statistics for the results in Table C.7a.[1]

Country	Diagnostic statistics			
	$\chi^2_{SC}(1)$	$\chi^2_{FF}(1)$	$\chi^2_N(2)$	$\chi^2_H(1)$
Bangladesh (0, 1, 0)	0.18	0.67	3.26	0.38
India (0, 0, 1)	5.23	2.34	0.76	1.19
Indonesia (1, 0, 0)	0.20	7.25	0.14	0.18
Korea (1, 0, 0)	2.45	0.26	0.62	1.01
Malaysia (1, 0, 0)	0.22	2.65	2.77	0.60
Pakistan (1, 0, 0)	0.24	0.32	0.92	2.00
Philippines (1, 0, 0)	2.72	12.99	15.68	9.33
Sri Lanka (0, 0, 0)	2.92	0.02	0.05	1.54
Taiwan (0, 0, 0)	3.61	7.99	9.51	0.13
Thailand (1, 0, 0)	2.99	2.01	0.13	0.00

[1] $\chi^2_{SC}(1)$, $\chi^2_{FF}(1)$, $\chi^2_N(2)$, $\chi^2_H(1)$, are Lagrange multiplier statistics for tests of residual serial correlation, functional form mis-specification, non-normal errors, and heteroskedasticity.

Table C.8a: Country-specific estimates of the long-run output and price elasticities of transportation energy demand based on ARDL(1, 0, 0, 0) specifications.[1]

Country	Parameter estimates						
	$\hat{\varphi}$	$\hat{\theta}_y$	$\hat{\theta}_p$	$\hat{\theta}_x$	$\hat{\sigma}$	$\bar{R}^2$	LL
Bangladesh	−0.731	1.608	−0.006	0.024	0.071	0.80	23.89
	(0.165)	(0.308)	(0.139)	(0.229)			
India	−0.860	0.287	−0.064	0.171	0.022	0.31	44.05
	(0.271)	(0.123)	(0.068)	(0.133)			
Indonesia	−0.422	1.092	−0.449	0.268	0.027	0.55	39.94
	(0.206)	(0.171)	(0.183)	(0.182)			
Korea	−0.757	1.396	−0.152	−0.172	0.094	0.56	18.99
	(0.196)	(0.102)	(0.159)	(0.382)			
Malaysia	−0.147	2.052	−1.064	0.525	0.042	0.17	32.60
	(0.226)	(3.363)	(2.059)	(1.375)			
Pakistan	−0.726	2.314	0.068	−0.542	0.033	0.41	37.04
	(0.249)	(0.318)	(0.087)	(0.196)			
Philippines	−0.184	5.681	−2.861	3.617	0.126	0.54	14.05
	(0.144)	(5.146)	(2.233)	(3.616)			
Sri Lanka	−0.816	0.182	0.033	0.285	0.054	0.61	28.55
	(0.205)	(0.224)	(0.084)	(0.130)			
Taiwan	−1.073	1.104	−0.114	0.346	0.062	0.53	26.06
	(0.262)	(0.077)	(0.122)	(0.278)			
Thailand	−0.796	1.298	−0.330	0.387	0.033	0.82	36.72
	(0.127)	(0.087)	(0.059)	(0.162)			

[1]All the regressions are estimated over the period 1974–1990 inclusive ($T = 17$). The figures in brackets are standard errors, $\hat{\sigma}$ is the estimated standard error of the regression, $\bar{R}^2$ is the adjusted squared multiple correlation coefficient of the error correction model, $\hat{\varphi}$ is the coefficient of the error correction term which is imposed to be equal to −1 in case of models without lagged dependent variables. LL is the maximized value of the log-likelihood of the estimated equation.

Table C.8b: Diagnostic statistics for the results in Table C.8a.[1]

Country	Diagnostic statistics			
	$\chi^2_{SC}(1)$	$\chi^2_{FF}(1)$	$\chi^2_{N}(2)$	$\chi^2_{H}(1)$
Bangladesh	1.83	0.99	1.17	0.49
India	0.78	0.00	0.72	4.85
Indonesia	4.97	2.49	3.86	1.59
Korea	2.33	0.23	0.64	1.08
Malaysia	0.34	2.91	2.58	0.64
Pakistan	1.88	0.23	0.90	0.01
Philippines	1.06	9.50	2.60	13.36
Sri Lanka	5.70	3.66	2.54	0.03
Taiwan	6.32	12.78	1.23	0.00
Thailand	0.66	0.09	0.14	0.46

[1] $\chi^2_{SC}(1)$, $\chi^2_{FF}(1)$, $\chi^2_{N}(2)$, $\chi^2_{H}(1)$, are Lagrange multiplier statistics for tests of residual serial correlation, functional form mis-specification, non-normal errors, and heteroskedasticity.

Table C.9a: Country-specific estimates of the long-run output and price elasticities of residential energy demand based on ARDL(1, 0, 0) specifications.[1]

Country	Parameter estimates					
	$\hat{\varphi}$	$\hat{\theta}_y$	$\hat{\theta}_p$	$\hat{\sigma}$	$\bar{R}^2$	LL
Bangladesh	−0.443	1.252	−0.043	0.063	0.38	25.11
	(0.186)	(0.494)	(0.235)			
India	−0.628	1.643	−0.005	0.042	0.59	31.90
	(0.170)	(0.160)	(0.219)			
Indonesia	−0.424	1.187	−0.569	0.029	0.75	38.43
	(0.089)	(0.161)	(0.115)			
Korea	−0.803	0.624	0.203	0.035	0.42	35.02
	(0.213)	(0.041)	(0.035)			
Malaysia	−0.474	1.004	−0.286	0.051	0.71	28.75
	(0.107)	(0.238)	(0.214)			
Pakistan	−0.599	2.947	−0.334	0.050	0.28	29.08
	(0.228)	(0.296)	(0.195)			
Philippines	−1.114	1.654	0.347	0.120	0.60	14.13
	(0.217)	(0.381)	(0.089)			
Sri Lanka	−0.697	0.376	−0.363	0.065	0.64	24.72
	(0.180)	(0.411)	(0.160)			
Taiwan	−0.240	0.811	−0.191	0.030	0.28	37.95
	(0.175)	(0.153)	(0.388)			
Thailand	−0.807	1.629	−0.114	0.064	0.23	24.79
	(0.339)	(0.117)	(0.118)			

[1] All the regressions are estimated over the period 1974–1990 inclusive ($T = 17$). The figures in brackets are standard errors, $\hat{\sigma}$ is the estimated standard error of the regression, $\bar{R}^2$ is the adjusted squared multiple correlation coefficient of the error correction model, $\hat{\varphi}$ is the coefficient of the error correction term which is imposed to be equal to −1 in case of models without lagged dependent variables. *LL* is the maximized value of the log-likelihood of the estimated equation.

Table C.9b: Diagnostic statistics for the results in Table C.9a.[1]

Country	Diagnostic statistics			
	$\chi^2_{SC}(1)$	$\chi^2_{FF}(1)$	$\chi^2_N(2)$	$\chi^2_H(1)$
Bangladesh	0.02	4.15	0.98	0.26
India	0.04	0.14	0.56	0.62
Indonesia	0.01	0.41	3.12	0.79
Korea	0.03	0.48	0.39	0.62
Malaysia	0.07	2.41	0.65	0.32
Pakistan	1.83	4.78	1.36	0.13
Philippines	0.42	4.05	0.28	0.25
Sri Lanka	2.64	1.01	1.33	0.07
Taiwan	0.17	2.16	0.69	2.39
Thailand	0.20	0.01	0.79	0.10

[1] $\chi^2_{SC}(1)$, $\chi^2_{FF}(1)$, $\chi^2_N(2)$, $\chi^2_H(1)$, are Lagrange multiplier statistics for tests of residual serial correlation, functional form mis-specification, non-normal errors, and heteroskedasticity.

Table C.10a: Country-specific estimates of the long-run output and price elasticities of residential energy demand based on ARDL(1, 1, 1) specifications.[1]

Country	Parameter estimates					
	$\hat{\varphi}$	$\hat{\theta}_y$	$\hat{\theta}_p$	$\hat{\sigma}$	$\bar{R}^2$	LL
Bangladesh	−0.458	1.633	−0.182	0.058	0.48	28.03
	(0.201)	(0.558)	(0.257)			
India	−0.561	1.584	0.077	0.044	0.56	32.76
	(0.244)	(0.217)	(0.321)			
Indonesia	−0.626	1.132	−0.468	0.024	0.83	42.97
	(0.117)	(0.104)	(0.072)			
Korea	−0.818	0.652	0.205	0.037	0.35	35.49
	(0.236)	(0.055)	(0.044)			
Malaysia	−0.442	0.995	−0.325	0.049	0.73	30.72
	(0.122)	(0.366)	(0.272)			
Pakistan	−0.651	2.898	−0.293	0.052	0.22	29.78
	(0.250)	(0.299)	(0.192)			
Philippines	−1.257	1.491	0.232	0.110	0.66	17.06
	(0.233)	(0.315)	(0.127)			
Sri Lanka	−0.885	0.272	−0.308	0.054	0.75	29.26
	(0.318)	(0.271)	(0.105)			
Taiwan	−0.313	0.703	0.064	0.019	0.69	46.58
	(0.118)	(0.111)	(0.154)			
Thailand	−0.710	1.560	−0.022	0.065	0.22	26.08
	(0.365)	(0.181)	(0.174)			

[1] All the regressions are estimated over the period 1974–1990 inclusive ($T = 17$). The figures in brackets are standard errors, $\hat{\sigma}$ is the estimated standard error of the regression, $\bar{R}^2$ is the adjusted squared multiple correlation coefficient of the error correction model, $\hat{\varphi}$ is the coefficient of the error correction term which is imposed to be equal to −1 in case of models without lagged dependent variables. *LL* is the maximized value of the log-likelihood of the estimated equation.

Table C.10b: Diagnostic statistics for the results in Table C.10a.[1]

Country	Diagnostic statistics			
	$\chi^2_{SC}(1)$	$\chi^2_{FF}(1)$	$\chi^2_N(2)$	$\chi^2_H(1)$
Bangladesh	1.28	2.93	0.17	0.26
India	0.05	0.18	0.43	0.31
Indonesia	0.00	3.39	0.82	0.13
Korea	0.05	0.21	0.60	1.38
Malaysia	0.16	0.86	4.34	0.26
Pakistan	1.64	5.62	0.92	0.57
Philippines	0.14	11.71	0.66	0.35
Sri Lanka	0.15	1.25	1.20	0.24
Taiwan	0.00	0.43	1.50	0.09
Thailand	0.02	0.34	1.22	0.67

[1] $\chi^2_{SC}(1)$, $\chi^2_{FF}(1)$, $\chi^2_N(2)$, $\chi^2_H(1)$, are Lagrange multiplier statistics for tests of residual serial correlation, functional form mis-specification, non-normal errors, and heteroskedasticity.

Table C.11a: Country-specific estimates of the long-run output and price elasticities of residential energy demand based on ARDL specifications selected using the Schwarz criterion.[1]

Country	Parameter estimates					
	$\hat{\varphi}$	$\hat{\theta}_y$	$\hat{\theta}_p$	$\hat{\sigma}$	$\bar{R}^2$	LL
Bangladesh	−0.393	1.627	−0.165	0.056	0.51	27.72
(1, 0, 1)	(0.168)	(0.632)	(0.285)			
India	−0.628	1.634	−0.005	0.042	0.59	31.90
(1, 0, 0)	(0.170)	(0.160)	(0.219)			
Indonesia	−0.650	1.176	−0.501	0.024	0.83	42.35
(1, 0, 1)	(0.113)	(0.087)	(0.061)			
Korea	−1.000	0.621	0.207	0.035	0.43	34.48
(0, 0, 0)	(N/A)	(0.032)	(0.028)			
Malaysia	−0.411	0.828	−0.227	0.048	0.74	30.42
(1, 0, 1)	(0.109)	(0.293)	(0.229)			
Pakistan	−0.599	2.947	−0.334	0.050	0.28	29.08
(1, 0, 0)	(0.228)	(0.296)	(0.195)			
Philippines	−1.000	1.525	0.256	0.107	0.68	16.13
(0, 0, 1)	(N/A)	(0.383)	(0.100)			
Sri Lanka	−1.000	0.221	−0.289	0.052	0.77	29.16
(0, 1, 1)	(N/A)	(0.187)	(0.074)			
Taiwan	−0.307	0.700	0.049	0.019	0.72	46.54
(1, 0, 1)	(0.111)	(0.109)	(0.141)			
Thailand	−1.000	1.603	−0.090	0.063	0.27	24.58
(0, 0, 0)	(N/A)	(0.081)	(0.084)			

[1] All the regressions are estimated over the period 1974–1990 inclusive ($T = 17$). The figures in brackets are standard errors, $\hat{\sigma}$ is the estimated standard error of the regression, $\bar{R}^2$ is the adjusted squared multiple correlation coefficient of the error correction model, $\hat{\varphi}$ is the coefficient of the error correction term which is imposed to be equal to −1 in case of models without lagged dependent variables. LL is the maximized value of the log-likelihood of the estimated equation.

Table C.11b: Diagnostic statistics for the results in Table C.11a.[1]

Country	Diagnostic Statistics			
	$\chi^2_{SC}(1)$	$\chi^2_{FF}(1)$	$\chi^2_N(2)$	$\chi^2_H(1)$
Bangladesh (1, 0, 1)	1.26	4.03	0.06	0.01
India (1, 0, 0)	0.04	0.14	0.56	0.62
Indonesia (1, 0, 1)	0.05	0.96	0.84	0.12
Korea (0, 0, 0)	0.51	11.77	0.46	0.15
Malaysia (1, 0, 1)	0.58	0.26	4.29	0.23
Pakistan (1, 0, 0)	1.83	4.78	1.36	0.13
Philippines (0, 0, 1)	0.79	17.53	0.04	4.97
SriLanka (0, 1, 1)	0.12	1.33	0.87	0.03
Taiwan (1, 0, 1)	0.00	0.14	1.33	0.06
Thailand (0, 0, 0)	1.25	1.71	0.87	0.04

[1] $\chi^2_{SC}(1)$, $\chi^2_{FF}(1)$, $\chi^2_N(2)$, $\chi^2_H(1)$, are Lagrange multiplier statistics for tests of residual serial correlation, functional form mis-specification, non-normal errors, and heteroskedasticity.

Table C.12a: Country-specific estimates of the long-run output and price elasticities of residential energy demand based on ARDL(1, 0, 0, 0) specifications.[1]

Country	Parameter estimates						
	$\hat{\varphi}$	$\hat{\theta}_y$	$\hat{\theta}_p$	$\hat{\theta}_x$	$\hat{\sigma}$	$\bar{R}^2$	LL
Bangladesh	−0.324	1.548	0.153	−0.509	0.063	0.39	25.86
	(0.217)	(0.868)	(0.356)	(0.723)			
India	−0.670	1.442	−0.088	0.235	0.043	0.57	32.20
	(0.185)	(0.319)	(0.232)	(0.341)			
Indonesia	−0.280	1.021	−0.854	0.326	0.029	0.75	39.20
	(0.162)	(0.338)	(0.467)	(0.475)			
Korea	−0.778	0.623	0.209	−0.057	0.036	0.38	35.19
	(0.225)	(0.043)	(0.039)	(0.119)			
Malaysia	−0.538	0.676	−0.171	0.392	0.050	0.72	29.84
	(0.116)	(0.313)	(0.190)	(0.281)			
Pakistan	−0.600	2.845	−0.314	0.055	0.052	0.23	29.10
	(0.237)	(0.636)	(0.226)	(0.305)			
Philippines	−1.248	1.999	0.215	0.397	0.113	0.65	15.91
	(0.218)	(0.378)	(0.106)	(0.222)			
Sri Lanka	−0.686	−0.009	−0.409	0.268	0.056	0.72	27.71
	(0.157)	(0.353)	(0.150)	(0.135)			
Taiwan	−0.448	1.058	−0.372	0.742	0.026	0.43	40.61
	(0.184)	(0.087)	(0.242)	(0.320)			
Thailand	−0.880	1.406	−0.132	0.618	0.053	0.48	28.81
	(0.280)	(0.112)	(0.092)	(0.287)			

[1] All the regressions are estimated over the period 1974–1990 inclusive ($T = 17$). The figures in brackets are standard errors, $\hat{\sigma}$ is the estimated standard error of the regression, $\bar{R}^2$ is the adjusted squared multiple correlation coefficient of the error correction model, $\hat{\varphi}$ is the coefficient of the error correction term which is imposed to be equal to −1 in case of models without lagged dependent variables. LL is the maximized value of the log-likelihood of the estimated equation.

Table C.12b: Diagnostic statistics for the results in Table C.12a.[1]

Country	Diagnostic statistics			
	$\chi^2_{SC}(1)$	$\chi^2_{FF}(1)$	$\chi^2_N(2)$	$\chi^2_H(1)$
Bangladesh	0.02	9.64	0.18	1.10
India	0.10	0.06	0.49	0.66
Indonesia	0.02	0.34	2.12	0.62
Korea	0.01	0.03	0.60	1.10
Malaysia	0.07	0.48	2.66	0.17
Pakistan	1.86	11.43	1.45	0.01
Philippines	0.54	4.28	1.66	0.00
Sri Lanka	0.22	0.60	1.88	1.04
Taiwan	0.00	1.45	0.50	2.68
Thailand	0.37	0.00	0.77	2.04

[1] $\chi^2_{SC}(1)$, $\chi^2_{FF}(1)$, $\chi^2_N(2)$, $\chi^2_H(1)$, are Lagrange multiplier statistics for tests of residual serial correlation, functional form mis-specification, non-normal errors, and heteroskedasticity.

Table C.13a: Country-specific estimates of the long-run output and price elasticities of commercial energy demand based on ARDL(1, 0, 0) specifications.[1]

Country	Parameter estimates					
	$\hat{\varphi}$	$\hat{\theta}_y$	$\hat{\theta}_p$	$\hat{\sigma}$	$\bar{R}^2$	LL
Bangladesh	−0.613	3.994	−0.015	0.1231	0.74	13.73
	(0.154)	(0.624)	(0.369)			
India	−0.443	2.762	−1.290	0.096	0.25	17.93
	(0.291)	(1.329)	(1.241)			
Indonesia	−0.728	3.042	−1.903	0.247	0.57	1.91
	(0.214)	(0.380)	(0.468)			
Korea	−0.961	0.881	−0.014	0.190	0.30	6.36
	(0.319)	(0.160)	(0.243)			
Malaysia	−0.126	1.777	−0.280	0.053	0.01	28.09
	(0.087)	(0.840)	(0.665)			
Pakistan	−1.058	−0.620	0.069	0.065	0.44	24.70
	(0.274)	(0.311)	(0.161)			
Philippines	−0.612	0.108	−0.629	0.182	0.11	7.08
	(0.289)	(1.110)	(0.458)			
Sri Lanka	−0.408	1.880	−0.040	0.038	0.31	33.65
	(0.130)	(0.408)	(0.146)			
Taiwan	−1.469	0.602	0.004	0.040	0.67	32.87
	(0.260)	(0.028)	(0.046)			
Thailand	−1.173	0.530	−0.095	0.049	0.71	29.53
	(0.194)	(0.071)	(0.066)			

[1] All the regressions are estimated over the period 1974–1990 inclusive ($T = 17$). The figures in brackets are standard errors, $\hat{\sigma}$ is the estimated standard error of the regression, $\bar{R}^2$ is the adjusted squared multiple correlation coefficient of the error correction model, $\hat{\varphi}$ is the coefficient of the error correction term which is imposed to be equal to −1 in case of models without lagged dependent variables. LL is the maximized value of the log-likelihood of the estimated equation.

Table C.13b: Diagnostic statistics for the results in Table C.13a.[1]

Country	Diagnostic statistics			
	$\chi^2_{SC}(1)$	$\chi^2_{FF}(1)$	$\chi^2_N(2)$	$\chi^2_H(1)$
Bangladesh	1.56	8.34	1.53	2.15
India	0.86	1.98	4.34	0.11
Indonesia	0.72	13.02	1.30	15.92
Korea	3.26	1.22	0.13	3.38
Malaysia	0.38	0.23	1.27	0.91
Pakistan	0.00	0.12	2.13	1.90
Philippines	0.69	0.82	20.50	0.00
Sri Lanka	2.52	3.30	1.42	2.03
Taiwan	0.06	1.04	15.35	0.21
Thailand	1.65	3.72	1.93	0.11

[1] $\chi^2_{SC}(1)$, $\chi^2_{FF}(1)$, $\chi^2_N(2)$, $\chi^2_H(1)$, are Lagrange multiplier statistics for tests of residual serial correlation, functional form mis-specification, non-normal errors, and heteroskedasticity.

Table C.14a: Country-specific estimates of the long-run output and price elasticities of commercial energy demand based on ARDL(1, 1, 1) specifications.[1]

Country	Parameter estimates					
	$\hat{\varphi}$	$\hat{\theta}_y$	$\hat{\theta}_p$	$\hat{\sigma}$	$\bar{R}^2$	*LL*
Bangladesh	−0.686	3.769	0.185	0.125	0.73	14.92
	(0.269)	(0.600)	(0.330)			
India	−0.495	1.938	−0.531	0.083	0.44	21.88
	(0.268)	(0.792)	(0.787)			
Indonesia	−0.549	2.914	−1.941	0.246	0.57	3.45
	(0.270)	(0.498)	(0.680)			
Korea	−0.740	0.655	−0.114	0.124	0.70	15.03
	(0.235)	(0.187)	(0.257)			
Malaysia	−0.098	1.994	−0.643	0.056	−0.10	28.62
	(0.115)	(1.404)	(1.219)			
Pakistan	−1.059	−0.588	0.052	0.070	0.34	24.75
	(0.306)	(0.383)	(0.200)			
Philippines	−0.767	0.075	−0.934	0.188	0.06	8.02
	(0.327)	(0.920)	(0.477)			
Sri Lanka	−0.485	2.111	−0.131	0.040	0.23	34.16
	(0.218)	(0.450)	(0.167)			
Taiwan	−1.291	0.573	0.031	0.039	0.68	34.74
	(0.281)	(0.037)	(0.056)			
Thailand	−1.199	0.549	−0.107	0.051	0.68	30.19
	(0.205)	(0.112)	(0.087)			

[1] All the regressions are estimated over the period 1974–1990 inclusive ($T = 17$). The figures in brackets are standard errors, $\hat{\sigma}$ is the estimated standard error of the regression, $\bar{R}^2$ is the adjusted squared multiple correlation coefficient of the error correction model, $\hat{\varphi}$ is the coefficient of the error correction term which is imposed to be equal to −1 in case of models without lagged dependent variables. *LL* is the maximized value of the log-likelihood of the estimated equation.

Table C.14b: Diagnostic statistics for the results in Table C.14a.[1]

Country	Diagnostic statistics			
	$\chi^2_{SC}(1)$	$\chi^2_{FF}(1)$	$\chi^2_N(2)$	$\chi^2_H(1)$
Bangladesh	4.66	6.99	1.37	0.29
India	0.20	0.01	0.43	0.01
Indonesia	0.18	14.49	0.62	14.71
Korea	3.54	2.44	0.85	0.23
Malaysia	0.33	2.22	0.88	4.71
Pakistan	0.02	0.27	1.79	2.06
Philippines	1.04	5.31	6.42	1.39
Sri Lanka	3.27	3.99	1.29	1.24
Taiwan	1.03	4.25	5.16	0.18
Thailand	2.24	3.59	1.84	0.01

[1] $\chi^2_{SC}(1)$, $\chi^2_{FF}(1)$, $\chi^2_N(2)$, $\chi^2_H(1)$, are Lagrange multiplier statistics for tests of residual serial correlation, functional form mis-specification, non-normal errors, and heteroskedasticity.

Table C.15a: Country-specific estimates of the long-run output and price elasticities of commercial energy demand based on ARDL specifications selected using the Schwarz criterion.[1]

Country	Parameter estimates					
	$\hat{\varphi}$	$\hat{\theta}_y$	$\hat{\theta}_p$	$\hat{\sigma}$	$\bar{R}^2$	LL
Bangladesh	−0.613	3.994	−0.015	0.123	0.74	13.73
(1, 0, 0)	(0.154)	(0.624)	(0.369)			
India	−0.495	1.938	−0.531	0.083	0.44	21.88
(1, 1, 1)	(0.268)	(0.792)	(0.787)			
Indonesia	−1.000	2.882	−1.605	0.253	0.55	0.92
(0, 0, 0)	(N/A)	(0.252)	(0.253)			
Korea	−1.000	0.664	−0.004	0.125	0.70	14.13
(0, 1, 1)	(N/A)	(0.139)	(0.163)			
Malaysia	−0.126	1.777	−0.280	0.053	0.01	28.09
(1, 0, 0)	(0.087)	(0.840)	(0.665)			
Pakistan	−1.000	−0.624	0.074	0.062	0.48	24.67
(0, 0, 0)	(N/A)	(0.317)	(0.163)			
Philippines	−1.000	0.182	−0.819	0.179	0.14	7.40
(0, 1, 0)	(N/A)	(0.663)	(0.328)			
SriLanka	−0.408	1.880	−0.040	0.038	0.31	33.65
(1, 0, 0)	(0.130)	(0.408)	(0.146)			
Taiwan	−1.000	0.573	0.012	0.038	0.70	33.81
(0, 0, 1)	(N/A)	(0.043)	(0.064)			
Thailand	−1.000	0.547	−0.119	0.048	0.71	29.02
(0, 0, 0)	(N/A)	(0.080)	(0.073)			

[1] All the regressions are estimated over the period 1974–1990 inclusive ($T = 17$). The figures in brackets are standard errors, $\hat{\sigma}$ is the estimated standard error of the regression, $\bar{R}^2$ is the adjusted squared multiple correlation coefficient of the error correction model, $\hat{\varphi}$ is the coefficient of the error correction term which is imposed to be equal to −1 in case of models without lagged dependent variables. *LL* is the maximized value of the log-likelihood of the estimated equation.

Table C.15b: Diagnostic statistics for the results in Table C.15a.[1]

Country	Diagnostic statistics			
	$\chi^2_{SC}(1)$	$\chi^2_{FF}(1)$	$\chi^2_N(2)$	$\chi^2_H(1)$
Bangladesh (1, 0, 0)	1.56	8.34	1.53	2.15
India (1, 1, 1)	0.20	0.01	0.43	0.01
Indonesia (0, 0, 0)	4.33	3.04	0.55	8.93
Korea (0, 1, 1)	1.21	1.28	1.21	0.05
Malaysia (1, 0, 0)	0.38	0.23	1.27	0.91
Pakistan (0, 0, 0)	0.26	0.13	3.31	1.94
Philippines (0, 1, 0)	0.04	11.35	2.41	2.61
Sri Lanka (1, 0, 0)	2.52	3.30	1.42	2.03
Taiwan (0, 0, 1)	9.58	1.91	2.75	0.06
Thailand (0, 0, 0)	0.30	9.74	1.20	2.12

[1] $\chi^2_{SC}(1)$, $\chi^2_{FF}(1)$, $\chi^2_N(2)$, $\chi^2_H(1)$, are Lagrange multiplier statistics for tests of residual serial correlation, functional form mis-specification, non-normal errors, and heteroskedasticity.

Table C.16a: Country-specific estimates of the long-run output and price elasticities of commercial energy demand based on ARDL(1, 0, 0, 0) specifications.[1]

Country	Parameter estimates						
	$\hat{\varphi}$	$\hat{\theta}_y$	$\hat{\theta}_p$	$\hat{\theta}_x$	$\hat{\sigma}$	$\bar{R}^2$	LL
Bangladesh	−0.606	4.022	0.003	−0.049	0.128	0.72	13.74
	(0.173)	(0.709)	(0.420)	(0.457)			
India	−0.479	2.318	−1.244	0.369	0.100	0.19	18.01
	(0.319)	(1.581)	(1.175)	(1.007)			
Indonesia	−0.779	2.068	−1.745	0.714	0.234	0.61	3.50
	(0.206)	(0.661)	(0.399)	(0.465)			
Korea	−0.952	0.882	−0.070	0.230	0.196	0.25	6.50
	(0.330)	(0.166)	(0.289)	(0.531)			
Malaysia	0.069	−3.046	1.904	6.343	0.052	0.03	28.99
	(0.188)	(10.131)	(4.408)	(12.821)			
Pakistan	−1.097	−0.786	0.097	0.083	0.067	0.40	24.80
	(0.302)	(0.521)	(0.176)	(0.209)			
Philippines	−0.724	−0.205	−0.311	−0.543	0.184	0.10	7.66
	(0.315)	(1.008)	(0.473)	(0.544)			
Sri Lanka	−0.411	1.910	−0.044	−0.010	0.040	0.25	33.65
	(0.142)	(0.611)	(0.162)	(0.155)			
Taiwan	−1.529	0.660	−0.068	0.186	0.038	0.70	34.44
	(0.250)	(0.046)	(0.064)	(0.119)			
Thailand	−1.264	0.637	−0.087	−0.312	0.041	0.79	33.03
	(0.168)	(0.073)	(0.052)	(0.124)			

[1] All the regressions are estimated over the period 1974–1990 inclusive ($T = 17$). The figures in brackets are standard errors, $\hat{\sigma}$ is the estimated standard error of the regression, $\bar{R}^2$ is the adjusted squared multiple correlation coefficient of the error correction model, $\hat{\varphi}$ is the coefficient of the error correction term which is imposed to be equal to −1 in case of models without lagged dependent variables. LL is the maximized value of the log-likelihood of the estimated equation.

Table C.16b: Diagnostic statistics for the results in Table C.16a.[1]

Country	Diagnostic statistics			
	$\chi^2_{SC}(1)$	$\chi^2_{FF}(1)$	$\chi^2_{N}(2)$	$\chi^2_{H}(1)$
Bangladesh	2.21	8.47	1.54	1.99
India	0.59	2.94	5.19	0.18
Indonesia	0.01	13.07	0.31	14.86
Korea	1.83	0.83	0.48	1.96
Malaysia	0.03	2.36	1.25	0.72
Pakistan	0.00	0.20	2.03	2.24
Philippines	0.39	4.07	11.20	0.51
Sri Lanka	2.59	3.44	1.44	2.00
Taiwan	0.00	2.87	9.76	0.21
Thailand	0.05	4.63	7.92	0.00

[1] $\chi^2_{SC}(1)$, $\chi^2_{FF}(1)$, $\chi^2_{N}(2)$, $\chi^2_{H}(1)$, are Lagrange multiplier statistics for tests of residual serial correlation, functional form mis-specification, non-normal errors, and heteroskedasticity.

Table C.17: Alternative pooled estimators of the long-run output and price elasticities of industrial energy demand in Asian developing economies (based on ARDL(1, 0, 0) specifications).

	Mean group estimators	Pooled mean group estimators	Dynamic fixed effects estimators	Static fixed effects estimators
Output elasticity ($\hat{\theta}_y$)	1.123 (0.201)	1.238 (0.081)	1.288 (0.177)	1.027 (0.061)
Price elasticity ($\hat{\theta}_p$)	−0.431 (0.090)	−0.518 (0.091)	−0.567 (0.170)	−0.165 (0.051)
Error correction coefficient ($\hat{\varphi}$)	−0.419 (0.090)	−0.285 (0.080)	−0.210 (0.042)	−1 (N/A)
Log-likelihood (LL)	251.69	236.93	195.29	96.10
$N \times T$	170	170	170	170
No. of est. parameters	50	32	14	13

Table C.18: Alternative pooled estimators of the long-run output and price elasticities of industrial energy demand in Asian developing economies (based on ARDL(1, 1, 1) specifications).

	Mean group estimators	Pooled mean group estimators	Dynamic fixed effects estimators	Static fixed effects estimators
Output elasticity ($\hat{\theta}_y$)	0.720 (0.318)	1.307 (0.084)	1.170 (0.204)	1.027 (0.061)
Price elasticity ($\hat{\theta}_p$)	0.006 (0.244)	−0.620 (0.082)	−0.496 (0.190)	−0.165 (0.051)
Error correction coefficient ($\hat{\varphi}$)	−0.428 (0.115)	−0.265 (0.097)	−0.188 (0.044)	−1 (N/A)
Log-likelihood (LL)	277.70	248.05	196.95	96.10
$N \times T$	170	170	170	170
No. of est. parameters	70	52	16	13

Table C.19: Alternative pooled estimators of the long-run output and price elasticities of industrial energy demand in Asian developing economies (based on ARDL-SBC specifications).

	Mean group estimators	Pooled mean group estimators	Dynamic fixed effects estimators	Static fixed effects estimators
Output elasticity ($\hat{\theta}_y$)	1.027 (0.229)	1.176 (0.052)		1.027 (0.061)
Price elasticity ($\hat{\theta}_p$)	−0.219 (0.210)	−0.498 (0.055)		−0.165 (0.051)
Error correction coefficient ($\hat{\varphi}$)	−0.444 (0.132)	−0.416 (0.134)		−1 (N/A)
Log-likelihood (LL)	269.34	232.20		96.10
$N \times T$	170	170		170
No. of est. parameters	52	34		13

Table C.20: Alternative pooled estimators of the long-run output and price elasticities of industrial energy demand in Asian developing economies (based on ARDL(1, 0, 0, 0) specifications).

	Mean group estimators	Pooled mean group estimators	Dynamic fixed effects estimators	Static fixed effects estimators
Output elasticity ($\hat{\theta}_y$)	0.940	1.091	1.166	0.998
	(0.436)	(0.073)	(0.166)	(0.063)
Price elasticity ($\hat{\theta}_p$)	−0.500	−0.530	−0.943	−0.256
	(0.218)	(0.090)	(0.244)	(0.068)
Real exchange rate elasticity ($\hat{\theta}_R$)	0.451	0.232	0.653	0.155
	(0.426)	(0.082)	(0.238)	(0.079)
Error correction coefficient ($\hat{\varphi}$)	−0.538	−0.319	−0.213	−1
	(0.092)	(0.085)	(0.041)	(N/A)
Log-likelihood (LL)	273.25	239.36	200.71	98.17
$N \times T$	170	170	170	170
No. of est. parameters	60	33	15	14

Table C.21: Alternative pooled estimators of the long-run output and price elasticities of transportation energy demand in Asian developing economies (based on ARDL(1, 0, 0) specifications).

	Mean group estimators	Pooled mean group estimators	Dynamic fixed effects estimators	Static fixed effects estimators
Output elasticity ($\hat{\theta}_y$)	1.375	1.406	1.449	1.191
	(0.248)	(0.051)	(0.109)	(0.050)
Price elasticity ($\hat{\theta}_p$)	−0.375	−0.364	−0.439	−0.138
	(0.204)	(0.042)	(0.095)	(0.039)
Error correction coefficient ($\hat{\varphi}$)	−0.628	−0.357	−0.346	−1
	(0.090)	(0.073)	(0.045)	(N/A)
Log-likelihood (LL)	278.93	254.39	191.71	120.13
$N \times T$	170	170	170	170
No. of est. parameters	50	32	14	13

Table C.22: Alternative pooled estimators of the long-run output and price elasticities of transportation energy demand in Asian developing economies (based on ARDL(1, 1, 1) specifications).

	Mean group estimators	Pooled mean group estimators	Dynamic fixed effects estimators	Static fixed effects estimators
Output elasticity ($\hat{\theta}_y$)	1.483	1.417	1.371	1.191
	(0.277)	(0.069)	(0.127)	(0.050)
Price elasticity ($\hat{\theta}_p$)	−0.528	−0.151	−0.389	−0.138
	(0.311)	(0.063)	(0.110)	(0.039)
Error correction coefficient ($\hat{\varphi}$)	−0.685	−0.281	−0.288	−1
	(0.113)	(0.083)	(0.049)	(N/A)
Log-likelihood (LL)	293.74	262.30	196.60	120.13
$N \times T$	170	170	170	170
No. of est. parameters	70	52	16	13

Table C.23: Alternative pooled estimators of the long-run output and price elasticities of transportation energy demand in Asian developing economies (based on ARDL-SBC specifications).

	Mean group estimators	Pooled mean group estimators	Dynamic fixed effects estimators	Static fixed effects estimators
Output elasticity ($\hat{\theta}_y$)	1.389 (0.249)	1.073 (0.039)	N/A	1.191 (0.050)
Price elasticity ($\hat{\theta}_p$)	−0.377 (0.204)	−0.147 (0.031)	N/A	−0.138 (0.039)
Error correction coefficient ($\hat{\varphi}$)	−0.682 (0.103)	−0.613 (0.117)	N/A	−1 (N/A)
Log-likelihood (*LL*)	287.37	206.80	N/A	120.13
$N \times T$	170	170		170
No. of est. parameters	48	30		13

Table C.24: Alternative pooled estimators of the long-run output and price elasticities of transportation energy demand in Asian developing economies (based on ARDL(1, 0, 0, 0) specifications).

	Mean group estimators	Pooled mean group estimators	Dynamic fixed effects estimators	Static fixed effects estimators
Output elasticity ($\hat{\theta}_y$)	1.701 (0.490)	1.287 (0.049)	1.346 (0.107)	1.156 (0.054)
Price elasticity ($\hat{\theta}_p$)	−0.494 (0.284)	−0.334 (0.041)	−0.591 (0.119)	−0.190 (0.047)
Real exchange rate elasticity ($\hat{\theta}_R$)	0.491 (0.361)	0.384 (0.087)	0.341 (0.124)	0.116 (0.062)
Error correction coefficient ($\hat{\varphi}$)	−0.651 (0.095)	−0.357 (0.087)	−0.346 (0.044)	−1 (N/A)
Log-likelihood (*LL*)	301.89	258.27	196.27	121.99
$N \times T$	170	170	170	170
No. of est. parameters	60	33	15	14

Table C.25: Alternative pooled estimators of the long-run output and price elasticities of residential energy demand in Asian developing economies (based on ARDL(1, 0, 0) specifications).

	Mean group estimators	Pooled mean group estimators	Dynamic fixed effects estimators	Static fixed effects estimators
Output elasticity ($\hat{\theta}_y$)	1.312 (0.229)	0.947 (0.092)	1.086 (0.165)	0.976 (0.070)
Price elasticity ($\hat{\theta}_p$)	−0.135 (0.087)	−0.475 (0.065)	−0.269 (0.126)	−0.056 (0.050)
Error correction coefficient ($\hat{\varphi}$)	−0.623 (0.078)	−0.197 (0.056)	−0.232 (0.039)	−1 (N/A)
Log-likelihood (*LL*)	289.88	251.65	191.08	85.83
$N \times T$	170	170	170	170
No. of est. parameters	50	32	14	13

Table C.26: Alternative pooled estimators of the long-run output and price elasticities of residential energy demand in Asian developing economies (based on ARDL(1, 1, 1) specifications).

	Mean group estimators	Pooled mean group estimators	Dynamic fixed effects estimators	Static fixed effects estimators
Output	1.292	0.730	0.870	0.976
elasticity ($\hat{\theta}_y$)	(0.231)	(0.079)	(0.199)	(0.070)
Price	−0.102	−0.234	−0.182	−0.056
elasticity ($\hat{\theta}_p$)	(0.078)	(0.056)	(0.146)	(0.050)
Error correction	−0.672	−0.245	−0.205	−1
coefficient ($\hat{\varphi}$)	(0.085)	(0.081)	(0.039)	(N/A)
Log-likelihood	318.74	275.86	197.14	85.83
(*LL*)				
$N \times T$	170	170	170	170
No. of est.	70	52	16	13
parameters				

Table C.27: Alternative pooled estimators of the long-run output and price elasticities of residential energy demand in Asian developing economies (based on ARDL-SBC specifications).

	Mean group estimators	Pooled mean group estimators	Dynamic fixed effects estimators	Static fixed effects estimators
Output	1.288	1.508	N/A	0.976
elasticity ($\hat{\theta}_y$)	(0.243)	(0.058)		(0.070)
Price	−0.110	−0.058	N/A	−0.056
elasticity ($\hat{\theta}_p$)	(0.076)	(0.050)		(0.050)
Error correction	−0.699	−0.528	N/A	−1
coefficient ($\hat{\varphi}$)	(0.089)	(0.149)		(N/A)
Log-likelihood	312.35	199.83	N/A	85.83
(*LL*)				
$N \times T$	170	170		170
No. of est.	53	35		13
parameters				

Table C.28: Alternative pooled estimators of the long-run output and price elasticities of residential energy demand in Asian developing economies (based on ARDL(1, 0, 0, 0) specifications).

	Mean group estimators	Pooled mean group estimators	Dynamic fixed effects estimators	Static fixed effects estimators
Output	1.261	0.877	1.056	0.975
elasticity ($\hat{\theta}_y$)	(0.251)	(0.107)	(0.168)	(0.071)
Price	−0.176	−0.691	−0.382	−0.059
elasticity ($\hat{\theta}_p$)	(0.105)	(0.105)	(0.164)	(0.063)
Real exchange rate	0.247	0.266	0.228	0.007
elasticity ($\hat{\theta}_R$)	(0.112)	(0.107)	(0.190)	(0.078)
Error correction	−0.645	−0.170	−0.229	−1
coefficient ($\hat{\varphi}$)	(0.090)	(0.051)	(0.039)	(N/A)
Log-likelihood	304.43	255.19	191.92	85.83
(*LL*)				
$N \times T$	170	170	170	170
No. of est.	60	33	15	14
parameters				

Table C.29: Alternative pooled estimators of the long-run output and price elasticities of commercial energy demand in Asian developing economies (based on ARDL(1, 0, 0) specifications).

	Mean group estimators	Pooled mean group estimators	Dynamic fixed effects estimators	Static fixed effects estimators
Output	1.495	0.616	2.377	1.360
elasticity ($\hat{\theta}_y$)	(0.459)	(0.029)	(0.524)	(0.125)
Price	−0.419	−0.078	−1.269	−0.123
elasticity ($\hat{\theta}_p$)	(0.211)	(0.042)	(0.487)	(0.097)
Error correction	−0.759	−0.403	−0.175	−1
coefficient ($\hat{\varphi}$)	(0.128)	(0.149)	(0.046)	(N/A)
Log-likelihood	195.85	158.31	71.46	−22.52
(*LL*)				
$N \times T$	170	170	170	170
No. of est.	50	32	14	13
parameters				

Table C.30: Alternative pooled estimators of the long-run output and price elasticities of commercial energy demand in Asian developing economies (based on ARDL(1, 1, 1) specifications).

	Mean group estimators	Pooled mean group estimators	Dynamic fixed effects estimators	Static fixed effects estimators
Output	1.399	0.593	1.943	1.360
elasticity ($\hat{\theta}_y$)	(0.431)	(0.041)	(0.500)	(0.125)
Price	−0.413	−0.101	−0.961	−0.123
elasticity ($\hat{\theta}_p$)	(0.203)	(0.044)	(0.454)	(0.097)
Error correction	−0.737	−0.393	−0.166	−1
coefficient ($\hat{\varphi}$)	(0.115)	(0.135)	(0.047)	(N/)
Log-likelihood	215.76	192.54	77.67	−22.52
(*LL*)				
$N \times T$	170	170	170	170
No. of est.	70	52	16	13
parameters				

Table C.31: Alternative pooled estimators of the long-run output and price elasticities of commercial energy demand in Asian developing economies (based on ARDL-SBC specifications).

	Mean group estimators	Pooled mean group estimators	Dynamic fixed effects estimators	Static fixed effects estimators
Output	1.381	0.609	N/A	1.360
elasticity ($\hat{\theta}_y$)	(0.436)	(0.036)		(0.125)
Price	−0.333	−0.127	N/A	−0.123
elasticity ($\hat{\theta}_p$)	(0.167)	(0.041)		(0.097)
Error correction	−0.764	−0.645	N/A	−1
coefficient ($\hat{\varphi}$)	(0.103)	(0.146)		(N/A)
Log-likelihood	207.30	152.09	N/A	−22.52
(*LL*)				
$N \times T$	170	170		170
No. of est.	50	32		13
parameters				

Table C.32: Alternative pooled estimators of the long-run output and price elasticities of commercial energy demand in Asian developing economies (based on ARDL(1, 0, 0, 0) specifications)

	Mean group estimators	*Pooled mean group estimators*	*Dynamic fixed effects estimators*	*Static fixed effects estimators*
Output	0.846	0.608	1.621	1.104
elasticity ($\hat{\theta}_y$)	(0.613)	(0.039)	(0.312)	(0.113)
Price	−0.157	−0.077	−1.232	−0.410
elasticity ($\hat{\theta}_p$)	(0.300)	(0.040)	(0.313)	(0.092)
Real exchange rate	0.701	−0.253	1.177	0.831
elasticity ($\hat{\theta}_R$)	(0.636)	(0.073)	(0.293)	(0.112)
Error correction	−0.777	−0.386	−0.258	−1
coefficient ($\hat{\varphi}$)	(0.146)	(0.141)	(0.050)	(N/A)
Log-likelihood	204.33	161.34	78.92	2.98
(*LL*)				
$N \times T$	170	170	170	170
No. of est.	60	33	15	14
parameters				

Bibliography

Ahn, S.C. and P. Schmidt (1995), "Efficient Estimation of Models for Dynamic Panel Data", *Journal of Econometrics*, 68, pp. 5–27.

Aigner, D.J. and S.M. Goldfeld (1974), "Estimation and Prediction from Aggregate Data when Aggregates are Measured More Accurately than their Components", *Econometrica*, 42, pp. 113–34.

Akaike, H. (1973), "Information Theory and the Extension of the Maximum Likelihood Principle", in *Proceeding of the Second International Symposium on Information Theory*, eds. B.N. Petrov and F. Csaki, Budapest, pp. 267–81.

Akaike, H. (1974), "A New Look at the Statistical Identification Model", *IEEE: Trans. Auto. Control*, 19, pp. 716–23.

Amemiya, T. (1980), "Selection of Regressors", *International Economic Review*, 21, pp. 331–54.

Anderson, G.J. and R.W. Blundell (1982), "Estimation and Hypothesis Testing in Dynamic Singular Equation Systems", *Econometrica*, 50, pp. 1559–71.

Anderson, G.J. and R.W. Blundell (1983a), "Testing Restrictions in a Flexible Dynamic Demand System: An Application to Consumers' Expenditure in Canada", *Review of Economic Studies*, 50, pp. 397–410.

Anderson, G.J. and R.W. Blundell (1983b), "Consumer Non-Durable in the UK: A Dynamic Demand System", *Economic Journal* (Conference Papers), pp. 35–44.

Anderson, T.W. and C. Hsiao (1981), "Estimation of Dynamic Models with Error Components", *Journal of American Statistical Association*, 76, pp. 598–606.

Anderson, T.W. and C. Hsiao (1982), "Formulation and Estimation of Dynamic Models using Panel Data", *Journal of Econometrics*, 18, pp. 47–82.

Arellano, M. (1990), "Testing for Autocorrelation in Dynamic Random Effects Models", *Review of Economic Studies*, 57, pp. 127–34.

Arellano, M. (1993), "On the Testing of Correlated Effects with Panel Data", *Journal of Econometrics*, 59, pp. 87–97.

Arellano, M. and S. Bond (1991), "Some Tests of Specification for Panel Data: Monte-Carlo Evidence and an Application to Employment Equations", *Review of Economic Studies*, 58, pp. 127–134.

Arellano, M. and O. Bover (1993), "Another Look at the Instrumental Variables Estimation of Error-Components Models", *Journal of Econometrics*, 68, pp. 29–52.

Atkinson, J. and N. Manning (1995) "A Survey of International Energy Elasticities", in Barker, T., P. Ekins, and N. Johnstone (1995), *Global Warming and Energy Demand*, Routledge, London.

Bacon, R. (1992), "Measuring the Possibilities of Interfuel Substitution", Policy Research Working Paper, Public Economics Division, Country Economics Department, *World Bank*, No. WPS 1031.

Baker, P., R. Blundell and J. Micklewright (1989), "Modelling Household Energy Expenditures Using Micro-Data", *The Economic Journal*, 99, pp. 220–238.

Balestra, P. and M. Nerlove (1966), "Pooling Cross Section and Time Series Data in the Estimation of a Dynamic Model: The Demand for Natural Gas", *Econometrica*, 34, 3, pp. 585–612.

Baltagi, B.H. (1995), *Econometric Analysis of Panel Data*, John Wiley.

Barker, T., P. Ekins and N. Johnstone (1995), *Global Warming and Energy Demand*, Routledge.

Barten, A.P. (1977), "The Systems of Consumer Demand Functions Approach: A Review", *Econometrica*, 45, pp. 23–51.

Bera, A.K. and M. McAleer (1989), "Nested and Non-Nested Procedures for Testing Linear and Log-Linear Regression Models", *Sankhya B: The Indian Journal of Statistics*, 51, pp. 212–24.

Bhargava, L. and J.D. Sargan (1983), "Estimating Dynamic Random Effects Models from Panel Data Covering Short Time Periods", *Econometrica*, 51, pp. 1635–59.

Binder, M. and M.H. Pesaran (1995), "Multivariate Rational Expectations Models and Macro-econometric Modeling: A Review and Some New Results", in *Handbook of Applied Econometrics*, Pesaran, M.H. and M. Wickens (eds), Blackwell.

Binder, M. and M.H. Pesaran (1997), "Decision-Making in the Presence of Heterogeneous Information and Social Interactions", *International Economic Review*, forthcoming.

Bohi, D.P. (1981), *Analyzing Demand Behaviour: A Study of Energy Elasticities*, John Hopkins University Press, Baltimore.

Burniaux, J., J.P. Martin, G. Nicoletti and J.O. Martins (1992), "The Costs of Reducing CO_2 Emissions: Evidence from GREEN", Economics Department Working Papers, No. 115, OECD, Paris.

Campbell, C.J. (1998), *The Coming of Oil Crisis*, Petroconsultants in Association with Multi-Science Publishing Co. Ltd. (forthcoming in *Scientific American*).

Chateau, B. (1991), "Description of Instruments for Historical Analysis", in *Sectoral Energy Demand Studies: Application of the End-Use Approach to Asian Countries*, Energy Resources Development Series, No. 33, United Nations.

Chateau, B. and B. Lapillonne (1982), *Energy Demand: Facts and Trends: A Comparative Analysis of Industrialized Countries*, Springer-Verlag, Wien.

Chateau, B. and B. Lapillonne (1991), Chapters 1 and 2 in *Sectoral Energy Demand Studies: Application of the End-Use Approach to Asian Countries*, Energy Resources Development Series, No. 33, United Nations.

Christensen, L.R., D.W. Jorgenson and L.J. Lau (1975), "Transcendental Logarithmic Utility Functions", *American Economic Review*, 65, pp. 367–83.

Dahl, C. (1993), "A Survey of Oil Demand Elasticities for Developing Countries", *OPEC Review*, Vol. XVII, pp. 399–421.

Dahl, C. (1994), "A Survey of Oil Product Demand Elasticities for Developing Countries", *OPEC Review*, Vol. XVII, pp. 47–86.

Dargay, J. (1992), "The Irreversible Effects of High Oil Prices: Empirical Evidence for the Demand for Motor Fuels in France, Germany, and the UK" in D. Hawdon (ed.), *Energy Demand: Evidence and Expectations*, London, Academic.

Dargay, J. and D. Gately (1994), "Oil Demand in the Industrialized Countries", *Energy Journal*, 15, pp. 39–67 (Special issue).

Dargay, J. and D. Gately (1995), "The Response of World Energy and Oil Demand to Income Growth and Changes in Oil Prices", *Annual Review of Energy and the Environment*, 20, pp. 145–78.

Davidson, R., and J.G. MacKinnon (1981), "Several Tests for Model Specification in the Presence of Alternative Hypothesis", *Econometrica*, 49, pp. 781–93.

Davidson, R., and J.G. MacKinnon (1984), "Model Specification Tests Based on Artificial Linear Regressions", *International Economic Review*, 25, pp. 485–502.

Deaton, A. and J. Muellbauer (1980), "An Almost Ideal Demand System", *American Economic Review*, 70, 312–26.

Dubin, J. (1985), *Durable Choice and the Demand for Electricity*, North-Holland, Amsterdam.

Dubin, J. and D. McFadden (1984), "An Econometric Analysis of Residential Electricity Appliance Holding and Consumption", *Econometrica*, 52, pp. 345–62.

Engle, R.F. and C.W.J. Granger (1987), "Co-integration and Error Correction: Representation, Estimation and Testing", *Econometrica*, 55, pp. 1–87.

Engle, R.F. and C.W.J. Granger (1991), *Long-Run Economic Relationships: Readings in Cointegration*, Oxford University Press, Oxford.

Fisher, F.M. and C. Kaysen (1962), *A Study in Econometrics: The Demand for Electricity in the United States*, North-Holland, Amsterdam.

Galli, R. (1997), "Dematerialization and Long term Trends in Energy Intensity: An Application to Asian Emerging Countries", unpublished paper, Birkbeck College, London.

van Garderen, K.J., K. Lee and M.H. Pesaran (1997), "Aggregation and Prediction Criteria in Nonlinear Models", Journal of Econometrics (forthcoming).

Gately, D. (1992), "Imperfect Price-Reversibility of Oil Demand: Asymmetric Responses of US Gasoline Consumption to Price Increases and Declines", *Energy Journal*, 13, pp. 179–207.

Gately, D. (1993), "Oil Demand in the US and Japan: Why the Demand Reductions Caused by the Price Increases of the 1970s won't be Reversed by the Price Declines of the 1980s", *Japanese World Economics*, 5, pp. 295–320.

Gately, D. and S. Streifel (1996), "Oil Product Demand in the Developing Countries", *World Bank*, unpublished paper.

Godfrey, L.G. and M.H. Pesaran (1983), "Test of Non-Nested Regression Models: Small Sample Adjustments and Monte Carlo Evidence", *Journal of Econometrics*, 21, pp. 133–54.

Granger, C.W.J. (1986), "Developments in the Study of Cointegrated Variables", *Oxford Bulletin of Economics and Statistics*, 48, pp. 213–27.

Granger, C.W.J. (1998), *Empirical Modeling in Economics, Specification and Evaluation*, Marshall Lectures delivered at Cambridge University, February 1998.

Greene, W.H. (1993), *Econometric Analysis*, Macmillan (2nd edition), New York.

Greene, W.H. (1995), *LIMDEP, Version 7.0*, Econometric Software Inc., NY, USA.

Griffin, J.M. (1979), *Energy Conservation in the OECD: 1980 to 2000*, Ballinger, Cambridge, Massachusetts.

Grunfeld, Y. and Z. Griliches (1960), "Is Aggregation Necessarily Bad?", *Review of Economics and Statistics*, 42, pp. 1–13.

Guo, C., and J.R. Tybout (1992), "Panel-Based Estimates of Fuel Demand Elasticities in Chilean Manufacturing", memo, *The World Bank*, Washington D.C.

Hausman, J. (1979), "Individual Discount Rates and the Purchase of and Utilisation of Energy – Using Durable", *The Bell Journal of Economics*, 10, pp. 33–54.

Hawdon, D. (ed.) (1992), *Energy Demand: Evidence and Expectations*, Surrey University Press, in association with Academic Press, London.

Hendry, D.F, A.R. Pagan and J.D. Sargan (1984), "Dynamic Specification", in *Handbook of Econometrics*, Vol. II, eds. Z. Griliches and M.D. Intriligator, Elsevier, Amsterdam, pp. 1023–1100.

Hogan, W.W. (1993), "OECD Oil Demand Dynamics: Trends and Asymmetries", *Energy Journal*, 14, pp, 125–157.

Holley, B.J. (1997), *Data Extractor for Time Series*, Oxford University Press, Electronic Publishing, Oxford.

Holtz-Eakin, D. (1988), "Testing for Individual Effects in Autoregressive Models", *Journal of Econometrics*, 39, pp. 297–307.

Holtz-Eakin, D., W. Newey and H.S. Rosen (1988), "Estimating Vector Autoregressions with Panel Data", *Econometrics*, 56, No. 6, pp. 1371–95.

Hsiao, C. (1986), *Analysis of Panel Data*, Cambridge University Press, Cambridge.

Hsiao, C., M.H. Pesaran and A.K. Tahmiscioglu (1997), "Bayes Estimation of Short-run Coefficients in Dynamic Panel Data Models," in the *Analysis of Panels and Limited Dependent Variables: A Volume in Honour of G.S. Maddala*, eds. Hsiao, C., K. Lahiri, L.-F. Lee and M.H. Pesaran, Cambridge University Press, Cambridge (forthcoming).

Ibrahim, B. and C. Hurst (1990), "Estimating Energy and Oil Demand Functions: A Study of Thirteen Developing Countries", *Energy Economics*, 12, pp. 93–102.

IEA (1996), *World Energy Outlook*, 1996 Edition, International Energy Agency, OECD, Paris.

Igbal, M. (1986), "Substitution of Labour, Capital and Energy in the Manufacturing Sector of Pakistan", *Empirical Economics*, 2.

Imran, M. and P. Barnes (1992), "Energy Demand in the Developing Countries: Prospects for the Future", World Bank Staff Commodity Working Paper, No.23, Washington, D.C.

Ishiguro, M. and T. Akiyama (1995a), "Energy Demand in Five Major Asian Countries: Structure and Prospects", *World Bank Discussion Paper*, World Bank.

Ishiguro, M. and T. Akiyama (1995b), "Electricity Demand in Asia and the Effects on Energy Supply and the Investment Environment", *World Bank Policy Research Working Paper* #1557, World Bank.

Judge, G.G. *et al.* (1985), *The Theory and Practice of Econometrics* (second edition), John Wiley.

Keane, M.P. and D.E. Runkle (1992), "On the Estimation of Panel-Data Models with Serial Correlation when Instruments are not Strictly Exogenous", *Journal of Business and Economic Statistics*, 10, pp. 1–29.

Lee, K., M.H. Pesaran and Ron Smith (1997), "Growth and Convergence in a Multi-Country Empirical Stochastic Solow Model", *Journal of Applied Econometrics*, 12, pp. 357–392.

Lütkepohl, H. (1991), *Introduction to Multiple Time Series Analysis*, Springer-Verlag.

Matyas, L. and P. Sevestre (1996), *The Econometrics of Panel Data: Handbook of Theory and Applications* (second edition), Kluwer Academic Publishers.

Moss, D.L. and J.R. Tybout (1992), "The Scope for Fuel Substitution in Manufacturing Industries: A Case Study of Chile and Colombia", Memo, Georgetown University.

Nickell, S. (1981), "Biases in Dynamic Models with Fixed Effects", *Econometrica*, 49, pp. 1417–26.

Pashardes, P. (1993), "Bias in Estimating the Almost Ideal Demand System with the Stone Index Approximation", *Economic Journal*, 103, pp. 908–915.

Pesaran, M.H. (1997), "The Role of Economic Theory in Modelling the Long Run", *Economic Journal*, 107, pp. 178–191.

Pesaran, M.H. and B. Pesaran (1995), "A Non-nested Test of Level-Differenced Versus Log-Differenced Stationary Models", *Econometric Reviews*, 14, pp. 213–27.

Pesaran, M.H. and B. Pesaran (1997), *Working with Microfit 4.0: Interactive Econometric Analysis*, Oxford University Press, Oxford.

Pesaran, M.H. and Y. Shin (1997a), "An Autoregressive Distributed Lag Modelling Approach to Cointegration Analysis," in *Centennial Volume of Ragnar Frisch, Econometric Society Monograph*, eds. Strom, S., A. Holly and P. Diamond, Cambridge University Press, Cambridge (forthcoming).

Pesaran M.H. and Y Shin (1997b) "Long-Run Structural Modelling," unpublished manuscript, University of Cambridge.

Pesaran, M.H. and R.P. Smith (1985), "Evaluation of Macroeconometric Models, *Economic Modelling*, 2, pp. 125–34.

Pesaran, M.H. and Ron Smith (1995), "Estimating Long-Run Relationships from Dynamic Heterogeneous Panels", *Journal of Econometrics*, 68, pp. 79–113.

Pesaran, M.H. and Z. Zhao (1997), "Bias Reduction in Estimating Long-run Relationships from Dynamic Heterogenous Panels," in the *Analysis of Panels and Limited Dependent Variables: A Volume in Honour of G.S. Maddala*, eds Hsiao, C., K. Lahiri, L.-F. Lee and M.H. Pesaran, Cambridge University Press, Cambridge (forthcoming).

Pesaran, M.H., R.G. Pierse and M.S. Kumar (1989), "Econometric Analysis of Aggregation in the Context of Linear Prediction Models", *Econometrica*, 57, pp. 861–88.

Pesaran, M.H., Y. Shin and Richard Smith (1996), "Testing for the Existence of a Long-Run Relationship", *Department of Applied Economics* (DAE) Working Paper No. 9622, Cambridge University.

Pesaran, M.H., Shin, Y. and Ron Smith (1997), "Pooled Estimation of Long-Run Relationships in Dynamic Heterogeneous Panels", unpublished manuscript, University of Cambridge.

Pesaran, M.H., R. Smith and K.-S. Im (1996), "Dynamic Linear Models for Heterogeneous Panels", in *The Econometrics of Panel Data*, eds Matyas, L. and P. Sevestre, Kluwer.

Pindyck, R.S. (1979), *The Structure of World Energy Demand*, MIT Press, Cambridge, Massachusetts and London, England.

Pindyck, R.S. and J.J. Rottemberg (1983), "Dynamic Factor Demands and the Effects of Energy Price Shocks", *American Economic Review*, 73, pp. 1066–79.

Sathaye, J., A. Ghirardi, and L. Schipper (1987), "Energy Demand in Developing Countries: A Sectoral Analysis of Recent Trends", *Annual Review of Energy*, 12, pp. 253–81.

Schwarz, G. (1978), "Estimating the Dimension of a Model", *Annals of Statistics*, 6, pp. 461–4.

Siddayao, C.M. (1985), *Energy Demand and Economic Growth: Measurement and Conceptual Issues in Policy Analysis*, Westview Press Boulder, Co.

Siddayao, C.M., M. Khaled, J.G. Ranada and S. Saicheua (1987), "Estimates of Energy and Non-Energy Elasticities in Selected Asian Manufacturing Sectors", *Energy Economics*, 9, pp. 115–28.

Sterner, T. (1989), "Factor Demand and Substitution in a Developing Country: Energy Use in Mexican Manufacturing", *The Scandinavian Journal of Economics*, 91, pp. 723–39.

Stone, J.R.N. (1954), "Linear Expenditure Systems and Demand Analysis: An Application to the Pattern of British Demand", *Economic Journal*, 64, pp. 511–27.

Streifel, S.S. (1995), *Review and Outlook for the World Oil Market*, World Bank Discussion Paper, Number 301, World Bank, Washington D.C.

Swamy, P.A.V.B. (1971), "Statistical Inference in Random Coefficient Regression Models", *Lecture Notes in Operations Research and Mathematical Systems*, 66, Springer-Verlag, Berlin.

Theil, H. (1975–1976), *Theory and Measurement of Consumer Demand, Vols. 1 and 2*, North-Holland, Amsterdam.

UN-FCCC (1998), *UN Framework Convention on Climate Change: Report of the Conference of the Parties on its Third Session,* held in Kyoto from 1 to 11 December 1997.

Uri, N.D. (1979), "Energy Demand and Interfuel Substitution in India", *European Economic Review,* 12, pp. 181–90.

Vouyoukas, E.L. (1992), "Carbon Taxes and CO_2 Emissions Targets: Results From the IEA Energy Model", *Economics Department Working Papers,* No. 114, OECD, Paris.

Watkins, G.C. (1992), "The Economic Analysis of Energy Demand: Perspectives of a Practitioner", in *Energy Demand: Evidence and Expectations,* Hawdon, D. (ed.), Surrey University Seminars, pp. 29–96.

Waverman, L. (1992), "Econometric Modelling of Energy Demand", in *Energy Demand: Evidence and Expectations,* Hawdon, D. ed., Surrey University Seminars, pp. 7–28.

Westley, G.D. (1992), *New Directions in Econometric Modelling of Energy Demand With Applications to Latin America,* Inter-American Development Bank, Distributed by John Hopkins University Press, Washington, D.C.

White, H. (1980), "A Heteroskedasticity-Consistent Covariance Matrix Estimator and a Direct Test for Heteroskedasticy", *Econometrica,* 48, pp. 817–38.

Wickens, M. and T.S. Breusch (1988), "Dynamic Specification, the Long Run Estimation of the Transformed Regression Models", *Economic Journal,* 98, pp. 189–205.

Williams, M. and P. Laumas (1981), "The Relationship between Energy and Non-Energy Inputs in India's Manufacturing Industries", *The Journal of Industrial Economics,* 30, pp. 113–22.

Zellner, A. (1962), "An Efficient Method of Estimating Seemingly Unrelated Regressions, and Tests for Aggregation Bias", *Journal of the American Statistical Association,* 57, pp. 348–68.

Data Sources

APEC Energy Statistics, Asia Pacific Economic Co-operation, October 1993, The Energy Data and Modelling Centre, *Institute of Energy Economics.*

Asia Pacific Consensus Forecasts: A Digest of Economic Forecast (1997), published by *Consensus Economics Inc.,* 53, Upper Brooke Street, London U.K.

Commodity Markets and Developing Countries (1997), *World Bank Publications,* May.

Heidarian, J. and G. Wu (1994), "Power Sector Statistics for Developing Countries, 1987–1991", Industry and Energy Department, *The World Bank,* Washington DC.

IEA (1990–1996), "Energy Statistics and Balances of Non-OECD Countries", *International Energy Agency,* OECD Paris, various issues.

Summers, R. and A. Heston (1991), The Penn World Table (Mark 5); An Extended Set of International Comparisons 1950–1988, *Quarterly Journal of Economics,* 106, pp. 327–68.

UNIDO (1994), *Industrial Commodity Statistics Yearbooks.*

Subject Index

Author Index

225